IMAGES
of America

CARENCRO

ON THE COVER: Horses charge from the starting gate at Evangeline Downs in Carencro. The track, featuring thoroughbred and quarter horse racing, opened on April 28, 1966. Evangeline Downs has moved to St. Landry Parish, but the careers of many jockeys were born on the legendary track in Carencro. (Ned Guiterrez.)

IMAGES
of America

CARENCRO

Stacey Comeaux Judice,
Kathy Blanchard Higginbotham,
and Donna Sonnier Latiolais

ARCADIA
PUBLISHING

ISBN 978-1-4671-1279-6

Published by Arcadia Publishing
Charleston, South Carolina

Printed in the United States of America

Library of Congress Control Number: 2014952620

For all general information, please contact Arcadia Publishing:
Telephone 843-853-2070
Fax 843-853-0044
E-mail sales@arcadiapublishing.com
For customer service and orders:
Toll-Free 1-888-313-2665

Visit us on the Internet at www.arcadiapublishing.com

This book is dedicated to the brave men and women who settled in the Carencro Prairie. Many descendants of the founding families still call the city of Carencro home. As women of Carencro, we are pleased to present the history of our city in this book. Enjoy!

Contents

Acknowledgments 6

Introduction 7

1. Rich Land 11
2. True Heroes 21
3. Leading the People 35
4. Heart of the Community 55
5. Learning and Faith 61
6. Homes with History 73
7. Good Times 85
8. Early Businesses 97
9. Pieces of the Past 119

Bibliography 127

About the St. Pierre Genealogical Society 127

Acknowledgments

We would like to take a moment to thank everyone in the community who played a role in the creation of this book. As we took a walk down memory lane with longtime residents of Carencro, we laughed, cried, and shared the special moments that will leave a legacy for future generations.

A special thank you to: members of the St. Pierre Genealogical Society, Charles Guilbeau, Janice Sonnier Martin, Cora Arceneaux Grossie, the late Woodly Hebert, Linda Tribe Conolly, City of Carencro, Carencro mayor Glenn Brasseaux, Jimmie and Catherine Brasseaux, Rita Prejean, Linda Hernandez, Lela Mouton, Rachel Mouton, North Regional Library (Lafayette Public Library), Edith Garland Dupré Library (University of Louisiana at Lafayette), Carroll Guilbeau, Albert Guilbeau, John Guilbeau, the Bechet family, Don Stemmans, the late Janet Stemmans, Gladys Borel Brock, Madeline Ghandour, Russell Boudreaux, Louis Perret and the Lafayette Parish Clerk of Court office, Carencro Catholic School, Our Lady of the Assumption Catholic Church, St. Peter Roman Catholic Church, Evelyn Robin, Jennifer Melancon Conolly, Gerald and Sandra Melancon, Eddie and Angela Melancon (and the entire Melancon family), Clara Baudoin, Landry Studios, Carlos Stout, Valentine Breaux, Carmen Perry, Robley Richard III, Haili Arsement, J.L. Richard, Emily Vizina, Murray Conque, Ray Landry, Suzie Perry, Jeff Guidry, and Lizzie Sonnier.

Most importantly, we give our heartfelt thanks to our husbands—Jason Judice, Marcus Higginbotham, Mark Latiolais—and our families for their support and for sharing our time spent working on this project.

Unless otherwise noted, all images appear courtesy of the St. Pierre Genealogical Society.

Introduction

In 1779, the Carencro Prairie was laid out by a man with the last name Milau who was a surveyor in the area. After the Acadians were deported from Nova Scotia they made their way south, and some eventually settled in the prairie. Jean and Marin Mouton were some of the first settlers. Successful ranchers like Louis Pierre Arceneaux, Ovignac Arceneaux, Dominique Babineaux, Joseph Babineaux, Michel Bernard, Treville Bernard, Rosemond Breaux, Silvain Broussard, Jean Guilbeau, Jean Baptiste Melancon, Andre Prejean, Joseph Sonnier, and Paul Thibodeaux claimed land and built new lives here.

The Carencro Prairie stretched from what is now North Lafayette towards the Opelousas area. Post Road was the main stretch traveled by residents. A defined separation of land came in the 1800s, when the area of the present-day city of Carencro became known as St. Pierre (for the downtown area), Carencro (for the outer country limits), and Prairie Basse (for the area near Beau Basin).

Legend has it that the name "Carencro" may be derived from the bird known as the "carrion crow," which could often be found in the area. Other speculation says the name came from a large number of the carrion crows feasting on a mastodon in the Beau Basin area. Yet another rumor suggests that the name Carencro came from the tribe of Indians called the Karaulcraw, who called the Carencro Prairie home.

The famous Henry Wadsworth Longfellow poem *Evangeline, A Tale of Acadie* speaks of the love between Evangeline and Gabriel, who were torn apart in the exile of the Acadians from their homeland of Nova Scotia. In 1907, Louisiana politician Felix Voorhies suggested that the man called Gabriel was really Louis Arceneaux, who lost his love as the Acadians traveled through America. Arceneaux settled in the Beau Basin area in Carencro Prairie and became one of the wealthiest cattle ranchers in the area. He is said to have had 2,572 arpents of land. Legend dictates that Evangeline and Gabriel eventually found each other again under an oak tree along the Bayou Teche in St. Martinville. At that time, Gabriel was married and had a family. Evangeline was left heartbroken, as many were in the pursuit to reunite with their loved ones.

All the Acadians fought to rebuild their lives after the exile; many thrived in South Louisiana. In the 1700s, during the Revolutionary War, Carencro Prairie settlers' land was threatened by British soldiers. The men of Carencro Prairie traveled for days to meet Gov. Bernardo de Galvez and his troops in order to fight for their new homes. The men from Carencro Prairie were more than willing to fight and had no qualms about warring against the British soldiers who had helped banish them from their land in Canada. They defeated the British army and returned to their homes and families.

Prior to the Civil War, the downtown Carencro Prairie area contained just a few homes and businesses. The area exploded after the railroad came through town. By the mid-1800s, the New Orleans, Opelousas & Great Western Railroad ran through the heart of Carencro Prairie as it carried travelers and goods from one region to the next. In the downtown area, J.P. Morgan's Louisiana and Texas Railroad and Steamship Company tracks came through in 1880.

Farming and ranching were the main ways of life for many in the Carencro Prairie, and the downtown area benefited from the area farmers. Many goods were sold and exchanged from farmers to merchants. The main local crops included cotton, sweet potatoes, and corn, and farmers also raised cattle. The crops of the Carencro Prairie were indicated by the many mills located in the area—cotton gins, syrup mills, dairy farms, and sweet potato kilns. Those traveling through Carencro's countryside today can still see pieces of the past in the old cotton gins, sweet potato kilns, and silos.

Carencro received its town charter in 1905. Rumor has it that this was the second charter received by the town; the first, obtained in New Orleans, was supposedly lost when the celebration on the boat back to Carencro became a little rowdy. The area, while always rich in population and home to successful businessmen and ranchers, quickly became a hub of activity. Businesses lined up along Main Street, including grocers, hardware stores, fabric and apparel stores, and a bank. All businesses surrounded the beautiful St. Peter Roman Catholic Church, which still can be seen today on St. Peter Street.

Many elderly residents of Carencro proudly say they are from St. Pierre. Pierre Cormier, who donated the land for the prairie's first church, is where the name St. Pierre originated. Cormier asked the townspeople to name the church after his patron saint, Pierre (the French name for Peter), in exchange for the land. The land intended for the church location was deemed too low, so a trade was made with the Coussan family around 1875, and the area's first church was constructed.

The history of St. Peter Roman Catholic Church began with the faith of the Acadians. Their Catholic faith carried them through many hard times and heartaches. Fire destroyed the church two years after the completion of construction in 1877. Over a span of 27 years, St. Peter Roman Catholic Church had to be rebuilt five times due to fire and storms. The current church—a beacon of hope in Carencro—was constructed in 1906 by a carpenter named Hector Connolly. The altar was constructed in Belgium in 1893. Prior to arriving in St. Pierre, the altar traveled from Germany to the 1893 World's Columbian Exposition in Chicago; it was also displayed in St. John's Cathedral before being donated to St. Peter Roman Catholic Church in 1936. The bells that notify parishioners of the beginning of Mass have been replaced several times over the decades. One set has the inscription "1893." Another set served as fire bells to notify area volunteer firefighters of an emergency. Another bell came from a mission on the island of Buna in the South Seas; it was shattered and later welded back together by a soldier who gave the bell to a priest in Lafayette. The bell was awarded to Bishop Jules B. Jeanmard, who said his first Mass in Carencro. In 1957, workers installed four electronic bells in the church—the first of their kind in the entire United States.

Our Lady of the Assumption Church was built in 1926; however, the parish was established in 1925 by Bishop Jeanmard, who personally oversaw the building of a Catholic church intended to serve the African American community. Bishop Jeanmard invited The Holy Ghost Fathers to oversee the parish. The first pastor of Our Lady of the Assumption was Rev. Joseph Dolan. Reverend Dolan purchased the six arpents of land on Michaud Street on which the church was to be constructed. For years, Christmas service at Our Lady of the Assumption was standing room only. As families reunited for the holiday, they would attend church together to worship. Many documents reveal that the singing and joyful sounds coming from the church could be heard down the road that led into downtown Carencro. Many in the African American community would walk miles from Prairie Basse to downtown Carencro to attend Our Lady of the Assumption Church. A mission church constructed in 1936 on the land of St. Elizabeth School allowed a shorter commute for those who had to walk miles to worship.

Education in the Carencro Prairie began in the homes. Many large families would hold combined classes in attic rooms above their Acadian-style family homes. A one-room public school—the first known public school in the Carencro Prairie—was constructed on the farm of Auguste C. Melchior in 1874. In 1889, workers built a community schoolhouse known as the Carencro Graded School. A second story was eventually added to this school to meet the needs of the increasing student population. A new building, which would sit adjacent to the older Carencro

Graded School, was approved for construction in 1917. Some photographs in this book show a single wood frame school; in others, two buildings stand tall and proud for all to see. The two school buildings stood for progress and growth in the Carencro area.

Mother Katherine Drexel built the St. Elizabeth School in Prairie Basse on land donated by Washington Hayes Gordon and Andrea LeBlanc Gordon. Mother Katherine Drexel oversaw the building and worked hand in hand with teachers who arrived to teach African American and Native American children at St. Elizabeth. Down the road, closer to what is now downtown Carencro, Assumption School was home to many young African American students. After the death of Mother Katherine Drexel, Assumption also became the school for students from St. Elizabeth.

St. Ann's Convent was built in the Carencro Prairie in 1897. The school provided an education centered on the Catholic faith—at the time, most of the people who lived in the prairie were Catholic. The school remained open until 1962, when St. Pierre Catholic School was constructed. When Assumption School closed in 1971, the two schools merged and became Carencro Catholic School, which still stands downtown.

The schools located in Carencro today are Carencro Heights Elementary School, Live Oak Elementary, Carencro Middle School (which is on the land where Carencro Graded School once stood), and Carencro High School. When the Lafayette Parish School System consolidated many of the small towns into one school in 1969, the names of the high schools were changed to a more generic name. For example, Scott High School and Judice High School became Acadiana High School. Carencro High School was moved to a new location on Butcher Switch Road for the 1970–1971 school year, but did not combine with other schools. However, the school board still wanted to see the name changed to a more neutral name to keep the peace with other towns that were having to change their names due to consolidation. The residents of Carencro rallied and fought to keep the name of their beloved high school.

Many pictures in this book are over 100 years old; time and nature have not been kind to some of these photographs. The St. Pierre Genealogical Society and residents of Carencro lost many historic photographs to floods on March 12, 2012. Two homes that housed many old photographs of the city were destroyed by fire. While historic photographs may be hard to come by in modern Carencro, the beautiful oaks on the grounds of St. Peter Roman Catholic Church (and others in the city) are a testament to the beautiful land that once was called a prairie, developed into a town, and then became a city. Downtown, there are still iron posts that were once used to tie horses when travelers came to town for business or enjoyment. Carencro has continued to grow into a place where history is celebrated and the roots of faith and family are embedded deep in the souls of its people.

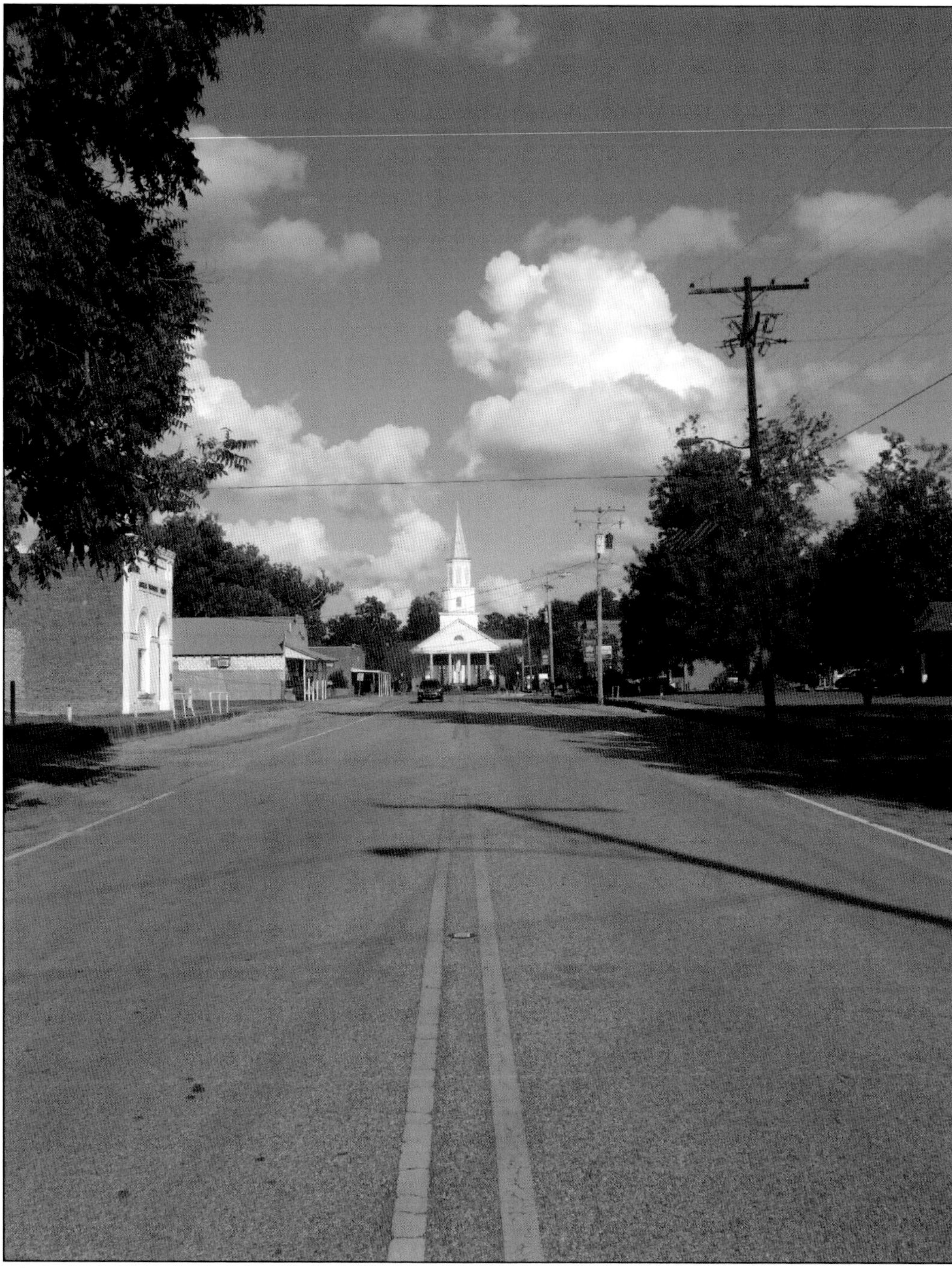

This current-day photograph looks toward St. Peter Roman Catholic Church from the corner of North University Avenue and St. Peter Street in downtown Carencro. While times have changed, Carencro has held on to its beauty and history.

One

RICH LAND

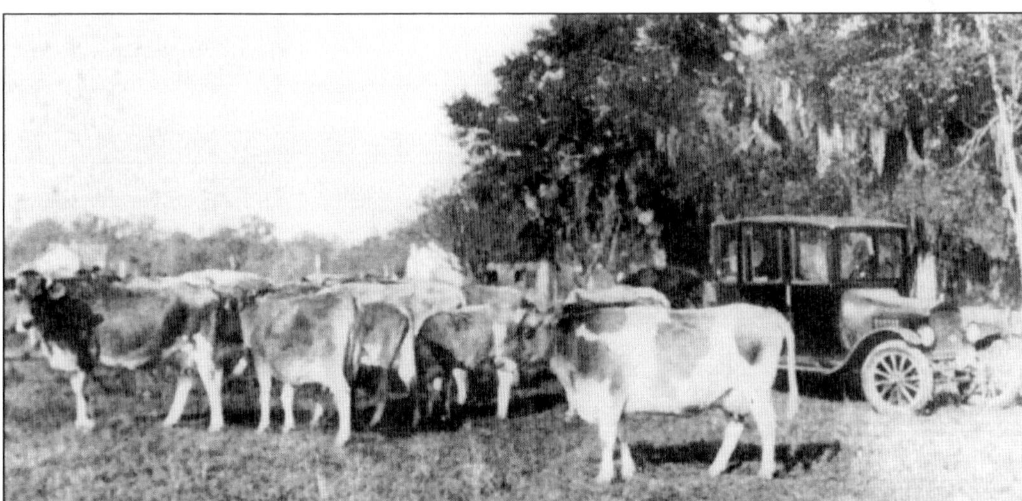

According to writings published by William Henry Perrin in 1891, the first settlers called this area Beau Basin, which means "pretty basin." The lands near the basin supported cattle and produced crops of cotton and corn. The area was known as a *vacherie*, or land for grazing cattle.

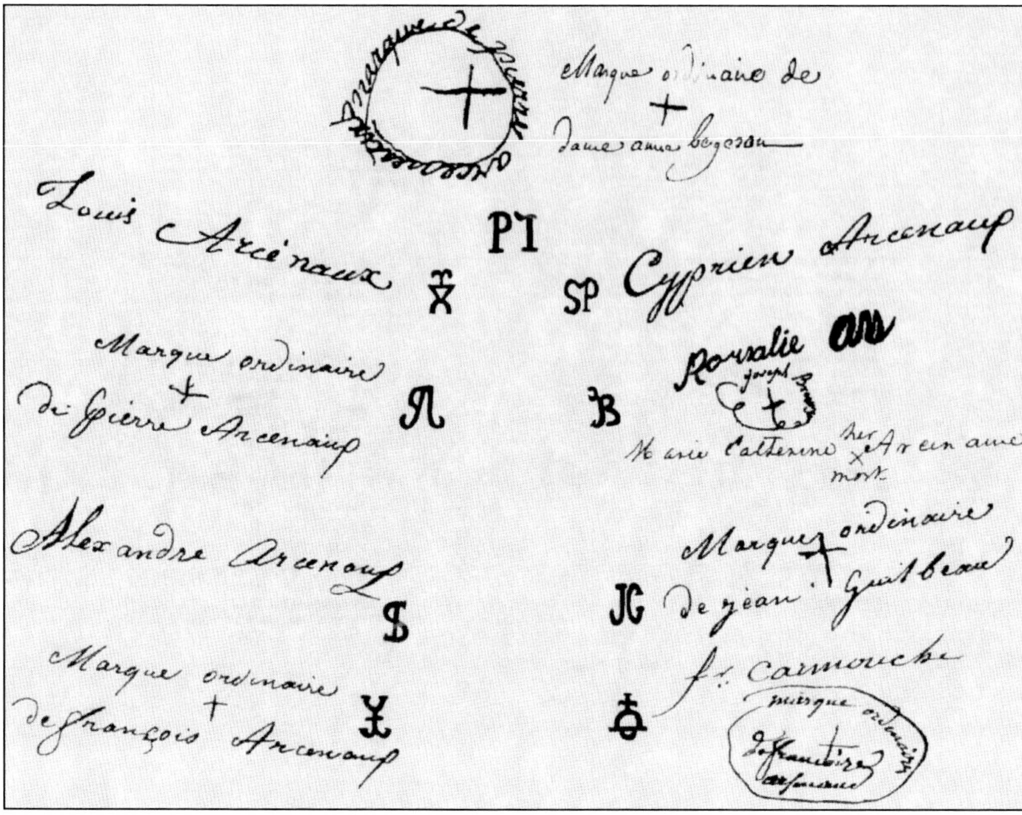

Some of the cattle brands shown here were owned by the first settlers in the Carencro Prairie. Louisiana passed its first cattle brand law in 1824. The Louisiana Livestock Brand Commission had to approve an application for a brand, then the commission sent a certificate to the farmer.

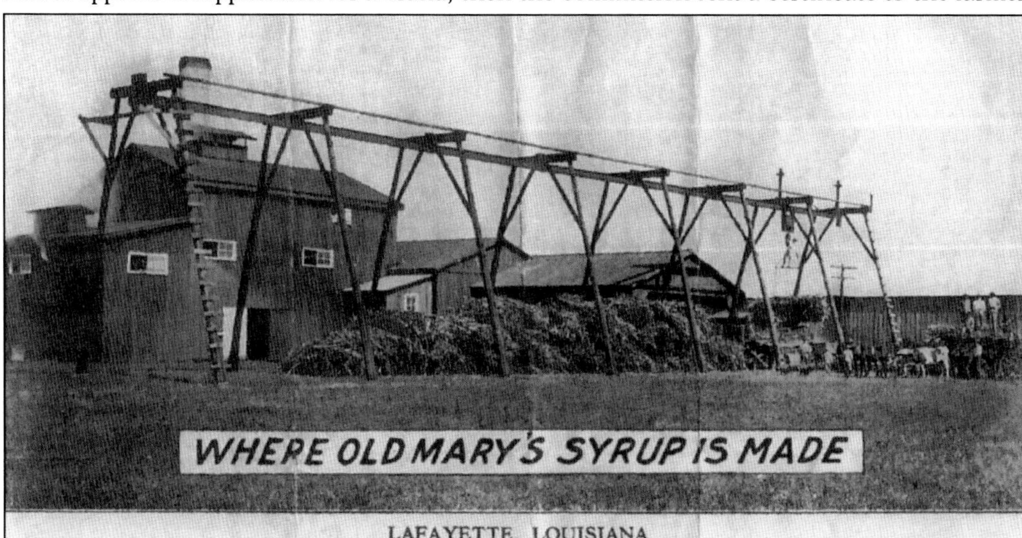

The Mary Syrup Mill was owned by the Mary family. James T. Mary hauled bricks from Washington to St. Landry Parish to build the mill. Mary Road ran alongside the syrup mill; the road has since been renamed Prejean Road.

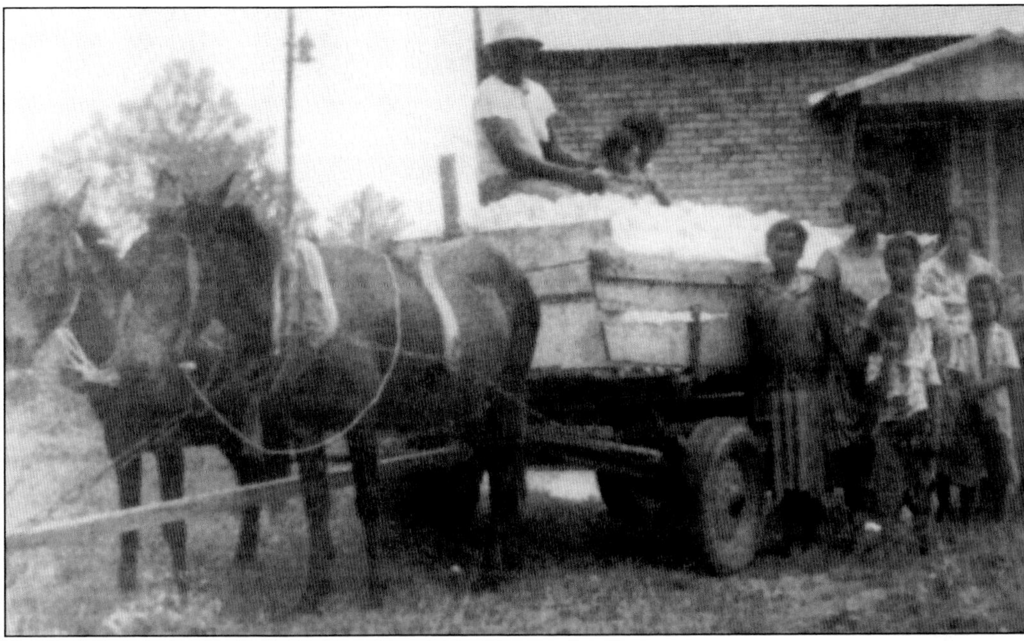

Several horse-powered cotton gins were in Carencro prior to 1876, when Ovignac Arceneaux built the first steam-powered gin in the parish. Four more gins went up in the 1880s and 1890s. Over 1,800 bales of cotton were shipped from Carencro Station in 1889. The last two cotton gins to stand in Carencro were Cotton Products Company, which was operated by Wallace Broussard, and Farmer's Gin Company, which closed around 1970. Pictured is a tenant farmer and his family after a day of picking cotton.

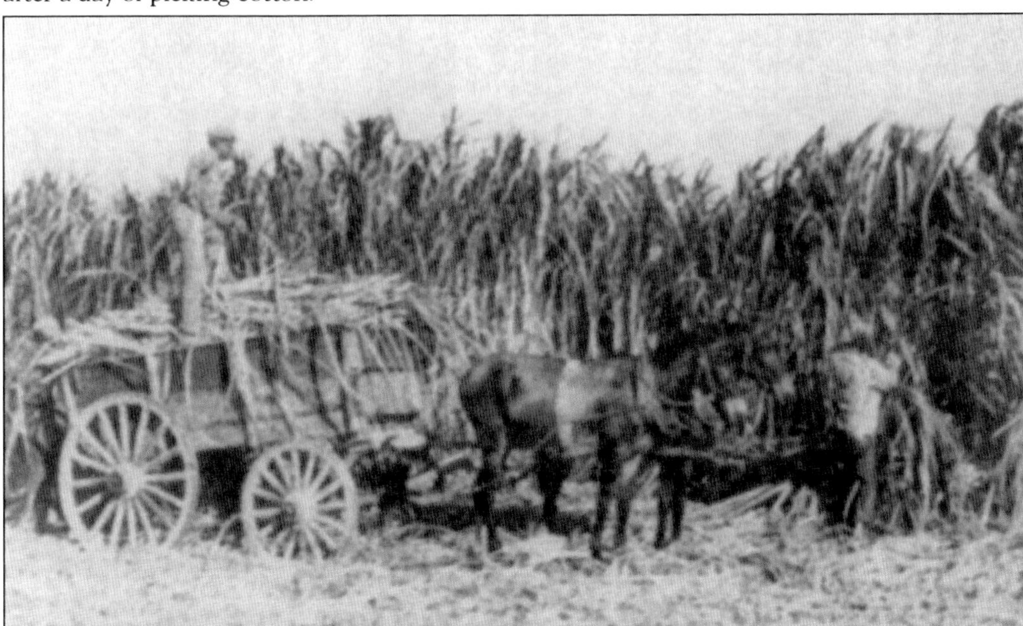

This c. 1910 photograph shows a farmer cutting sugar cane by hand. In 1889, Carencro had two sugar factories. One was operated by J.C. Couvillion and the other by G.L. Singleton. In 1894, Victor E. Dupuis formed Carencro Sugar Company next to the Morgan's Louisiana and Texas Railroad.

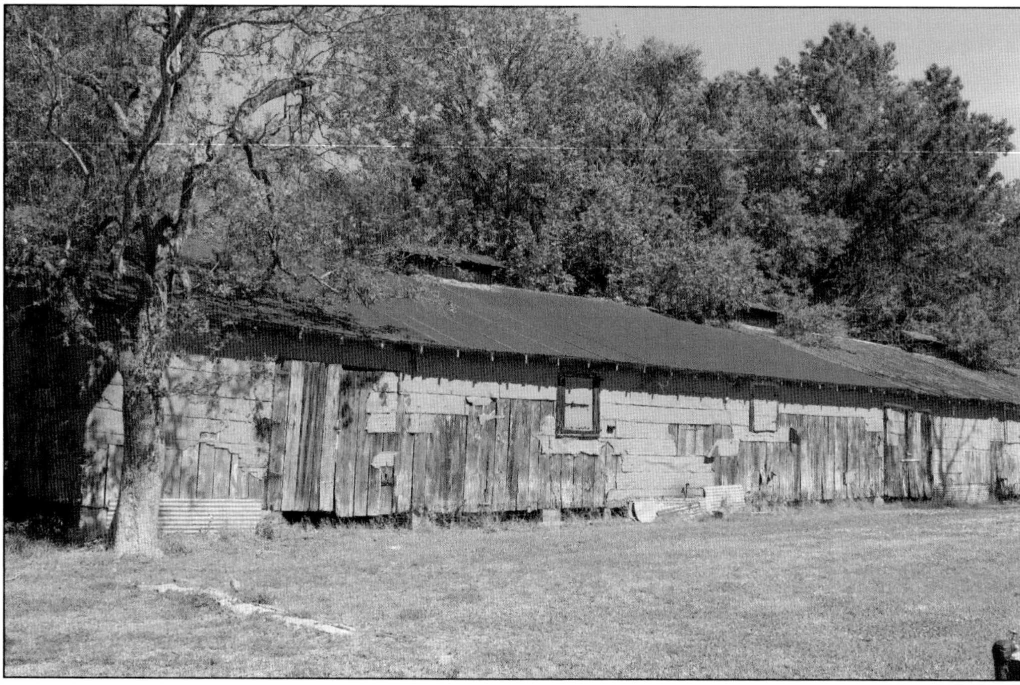

Sweet potatoes were a big part of farm life in Carencro. The railroad tracks ran behind several potato barns (kilns). More sweet potatoes were shipped from Carencro and Sunset than any other part of the state. In Carencro, Carencro Sweet Potato Co-Op, Artus "Fils" Angelle, Will Angelle, Theo Breaux, Simon Latour, Edwin Guilbeau, Cyprien Roy, Jean Conques & Sons, Christopher Dupuis, John Guilbeau, and Paul Breaux were all owners of sweet potato kilns.

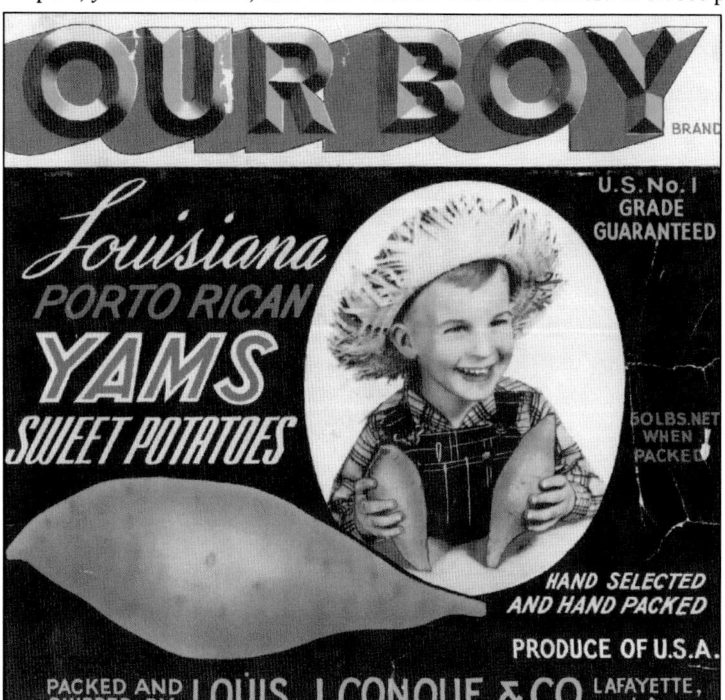

Louis Conque & Co. was one sweet potato broker in the Carencro area. Pictured on the label attached to the company's sweet potato crates was Conque's five-year-old son, Durwood J. Conque, who later became a district judge. (Conque family.)

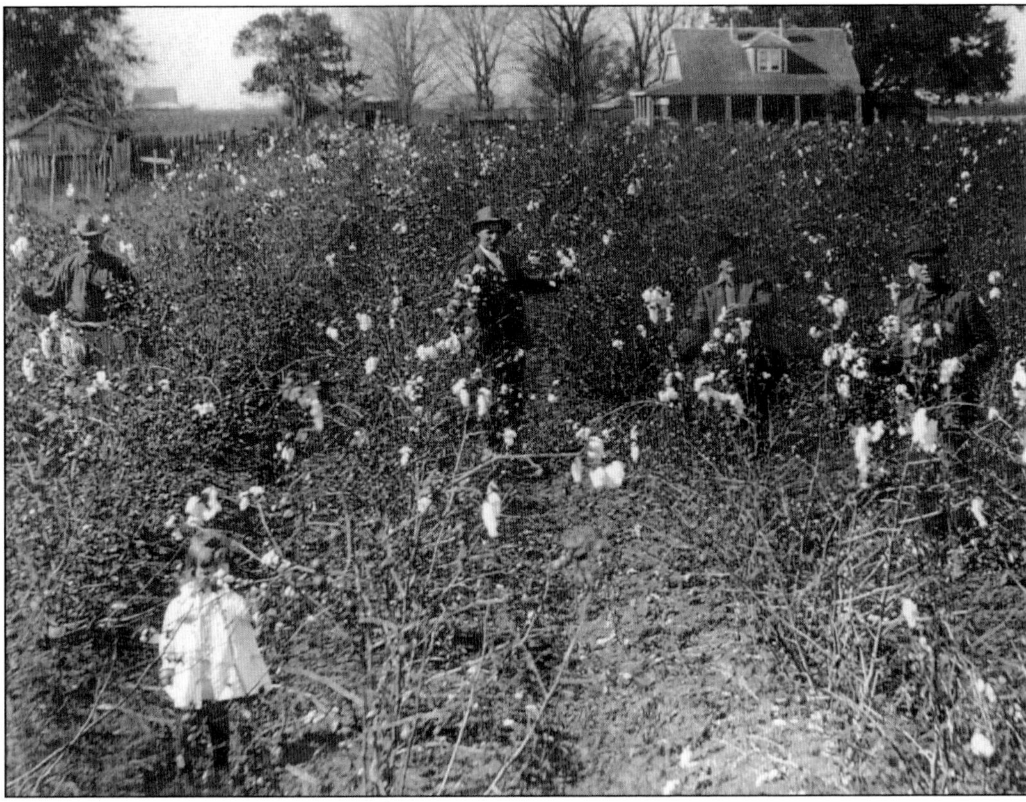

This is the home of Jules Mamer, who was paid a visit from government agents to help solve the beetle problem that affected area crops. Around the 1920s, the boll weevil, a beetle that feeds on cotton buds, ruined many cotton crops in the village of Carencro and across the South. In 1921, Mamer experimented with using Argentine ants, predators of boll weevils, to help control the infestation. The little girl is Anna Grace Martin Richard.

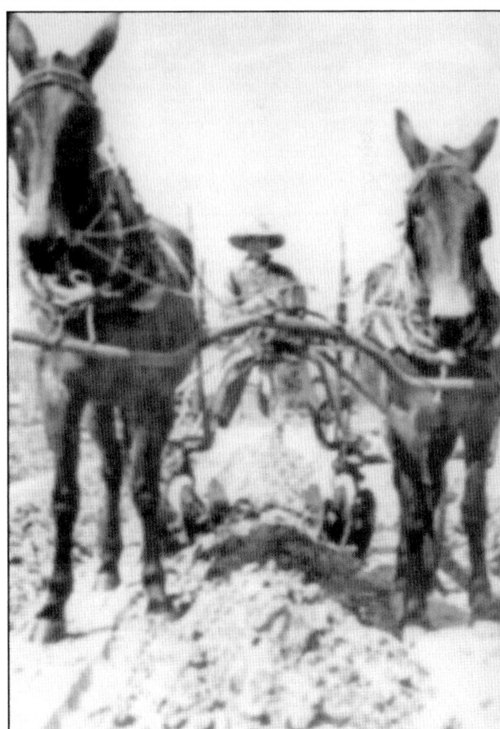

This Carencro Prairie farmer is getting his land ready for the planting of crops.

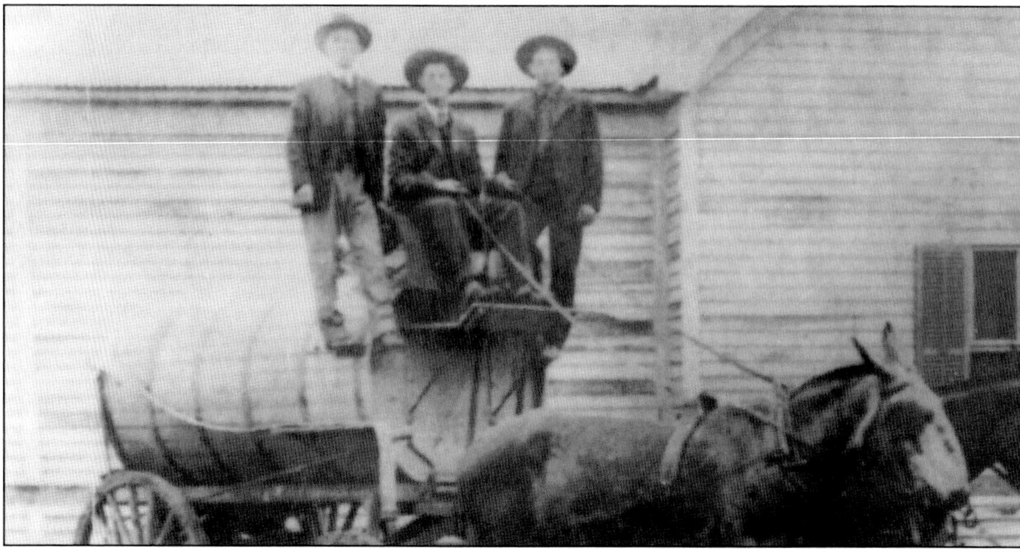

Water wagons were used to wet the dirt roads. Pictured here in 1912 are, from left to right, Overton Rowan, Cyprien Ploett, and Amar Kidder.

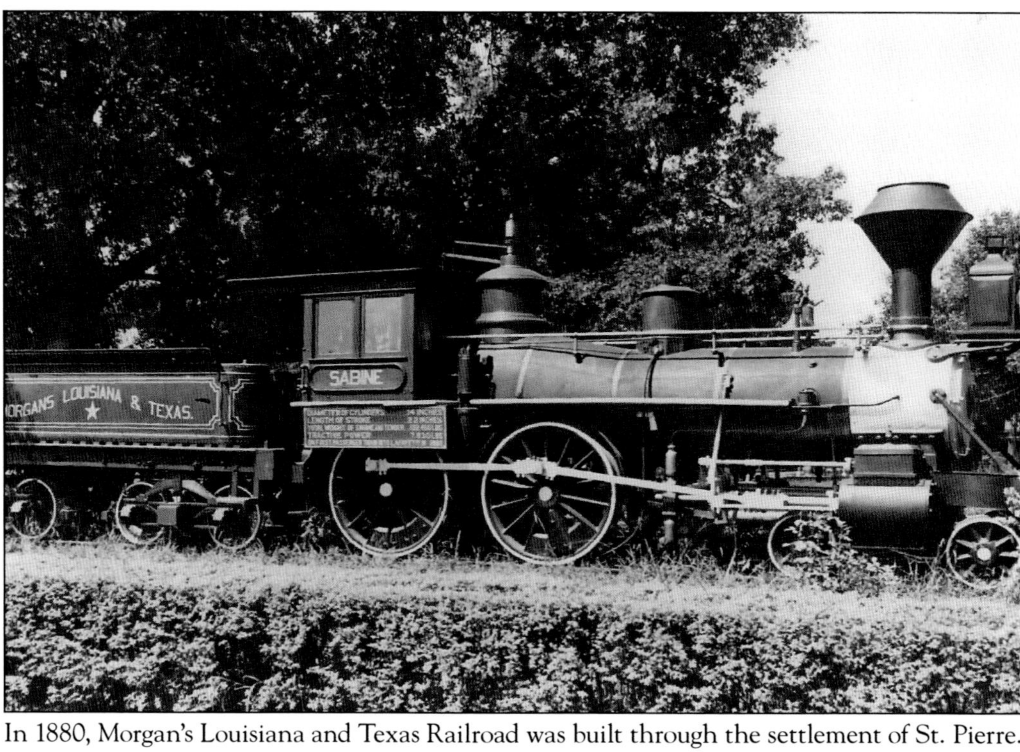

In 1880, Morgan's Louisiana and Texas Railroad was built through the settlement of St. Pierre.

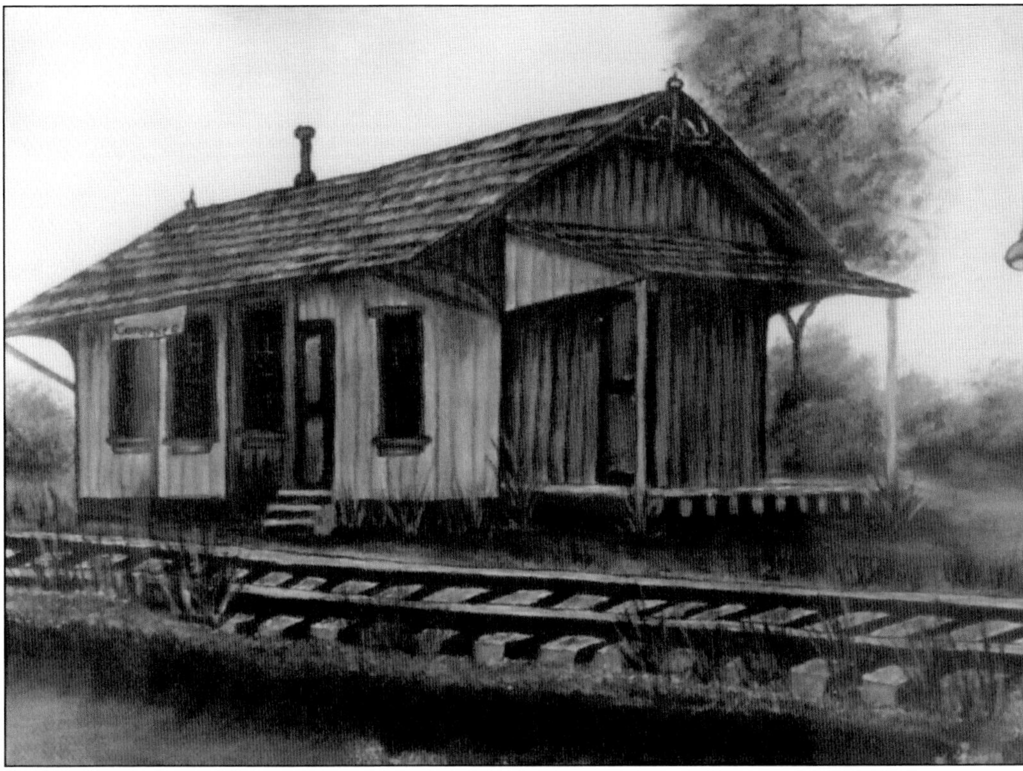

The train depot in the Carencro Prairie was full of activity as visitors traveled in and out of the area. It was also used for the shipping of goods. In 1898, there was a huge train accident in which nine freight cars were derailed on Alexandria Branch near Carencro. (Janice Martin.)

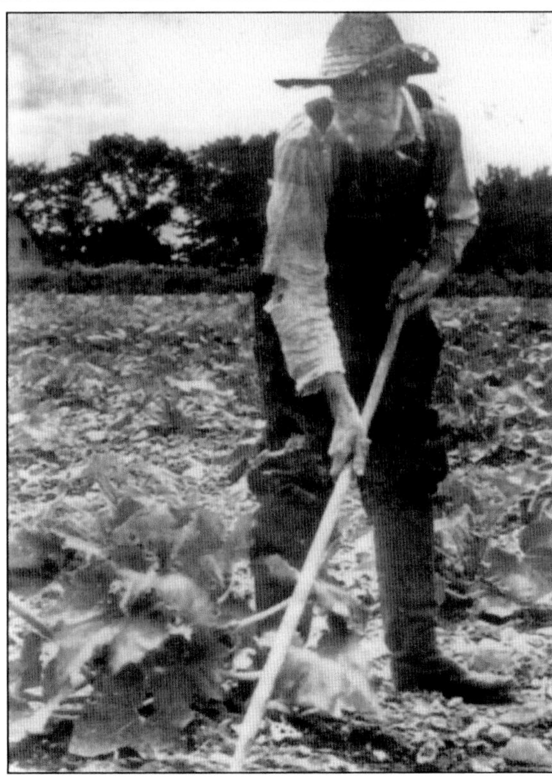

Mable Prejean works in his tobacco field in the Carencro Prairie.

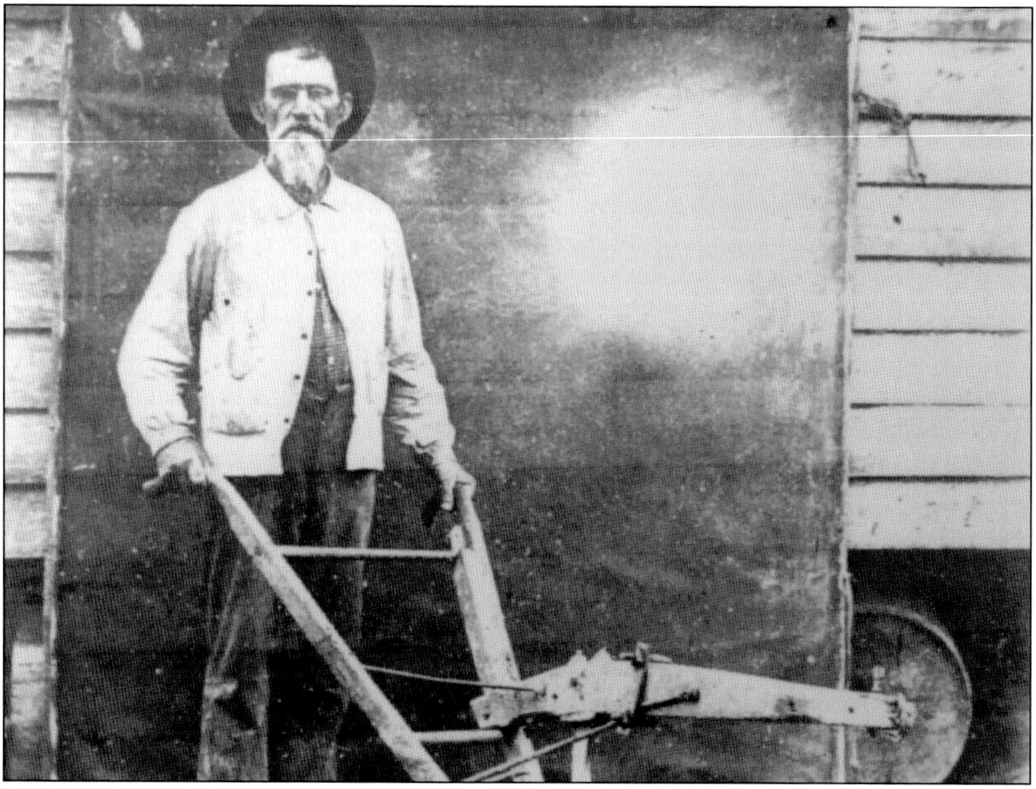

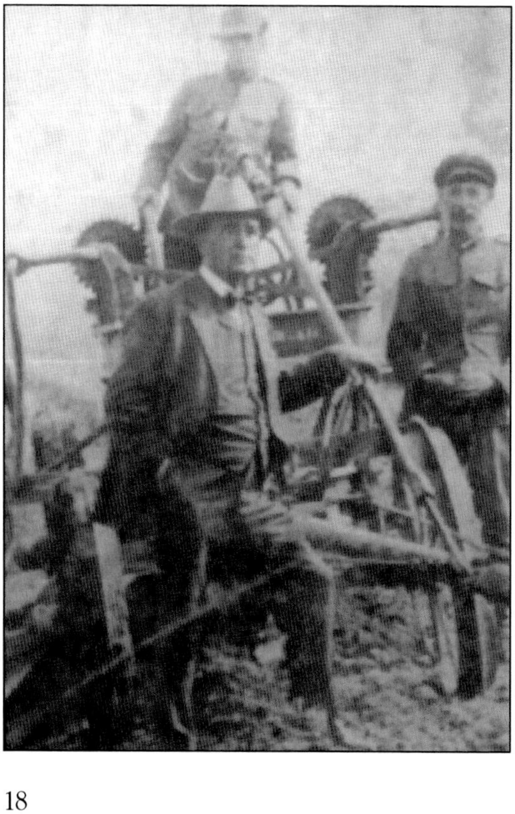

Vincent Hernandez was a farmer in the Carencro Prairie. He is shown here with a plow that he invented. He attached a contraption to the plow to ease the job of digging sweet potatoes from the ground. The device cleared the vines on the sides of the rows, leaving the potatoes more manageable for picking. (St. Pierre Genealogical Society and Daisy Hernandez.)

This early 1900s road-grading crew included, from left to right, John Latour, Simonette Breaux, and Felix Bacque. (Louis Perret.)

The grounds of Evangeline Memorial Gardens, the cemetery next to Melancon Funeral Home on University Avenue, once featured oak trees lined up in rows along a dirt road that led to a beautiful sugar plantation home. Gilbert Borel Sr. (pictured on the plantation) was born in 1877; he purchased the property—with the sugar plantation and its many acres of farmland—from a man with the last name Jones.

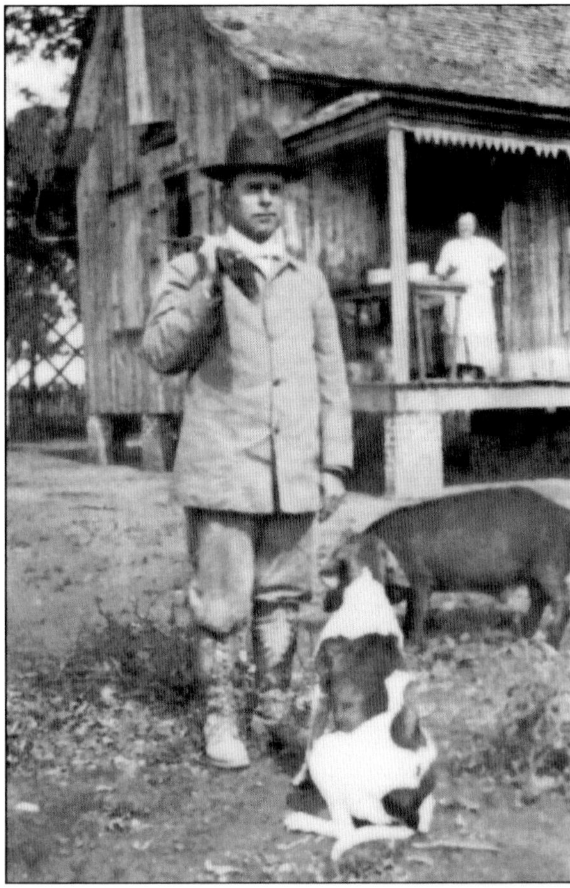

In 1940, Borel decided that the plantation was set too far back and had it torn down. He built a new home (pictured) closer to University Avenue in order to have easier access to the main road. Along with the new homestead, Borel constructed a potato kiln and a general dry goods store to meet the needs of the tenant farmers on his land. The land was eventually transferred to Gilbert Borel Jr. Another piece of history was born when Borel rented out a piece of the land and Carencro Raceways was constructed in 1960.

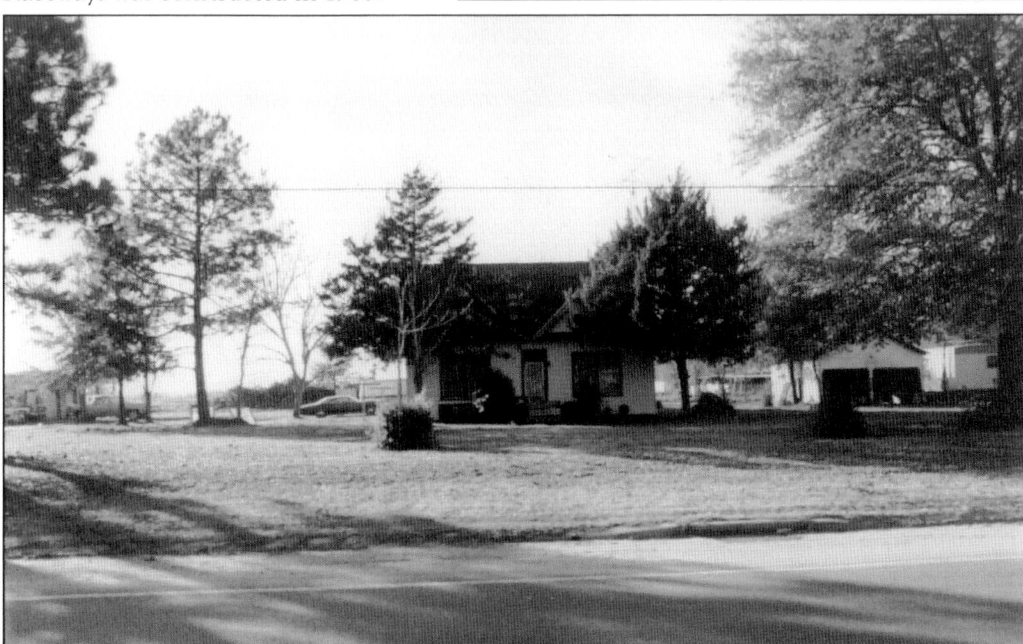

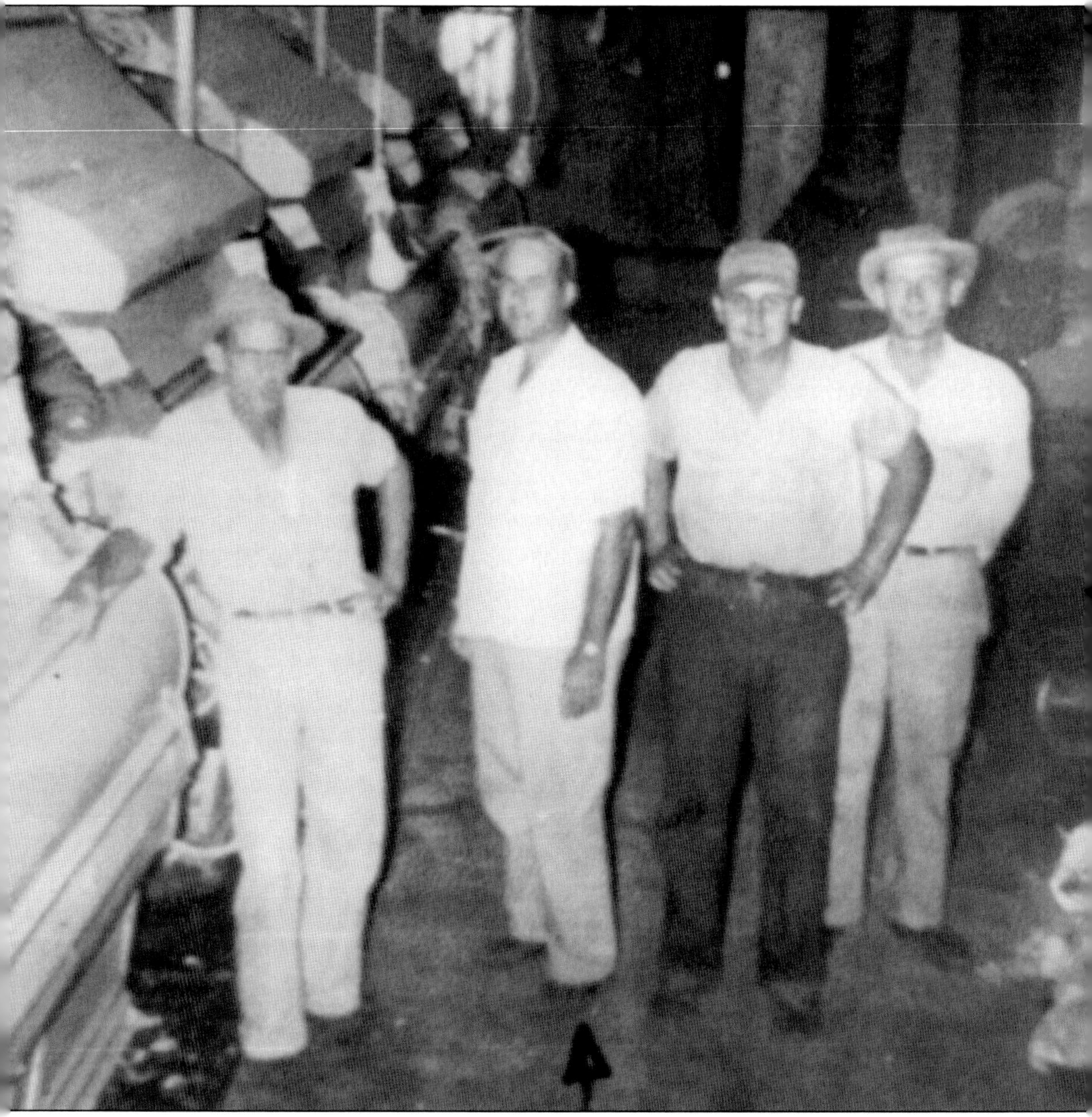

Pictured at the Cotton Gin Company are, from left to right, Marcel Roger; Wallace Broussard, manager of the gin; Elton "B-Root" Arceneaux; and Alfin Courville. Throughout the countryside of Carencro, historic barns and silos stand as reminders of the rich land that was farmed by many. Crops such as corn, soybeans, figs, peaches, pecans, rice, sweet potatoes, cotton, sugar cane, and even tobacco have grown in Carencro soil.

Two

TRUE HEROES

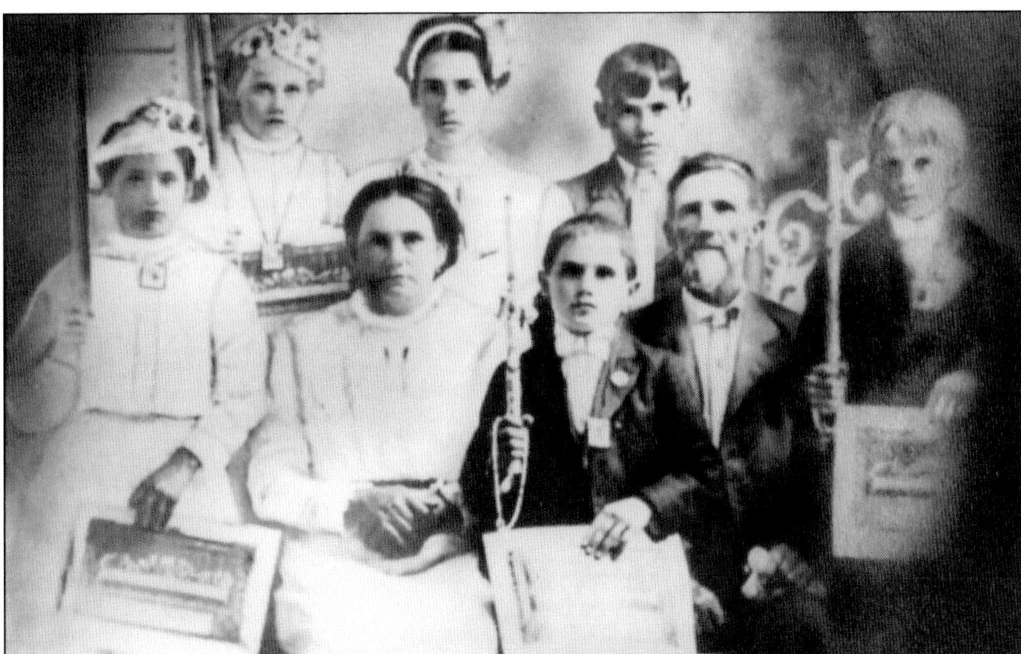

Victor Kilchrist was born in 1841 in Lafayette Parish. Kilchrist served in the Civil War in the 18th Louisiana Regiment under the command of Valein Fournet. Kilchrist filed for pension after he was accidentally injured during the war. His form reads, "Received an accidental flesh wound" and also states that he and his wives (married four times) had 18 children. He stated that he earned a living by working crops. Pictured here are, from left to right, (first row) Augustine, Josephine, Auguste, Victor, and Edmond; (second row) Edmondia, Antoinette, and Antoine.

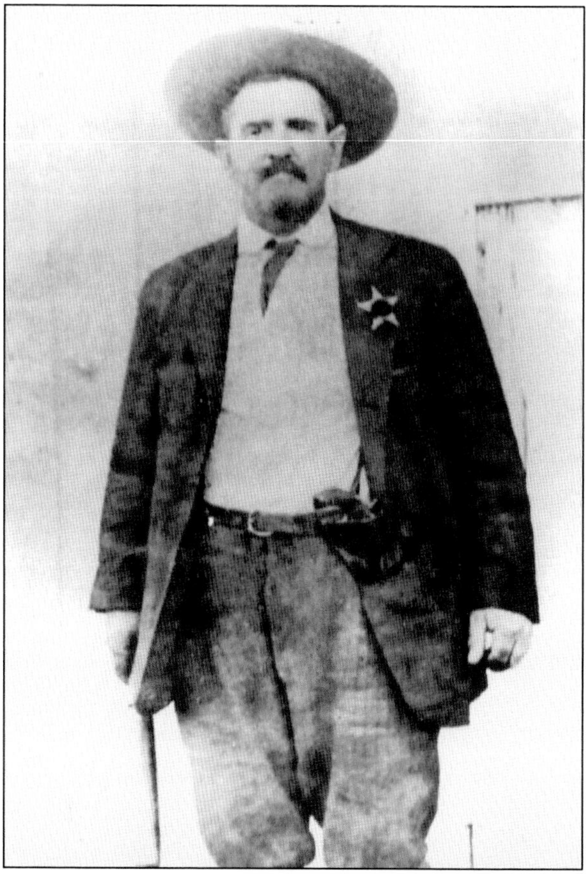

Armand Guidry was born during the Battle of Bayou Bourbeau around November 3, 1863. Guidry's mother was in the process of giving birth to him as the battle raged in a neighboring field. Many local residents feared for their lives with the battles so close to home; they packed up many of their belongings and their families with plans to flee. However, the civilians and the Union Army met on the road when traveling toward Carencro. (Susie Perry.)

The David Guidry home served as a field hospital for Union troops during the Civil War. The home was then located in the Carencro Prairie on L'Isle de Carencro property. Today, it is located in St. Landry Parish just outside of Carencro due to the rezoning of lands between Lafayette and St. Landry Parishes. The Battle of Bayou Bourbeau was fought near the home.

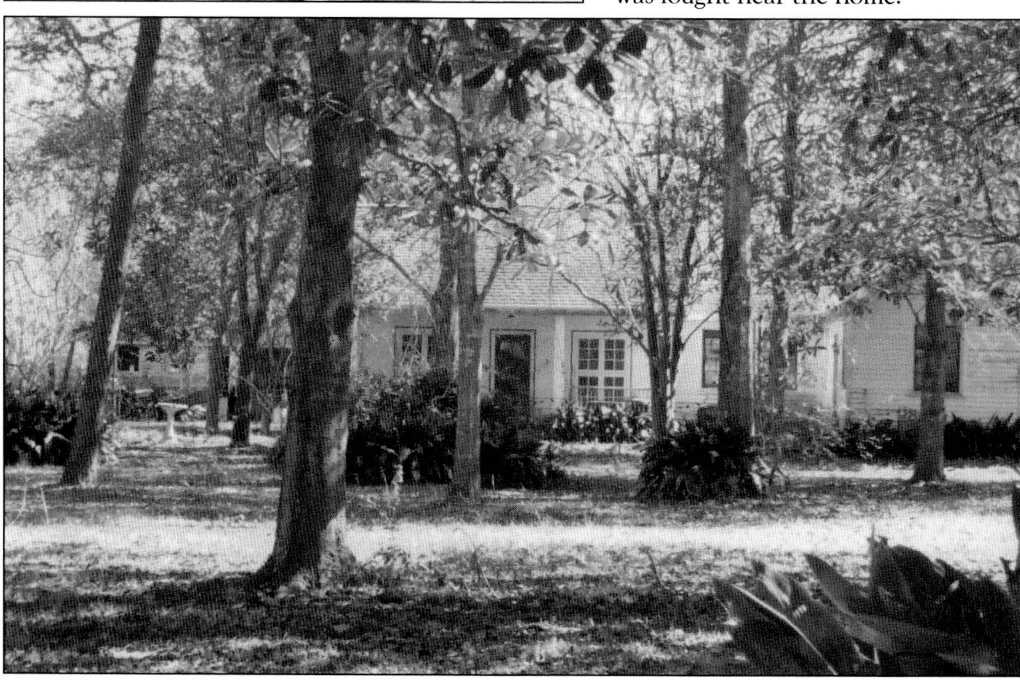

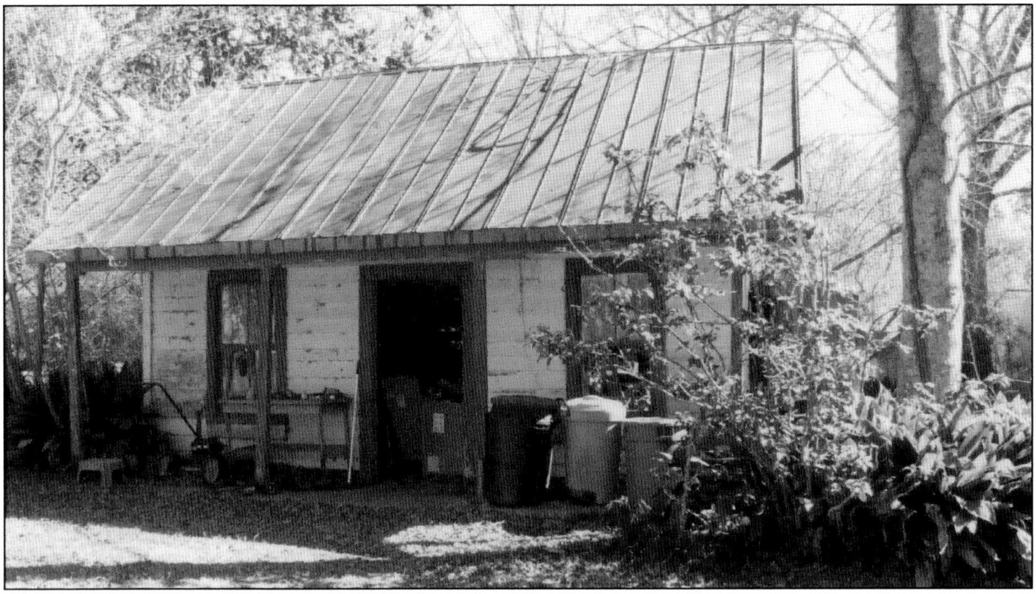

This building on the grounds of the Guidry Home is worn and dated. In researching accounts of the village of Carencro mentioned in Civil War History, this journal entry was discovered in the diary of Confederate soldier First Sgt. H.N. Connor: "Oct. 10, 1863: Enemy advanced across bayou. We fell back some 8 miles and formed line of battle, having a battery [of artillery] to support. Enemy fell back to Vermilion. We encamped for night on Carron Crow [Carencro Bayou]. Oct. 13, 14, 1863: Enemy falling back to Carencro with 'plunder.' Saddled up and advanced on enemy. Green's Brigade drove in their pickets near Grand Coteau Bayou or Boggy Bayou. Enemy fell back to Carencro. We camped near Boggy Bayou."

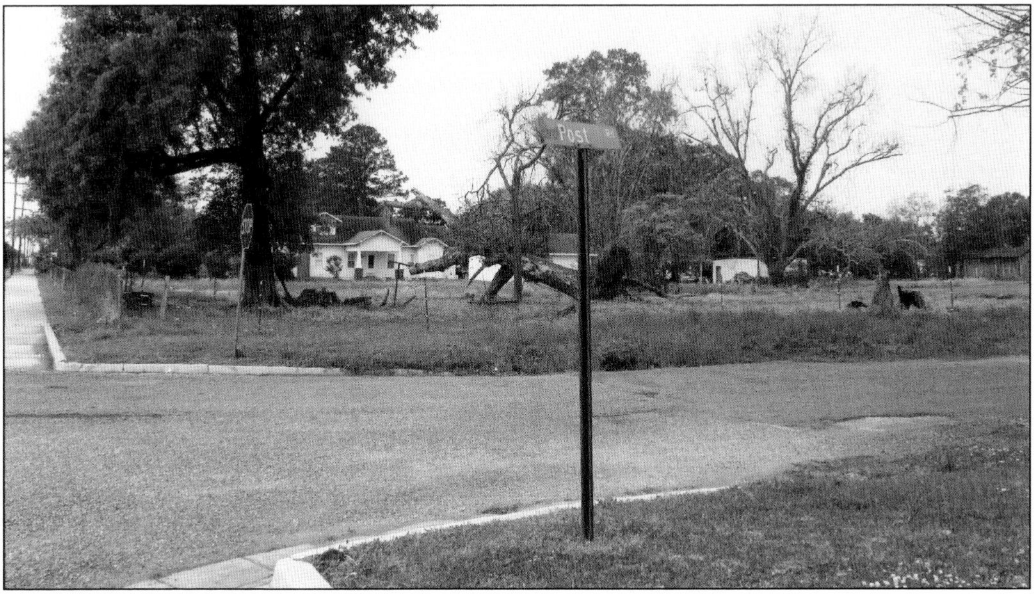

During the Civil War, the Battle of Bayou Bourbeau was fought in the areas of Carencro and Grand Coteau on November 3, 1863. Over 25,000 soldiers traveled along what is now Highway 182. Post Road's historic oaks (pictured) offered shade to federal soldiers traveling from Donaldsonville prior to the battle in the Carencro Prairie. Official records call it the Battle of Carrion Crow.

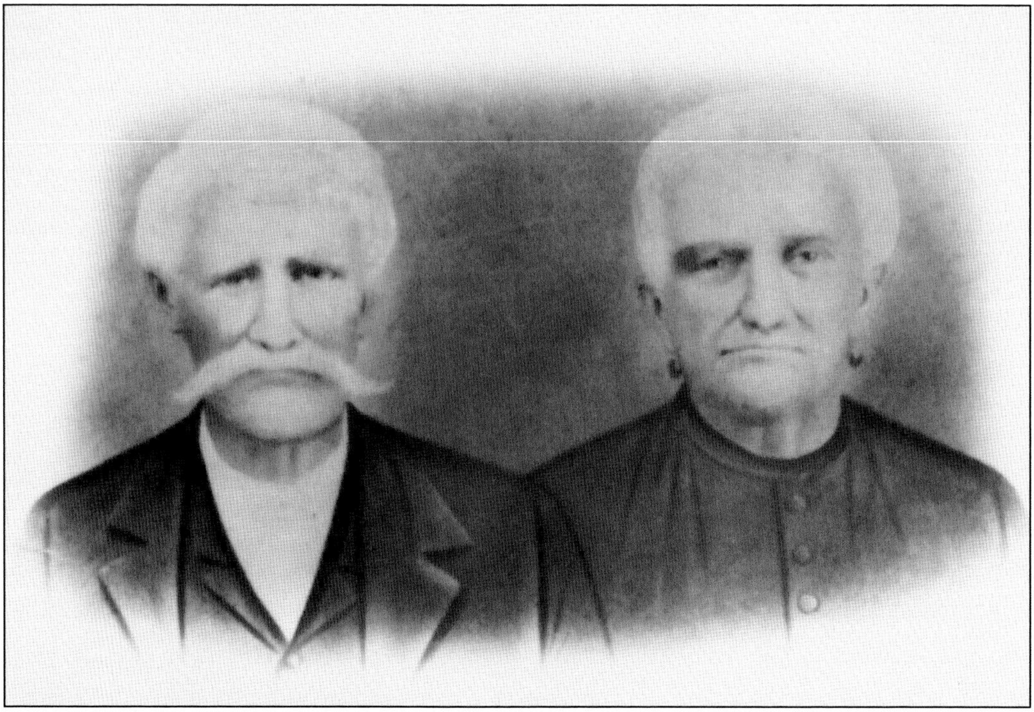

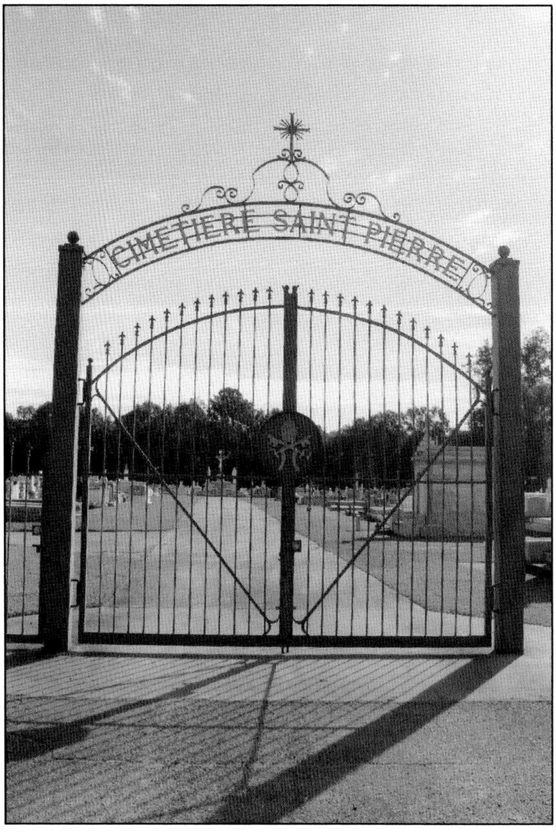

Hypolite Arceneaux (left) was a descendant of Louis Pierre Arceneaux, a founding father of the Carencro Prairie. He was born in 1860 and married Azelema Benoit (right), daughter of Augustin Benoît and Anastasie Babineaux, in 1857. Hypolite served in the Civil War under Company K, 18th Louisiana Infantry. Hypolite and Azelema had 10 children. (Roy and Bernadine Comeaux.)

St. Pierre Cemetery, on the side of the historic St. Peter Roman Catholic Church, holds over 60 Civil War veterans and over 70 World War I veterans. It is also home to Korean, Vietnam, and Iraq war veterans. Many veterans have also been laid to rest down the road at Our Lady of the Assumption Church Cemetery.

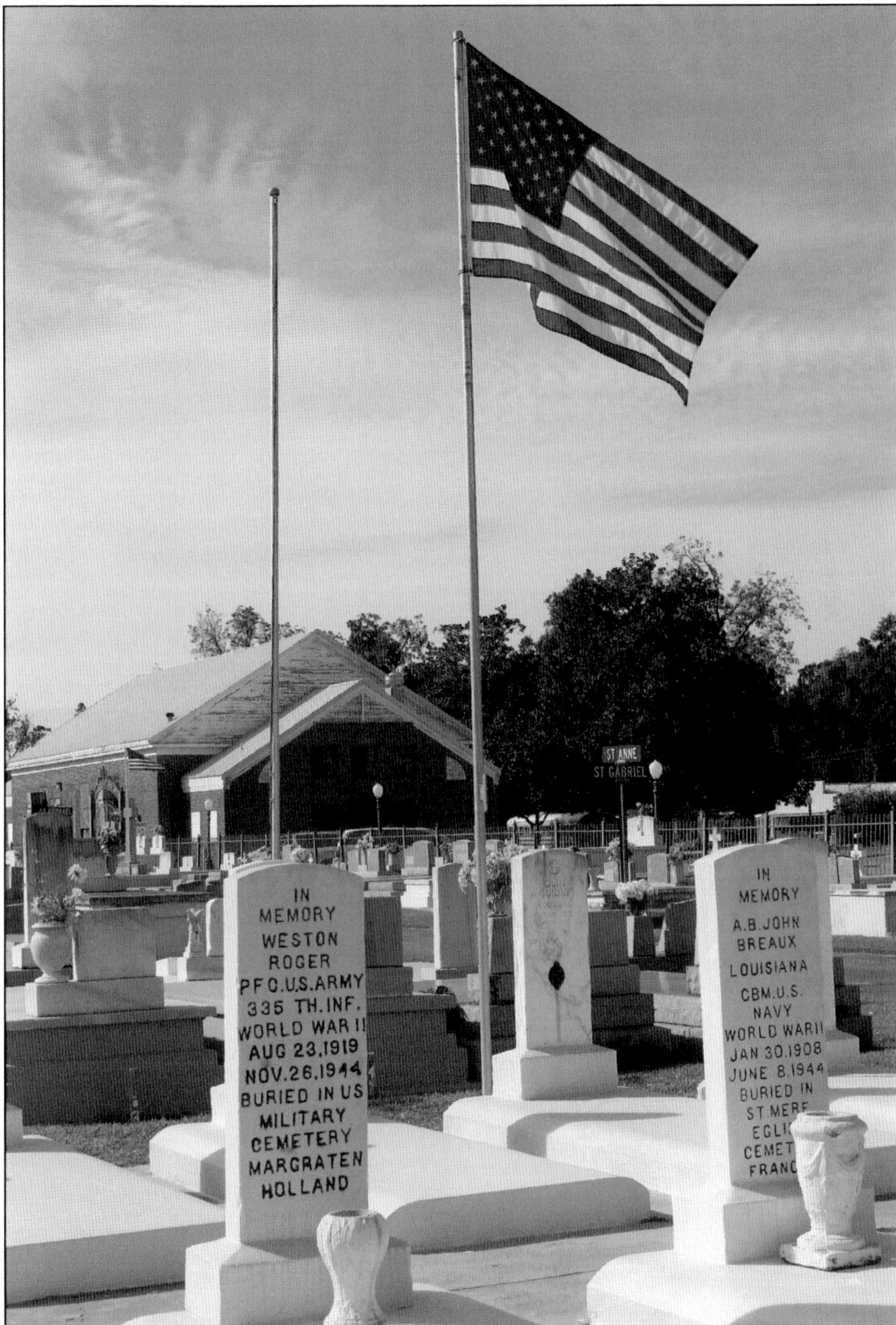

The designated veterans' area of St. Pierre Cemetery was donated by Fr. Auguste Wassler when he was pastor of the church. These headstones honor soldiers who died in service but whose bodies were buried elsewhere. These soldiers' graves offer a glimpse of the true heroes of Carencro. The headstone of Weston Roger, pictured here, tells of the pain that a family endured upon hearing their son had passed away. A solider from Carencro who died in battle is laid to rest thousands of miles away but is remembered here by a family who had to say goodbye too soon.

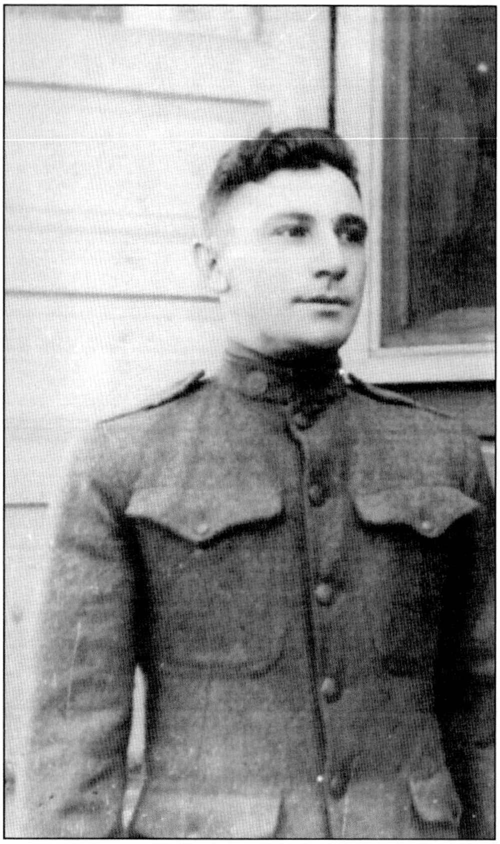

The names of these soldiers have been lost to time. However, the city of Carencro honors veterans yearly with the Carencro Veterans Day Program in November. This reminds the community that veterans from Carencro and beyond will always live in the hearts of the people.

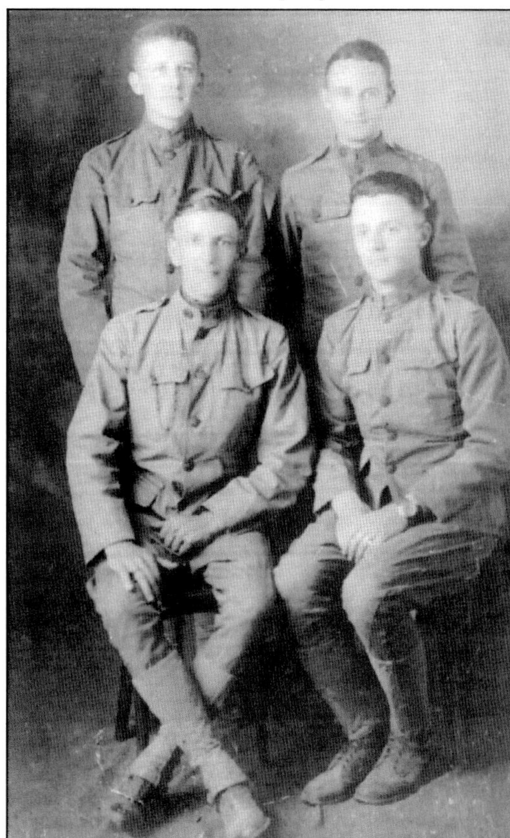

Aldus Roger was a soldier from the Carencro area.

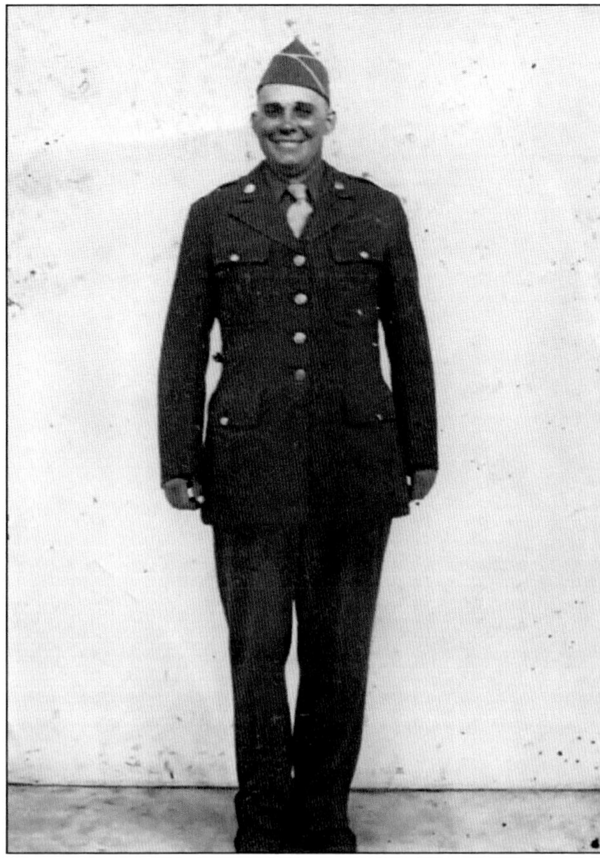

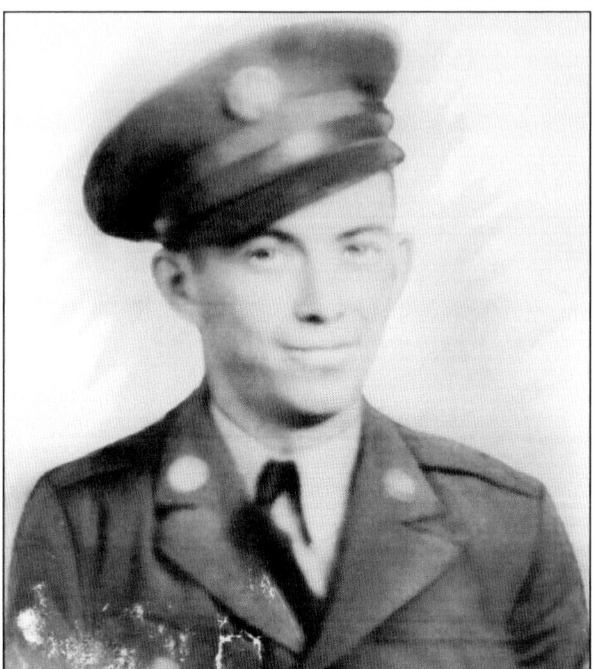

Olin Guidry, a Carencro resident, served the United States in World War II.

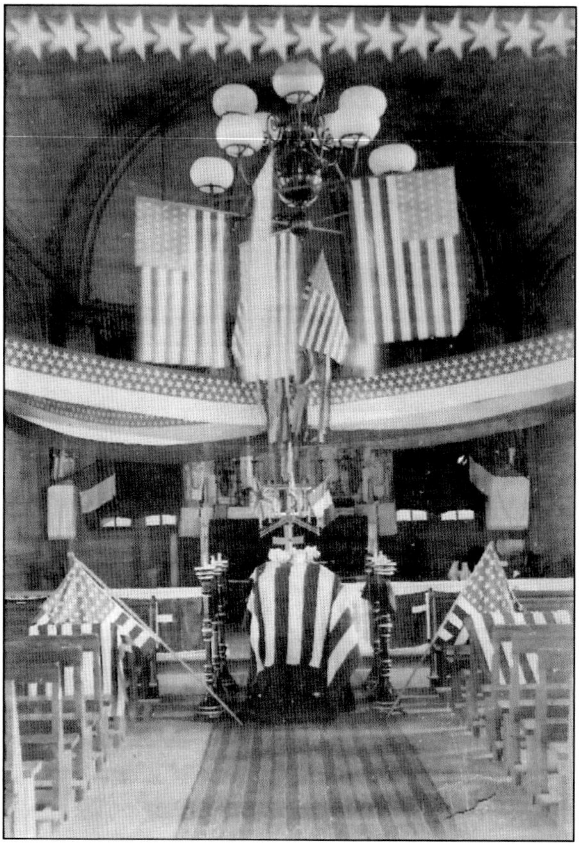

Olin Guidry's funeral was held at St. Peter Roman Catholic Church in downtown Carencro. The tribute to a fallen soldier is evident in this photograph.

This building, located on 107 North Church Street, served as a small grocery store during World War II. It later became the first Carencro library. Duchesene Guidry was the first librarian. (Louis Perret.)

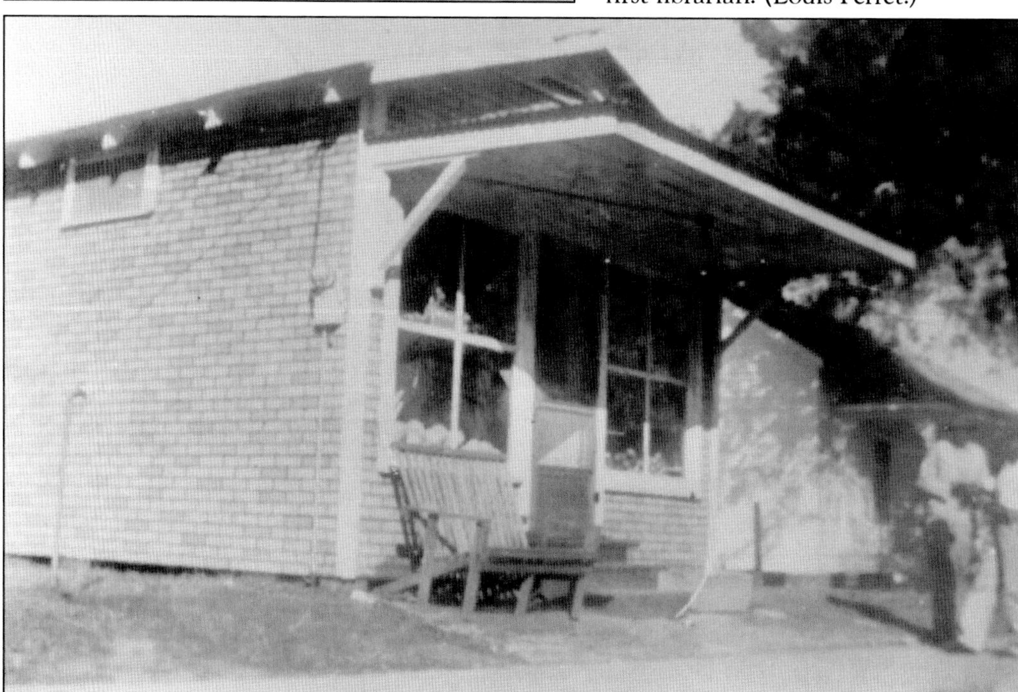

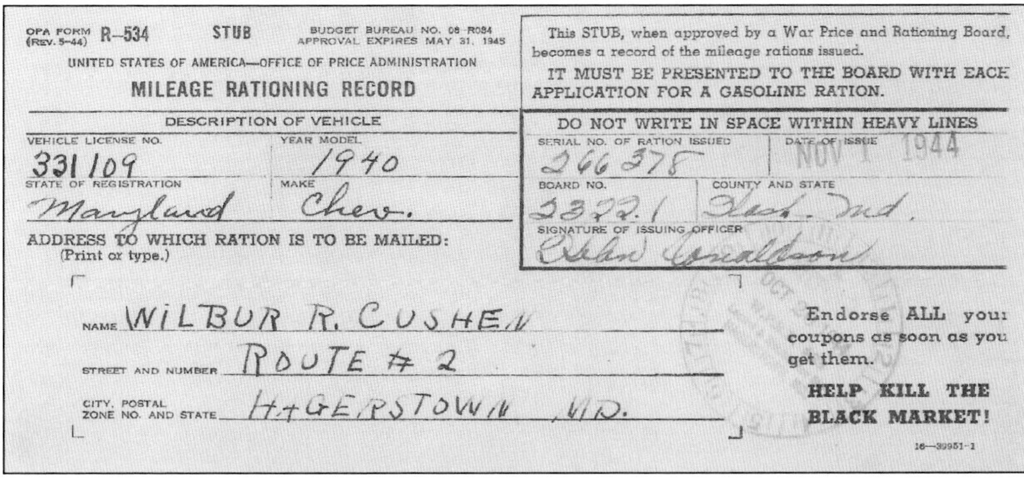

OPA FORM R-534 (REV. 5-44) STUB BUDGET BUREAU NO. 08-R084 APPROVAL EXPIRES MAY 31, 1945

UNITED STATES OF AMERICA—OFFICE OF PRICE ADMINISTRATION

MILEAGE RATIONING RECORD

This STUB, when approved by a War Price and Rationing Board, becomes a record of the mileage rations issued.

IT MUST BE PRESENTED TO THE BOARD WITH EACH APPLICATION FOR A GASOLINE RATION.

DESCRIPTION OF VEHICLE

VEHICLE LICENSE NO. 331109 YEAR MODEL 1940

STATE OF REGISTRATION Maryland MAKE Chev.

DO NOT WRITE IN SPACE WITHIN HEAVY LINES

SERIAL NO. OF RATION ISSUED 266378 DATE OF ISSUE NOV 1 1944

BOARD NO. 3322.1 COUNTY AND STATE [illegible] Ind.

SIGNATURE OF ISSUING OFFICER [illegible]

ADDRESS TO WHICH RATION IS TO BE MAILED: (Print or type.)

NAME WILBUR R. CUSHEN

STREET AND NUMBER ROUTE # 2

CITY, POSTAL ZONE NO. AND STATE HAGERSTOWN, MD.

Endorse ALL your coupons as soon as you get them.

HELP KILL THE BLACK MARKET!

16—30951-1

During World War II, the federal government distributed ration cards in order to conserve items such as food, gas, and clothing. Rationing helped bring neighbors together, since they could share ration coupons. In Mouton's Grocery Store, a special phone was installed under lock and key to assist in the country's civil air defense. The store owner was only to use the phone if someone spotted strange activity in the sky around the area.

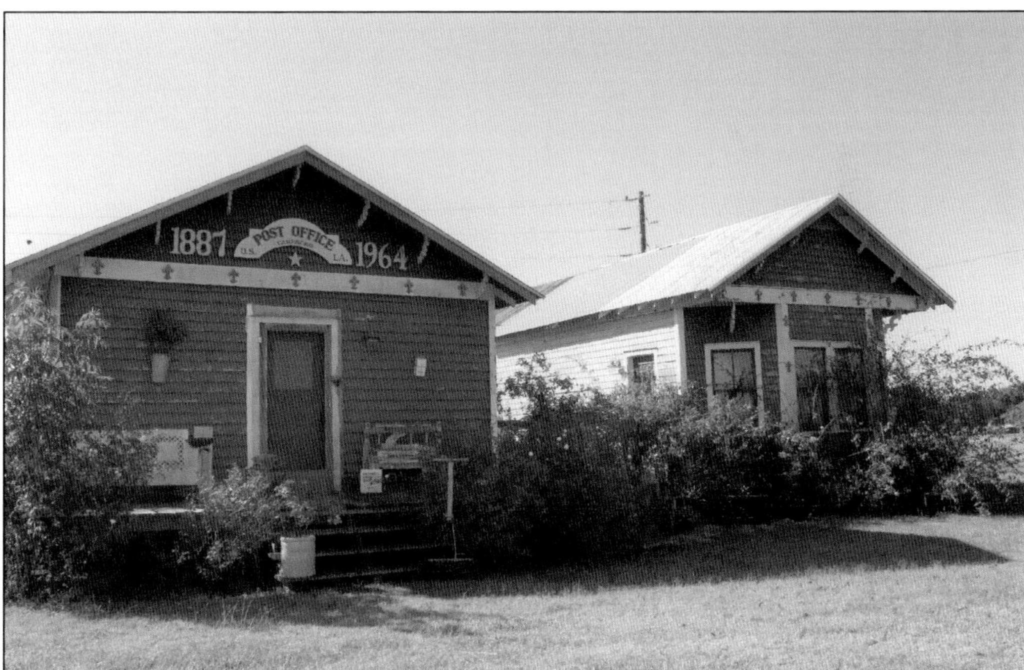

During World Wars I and II, residents lined up to receive mail at the old Carencro Post Office, pictured here on the left. The gathering was always filled with hope that loved ones overseas were alive and well.

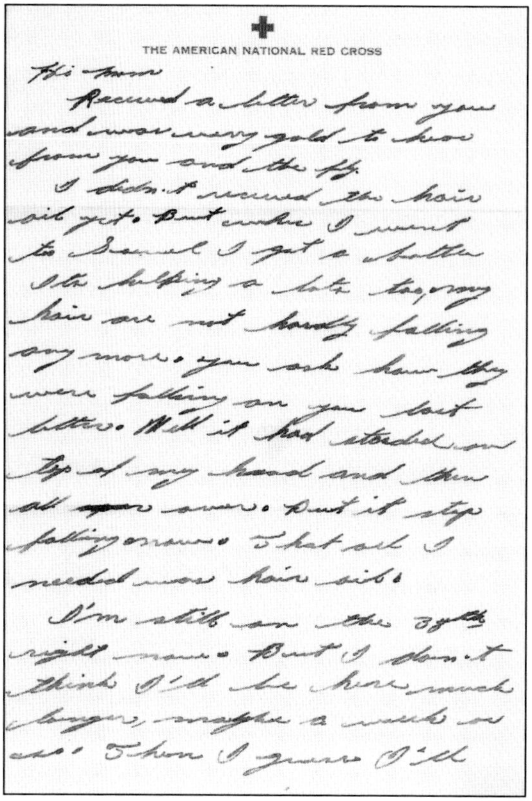

THE AMERICAN NATIONAL RED CROSS

Hi-mom

Received a letter from you and was very glad to hear from you and the fly.

I didn't received the hair oil yet. But when I went to Daniel I got a bottle. Its helping a lots to my hair are not hardly falling any more. you ask how they were falling on you last letter. Well it had started on top of my head and then all over. But it stop falling now. That all I needed was hair oil.

I'm still on the 39th right now. But I don't think I'll be here much longer, maybe a week or so. Then I guess I'll

The American Red Cross supplied stationery to soldiers. This is a soldier's letter to his mother on Red Cross stationery.

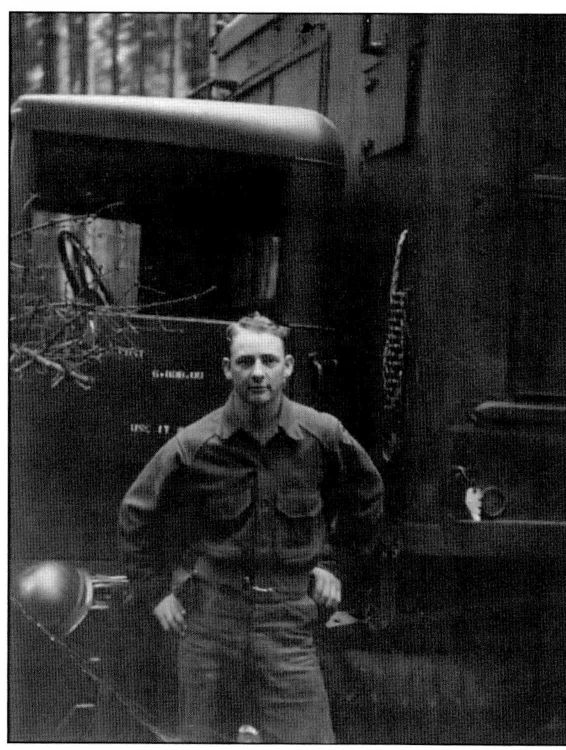

Soldier Wibert Roger is standing in front of an Army vehicle.

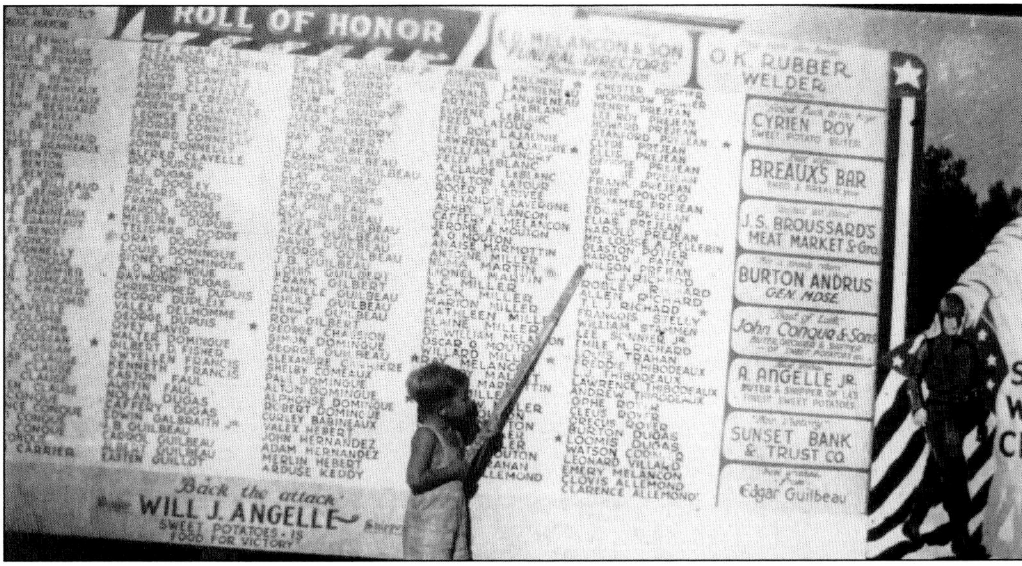

This board stood in front of St. Peter Roman Catholic Church during World War II. It listed all the boys from Carencro in service. Charles Richard is pointing to his father's name, C.J. Richard Jr. In this 1943 photograph, Charles is three years old. (Janice Martin.)

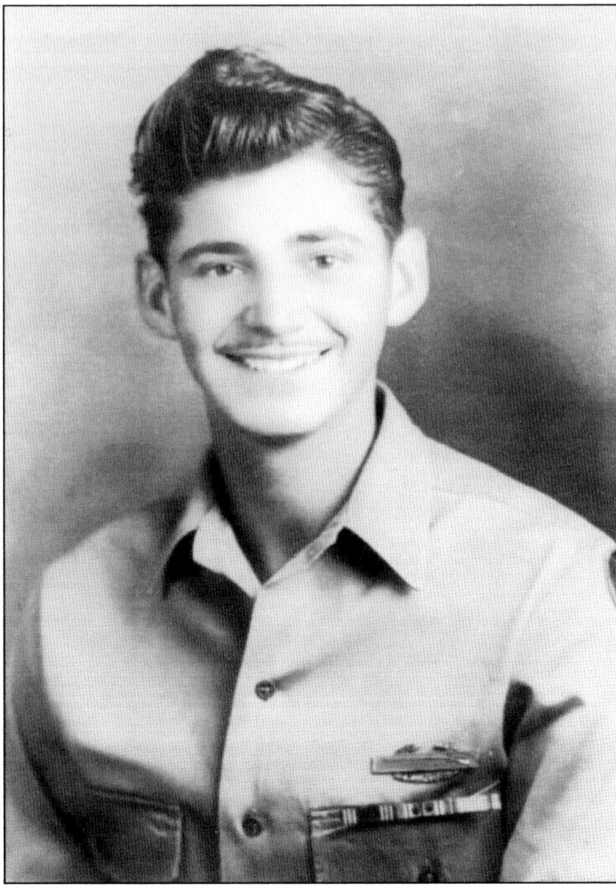

The Battle of Iwo Jima occurred from February 19 to March 26, 1945. This was a major battle in which the US armed forces captured the island of Iwo Jima from Japan. E.J. Guilbeau, pictured here, fought in the battle.

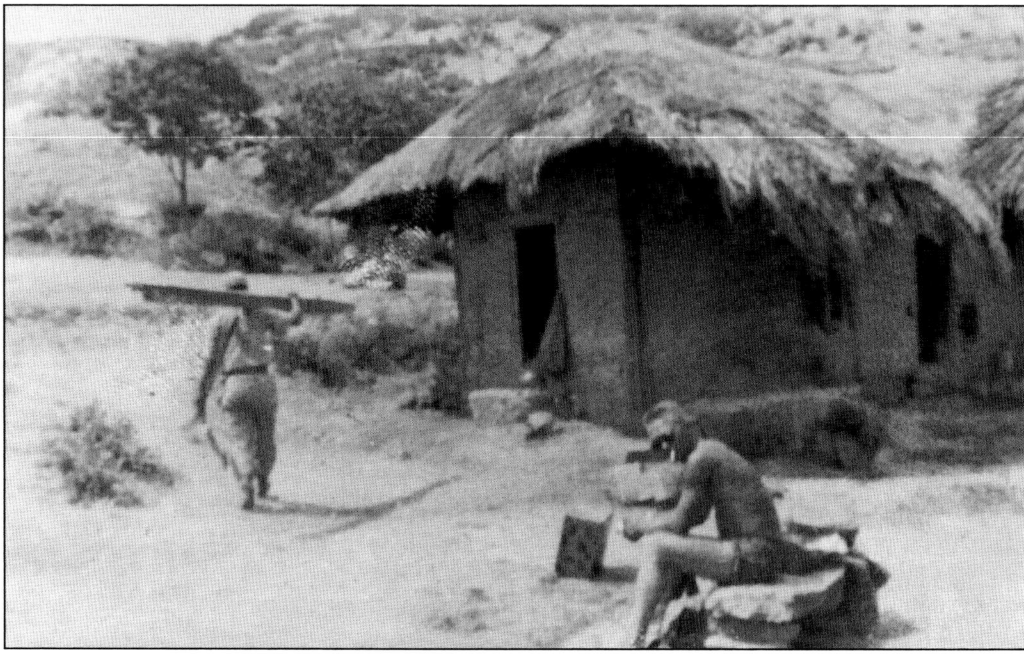

Floyd LeBouef relaxes in camp during the Korean War.

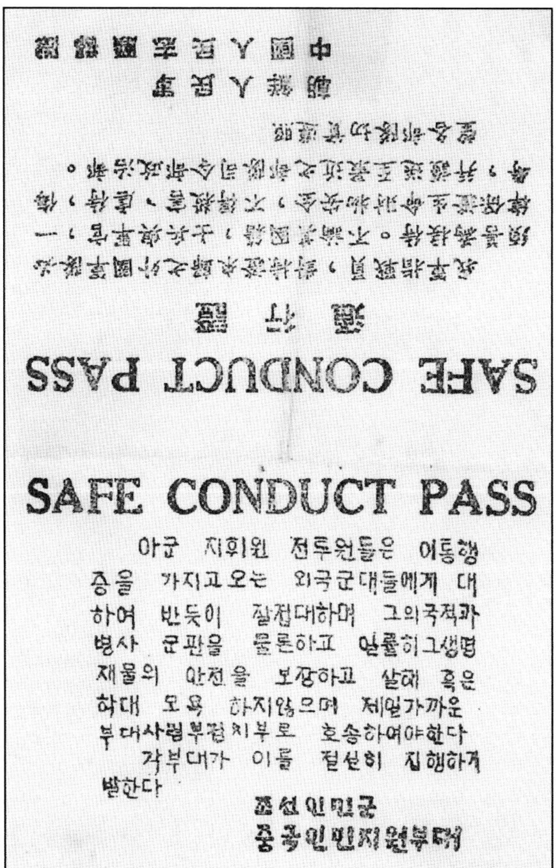

The Safe Conduct Pass was used during the Korean War by US troops. This card was issued to a Carencro soldier. It reads: "The bearer, regardless of his military rank or nationality, is hereby unconditionally guaranteed freedom from personal injury, maltreatment or abuse."

Douglas N. Harper, a US Navy veteran, experienced the bombings at Pearl Harbor and the Battle of Okinawa. He passed away in 2014 at age 90. In his memoir *Pearl Harbor*, Harper wrote, "I worked the Naval Receiving Station at Pearl Harbor. On December 7, 1941, we awoke to a cloud of smoke from the bombings. I noticed a plane flying above with what I thought looked like a meatball on its wing. I looked up and actually saw the pilot shaking his fist at us." (Velma Harper.)

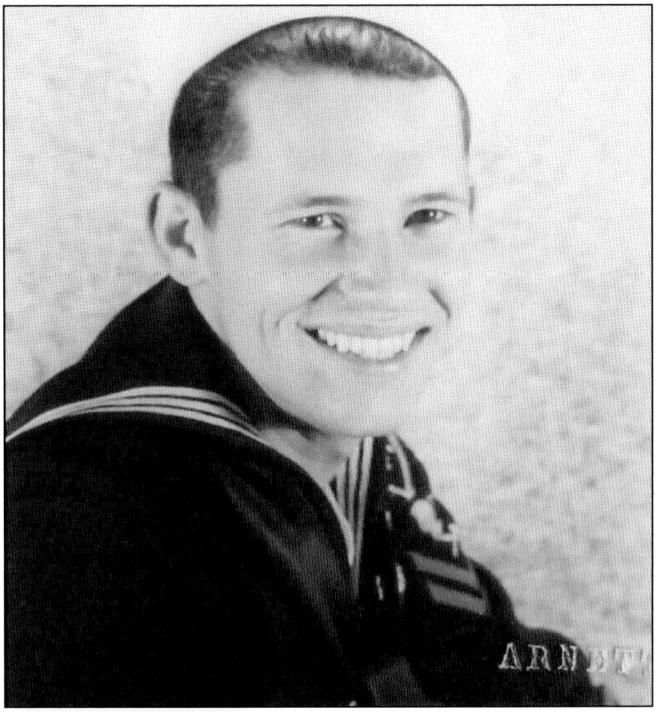

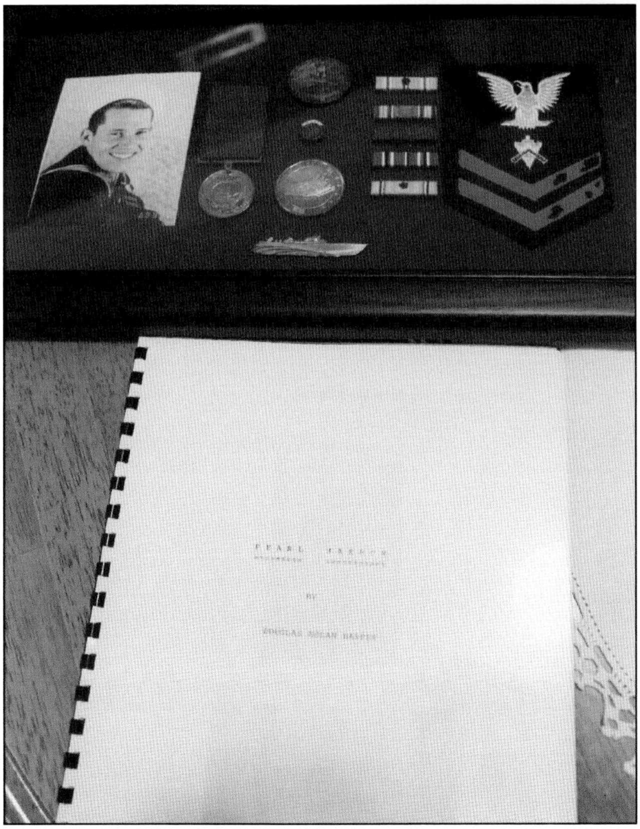

By the afternoon, the attacks had stopped, but the Americans were sure that more attacks would come. That evening, Harper, along with others, saw the lights of six planes coming towards them. He recognized them as American planes, but others—who thought the enemy had returned—did not, and five of the American planes were shot down. Harper said, "This was my first real initiation in dealing with death. On that day, I saw the USS *Arizona* when the bomb hit her lifting her out of the water about 8ft. I saw the dog fights over Wheeler Field." Harper spent two more years at Pearl Harbor after the attack. (Velma Harper.)

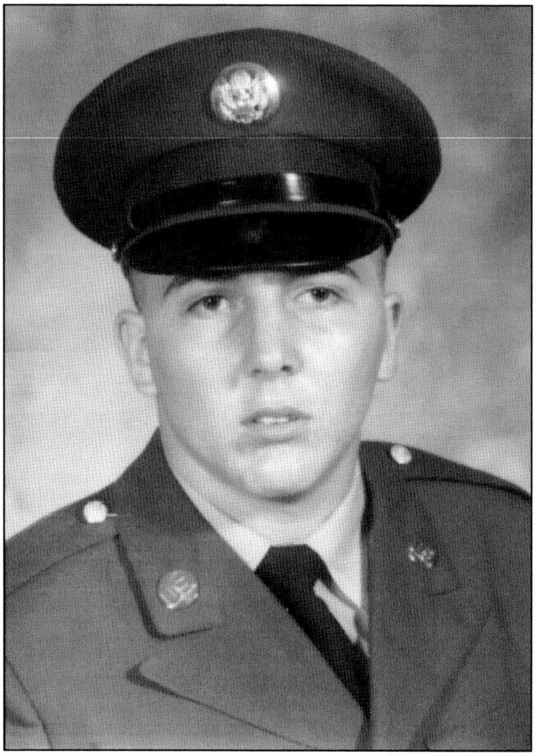

Kent A. Lee was stationed in Germany during the Vietnam War. He was enlisted from 1969 to 1971. (Carencro Veterans Day Program.)

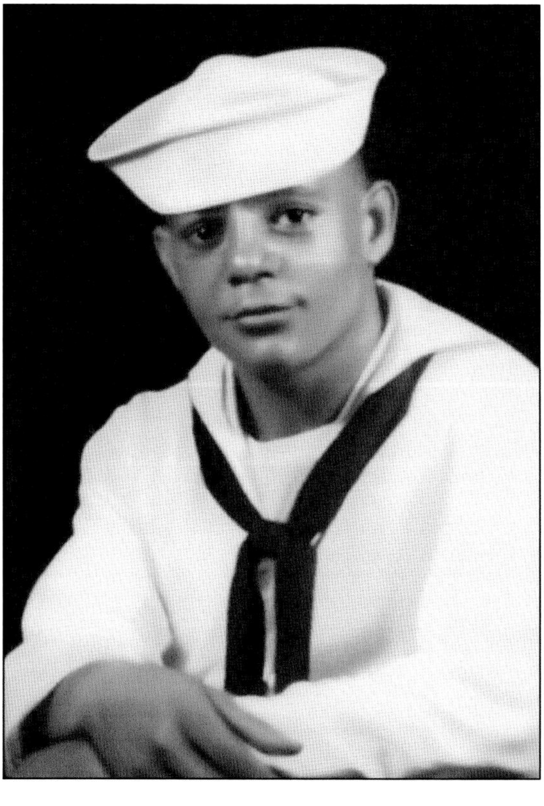

This is John Bordelon from Carencro. Across the street from St. Pierre Cemetery, construction began in April 2014 on the Carencro Veterans Memorial. Designed by Lynn Guidry Architects, the memorial will include a base of brick pavers engraved with the names of veterans, 16 granite "soldiers" (small pillars engraved with the names of veterans killed in action), and marble benches. The memorial is a tribute to the brave men and women who fought for their country and called Carencro home. (Carencro Veterans Day Program.)

Three

Leading the People

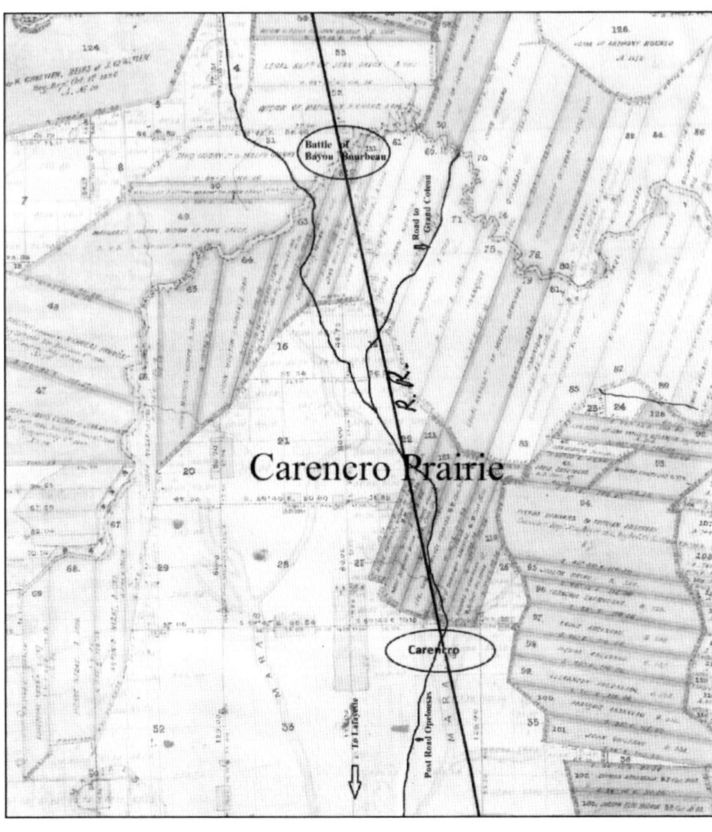

The map shows the Carencro Prairie around 1830. Post Road is shown going towards Opelousas, and the path to Lafayette is also marked. The darker shaded rectangles show the arpents of area landowners. The oval identifies downtown Carencro. Carencro received its official charter on July 6, 1905. At the time, the population was a little over 200. It is said that this was the second charter received for the region. The first was believed to have been lost when the men retrieving it misplaced it on their travels home. The charter was from Newton Crain Blanchard, governor of Louisiana. (State of Louisiana.)

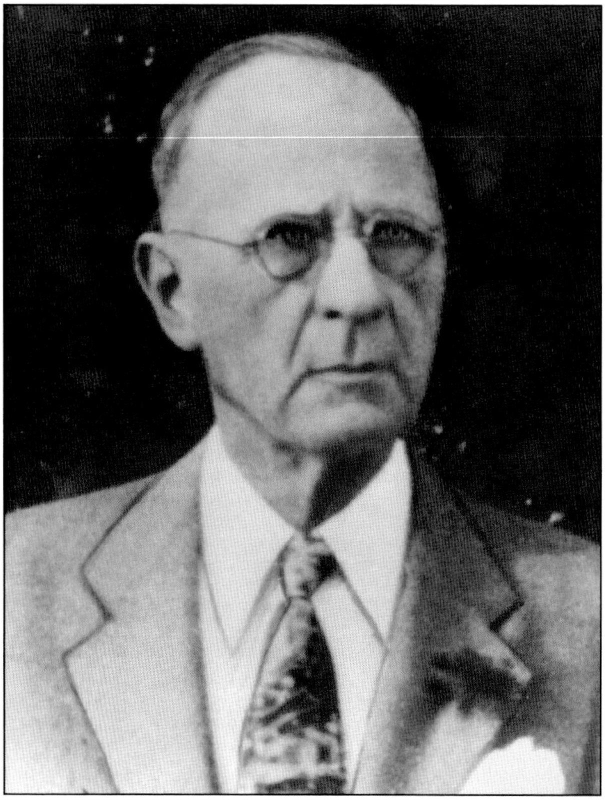

Carencro's first mayor was George J. Melchior (pictured). He served from 1905 to 1914, when Carencro was incorporated as a village. He was elected mayor once again in 1920 and ended his career as mayor in 1928. Between Melchior's first and second term, Dr. A.C. Prejean was elected and served as mayor from 1914 to 1920. From 1905 to 1912, C.F. Latiolais served as the town clerk/city clerk. V.A. Guidroz served as the town clerk for five months in 1912 before being replaced by S.P. Brown, who served from 1912 to 1914. (City of Carencro.)

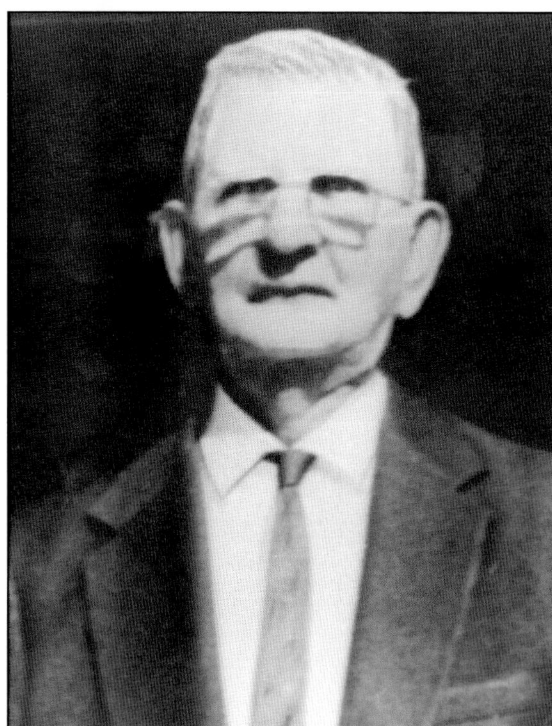

A.C. Prejean (pictured) was Carencro's second mayor, serving from 1914 to 1920. V.A. Guidroz served as town clerk for Mayor Prejean from 1914 to 1924. Prejean was elected into office again in 1947 and served until 1970. (City of Carencro.)

R.A. Richard Sr. served as mayor from 1928 to 1934. John P. Crouchet became town clerk in 1924 and remained in that position until 1946. (City of Carencro.)

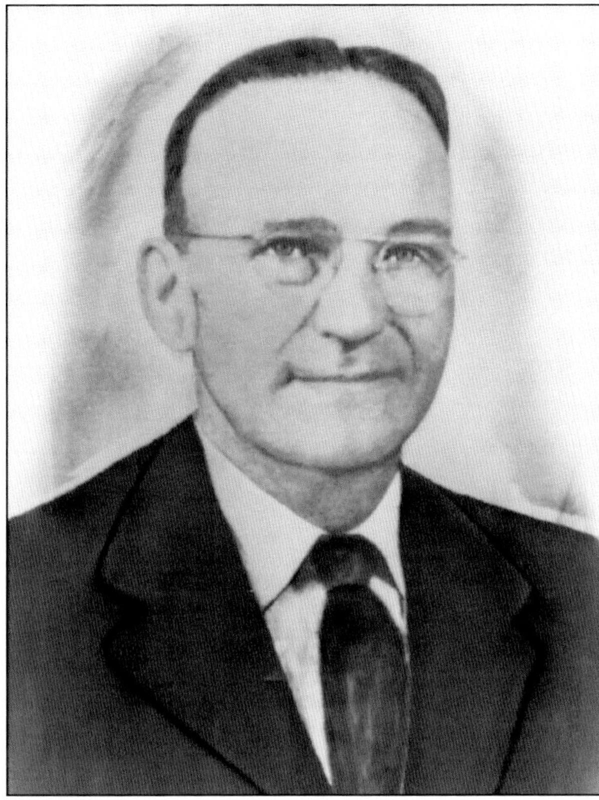

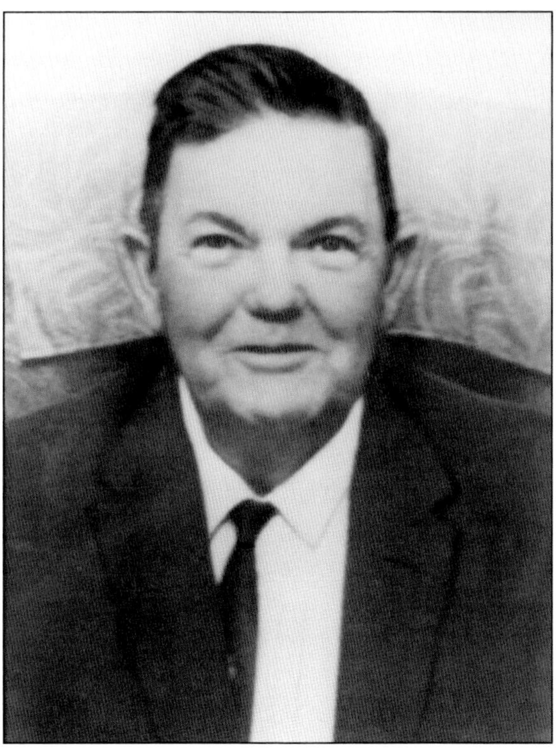

L.L. Breaux (pictured) was elected mayor of Carencro in 1934 and served until 1947. While Mayor Breaux was in office, the village of Carencro incorporated as a town in July 1947. Town clerk Joseph P. Arceneaux served under Breaux from 1946 to 1947. Carroll E. Guilbeau served as town clerk under Mayor Breaux for one year, beginning in 1948, and stayed in that position until 1974. (City of Carencro.)

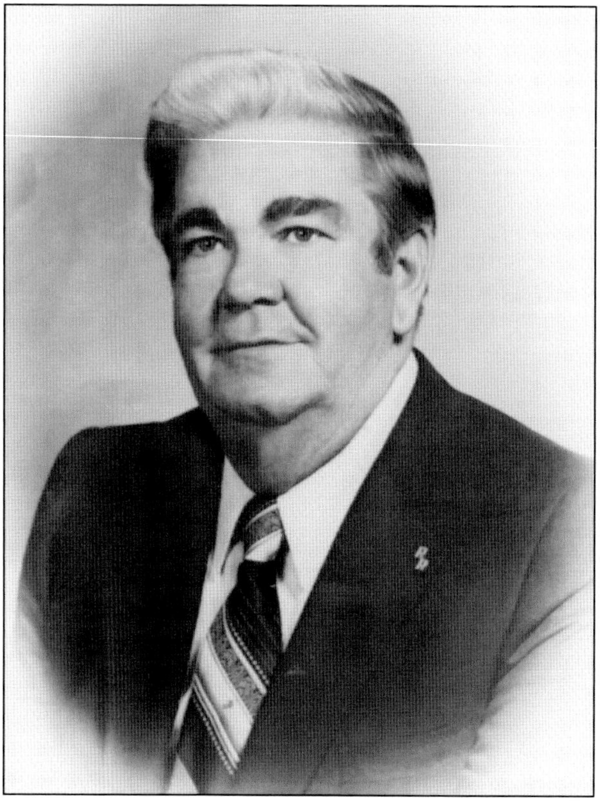

Robley Richard Jr. was mayor of Carencro from 1970 until 1978. Marie D. Lemaire became town clerk in 1974 and stayed in that office until 2003; her title changed from town clerk to city clerk when Carencro changed from a town to a city in 1984. (City of Carencro.)

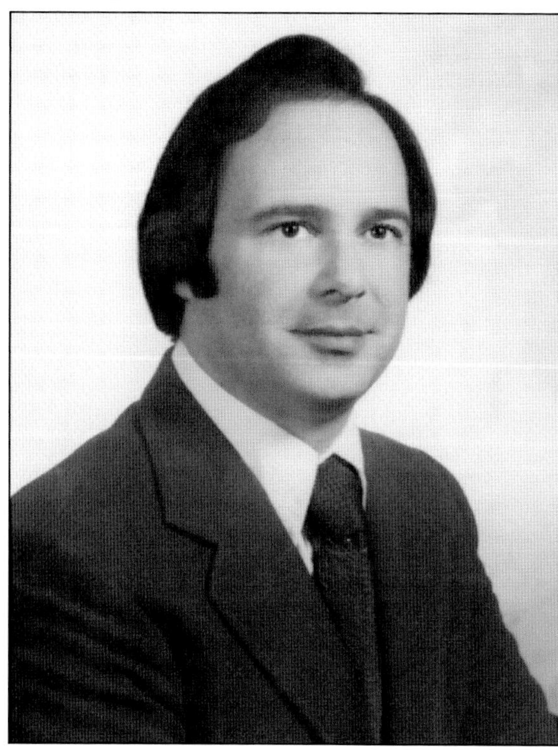

Tommy Angelle was elected mayor in 1978 and stayed in office until 2002. While he was in office, the town of Carencro became the city of Carencro in April 1984. (City of Carencro.)

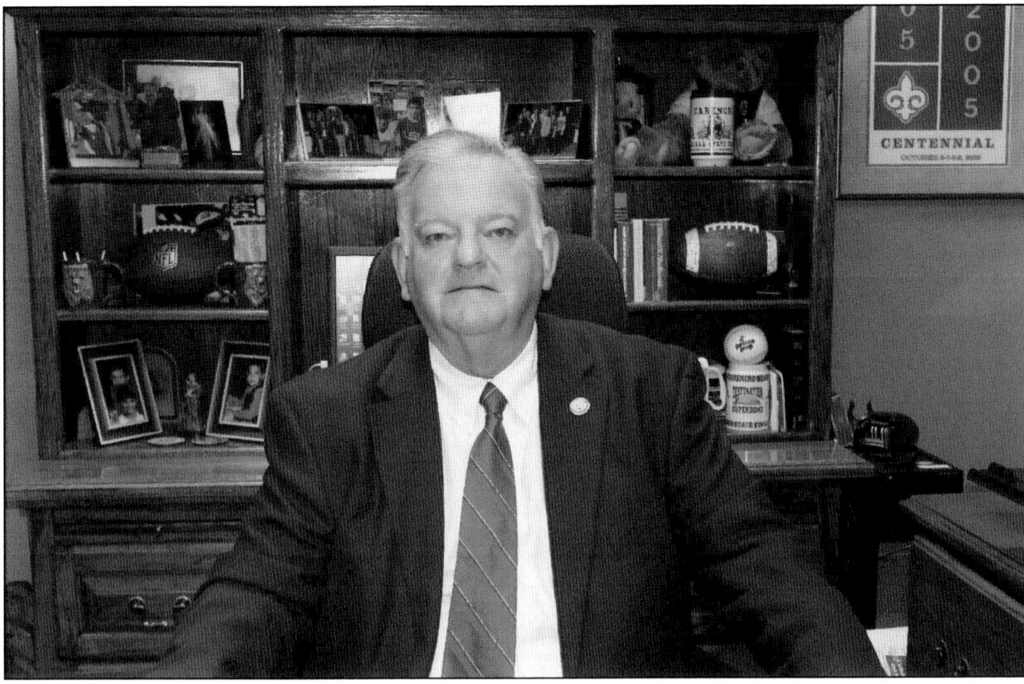

Glenn L. Brasseaux was elected mayor in 2003. As of 2014, when this book went to print, Mayor Brasseaux was still serving the city. Gwen B. Martin has served as city clerk for Carencro since Mayor Brasseaux was elected in 2003. (City of Carencro.)

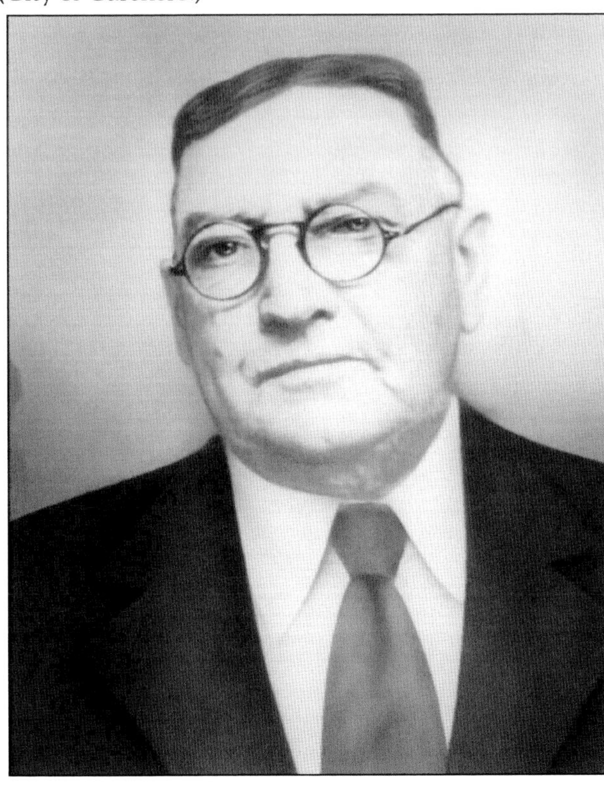

Marshal A.X. Lamulle served for only one month in 1905. Marshal A.B. Trahan (pictured) was in office from 1905 until 1914. Marshal Lambert Breaux wore his badge proudly from 1914 to 1916. Marshal Trahan served the village of Carencro from 1916 to 1928. (City of Carencro.)

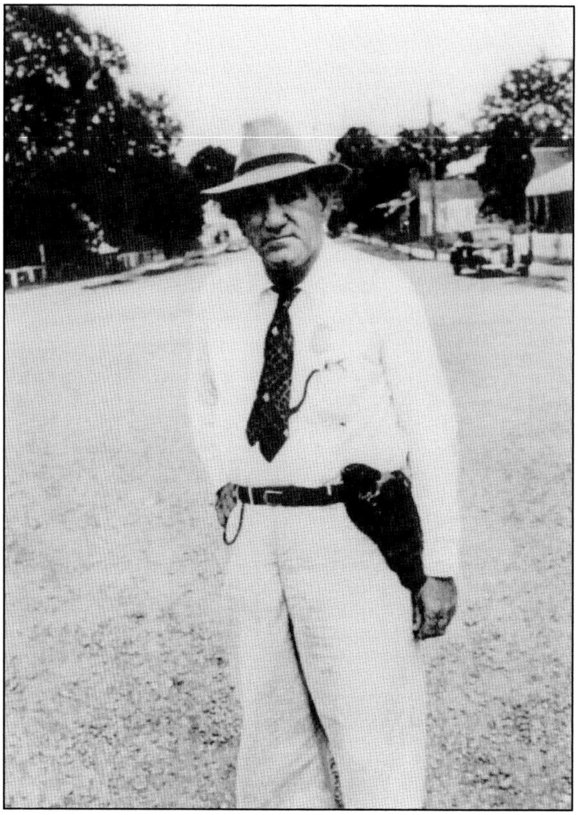

Marshal Joseph A. Dugas was in office from 1928 to 1930. Marshal A.B. Trahan once again became the leader in law from 1930 to 1932. Marshal Dugas served from 1932 to 1947. (City of Carencro.)

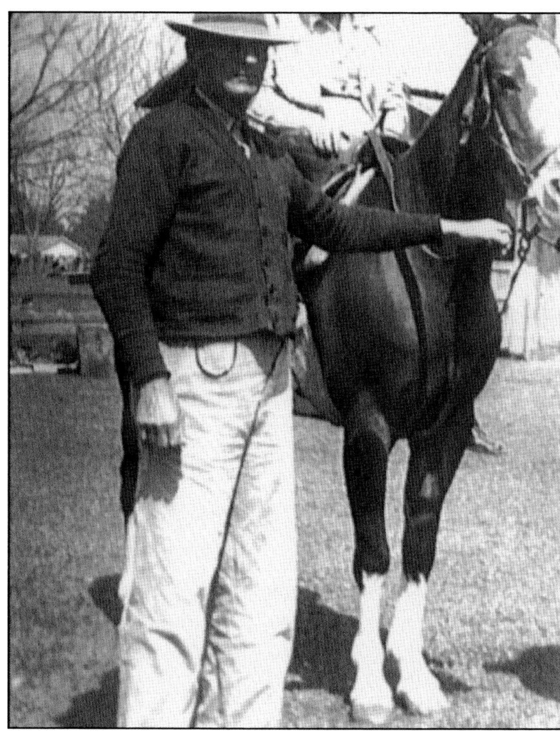

Marshal Jules Arceneaux was only in office for one year—from 1947 to 1948. (City of Carencro.)

Marshal Pierre Pourcio held office for many years, from 1948 to 1976. His title changed from marshal to police chief in 1974. (City of Carencro.)

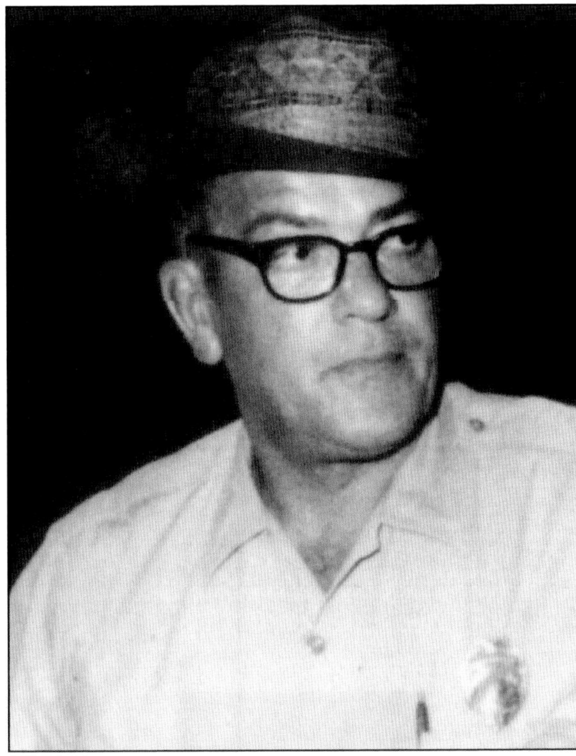

Chief Wallace Latiolais was in office from 1976 to 1979. Pictured are Latiolais (left) and officer Leroy Duffey. (City of Carencro.)

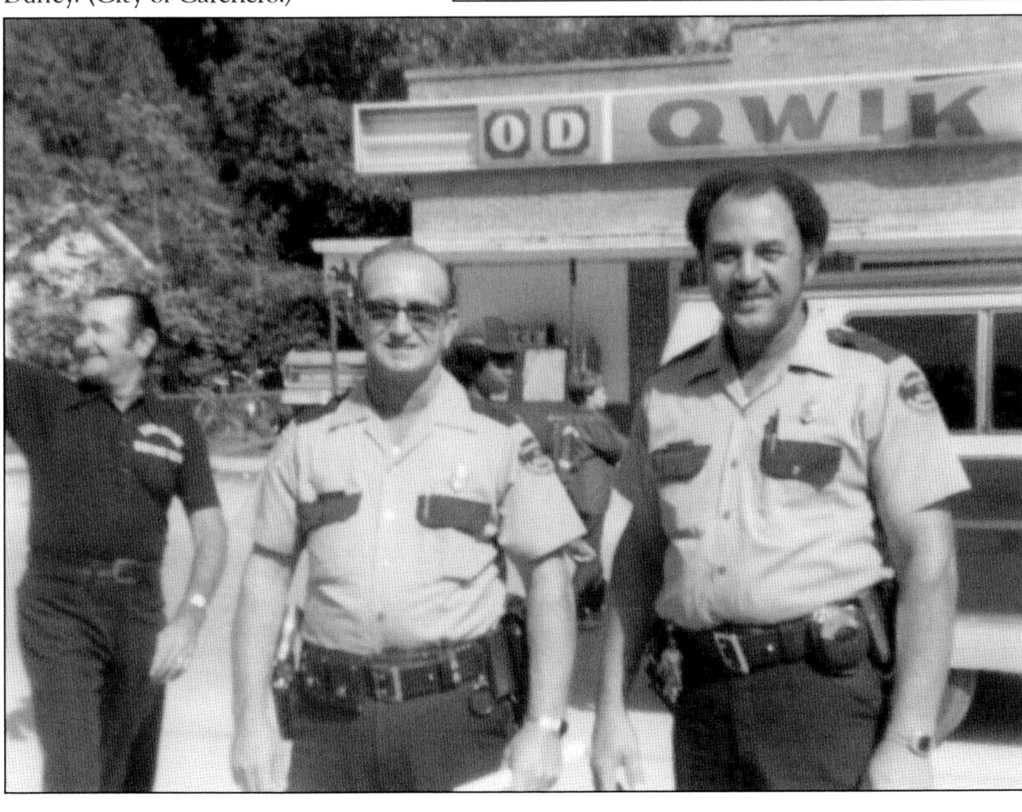

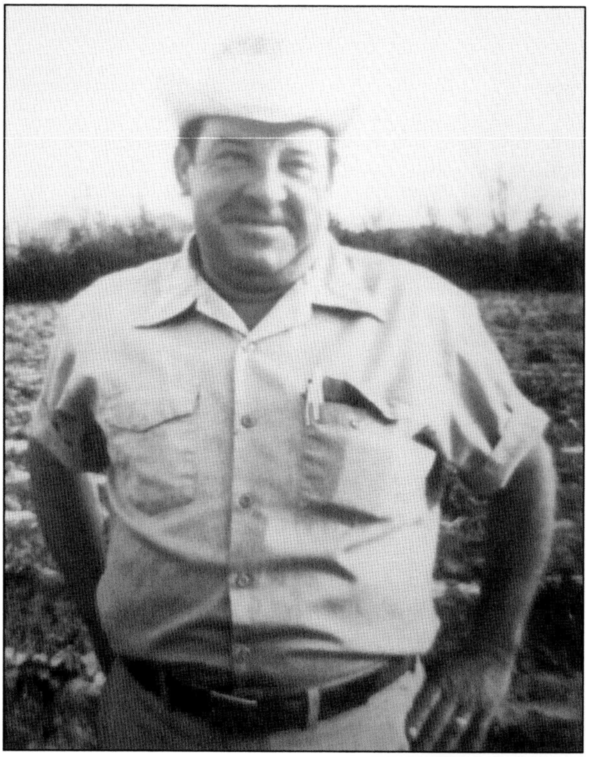

Chief Sosthene Arceneaux served from 1979 until he passed away in 1981. (City of Carencro.)

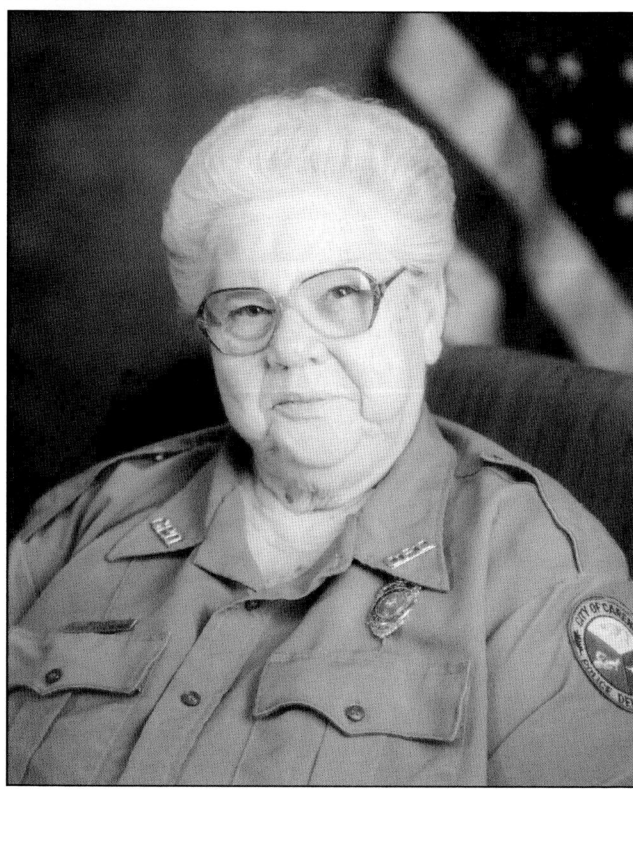

After the death of Chief Sosthene Arceneaux, his wife, Geraldyne Arceneaux, took over his office and served as Carencro's police chief from 1981 to 1998. Timmy Duhon was police chief from 1998 to 2002. Carlos Stout has been police chief since 2003, and as of 2014, he is still serving. (City of Carencro.)

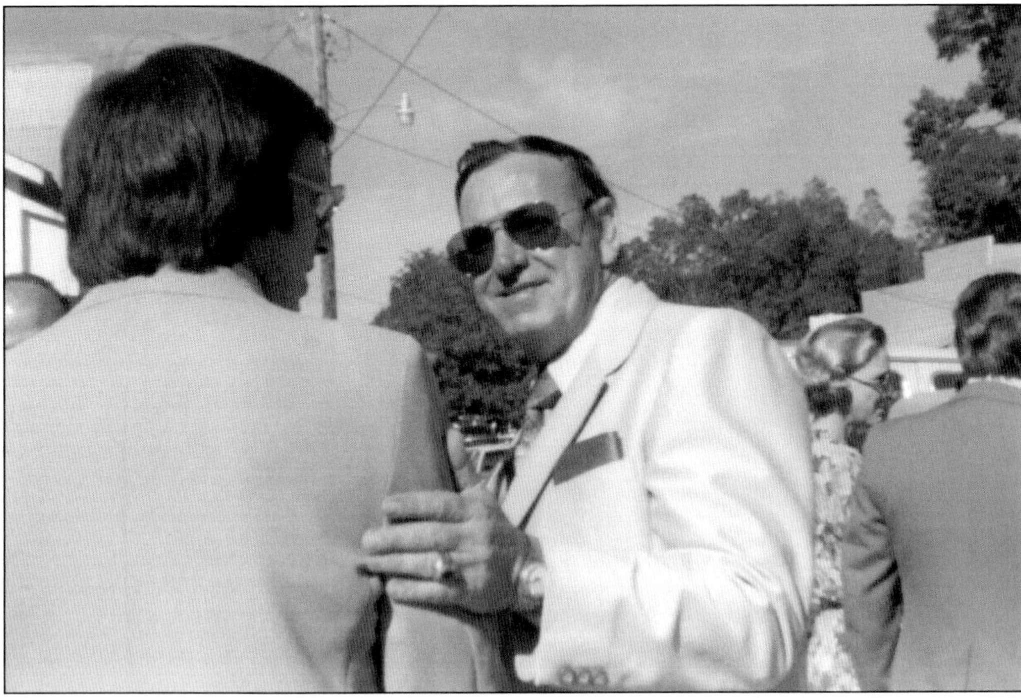

Pictured is J.L. Richard, who took office as alderman in 1977. He is one of many who have served the village, town, and city of Carencro as an alderman or city council member. (City of Carencro.)

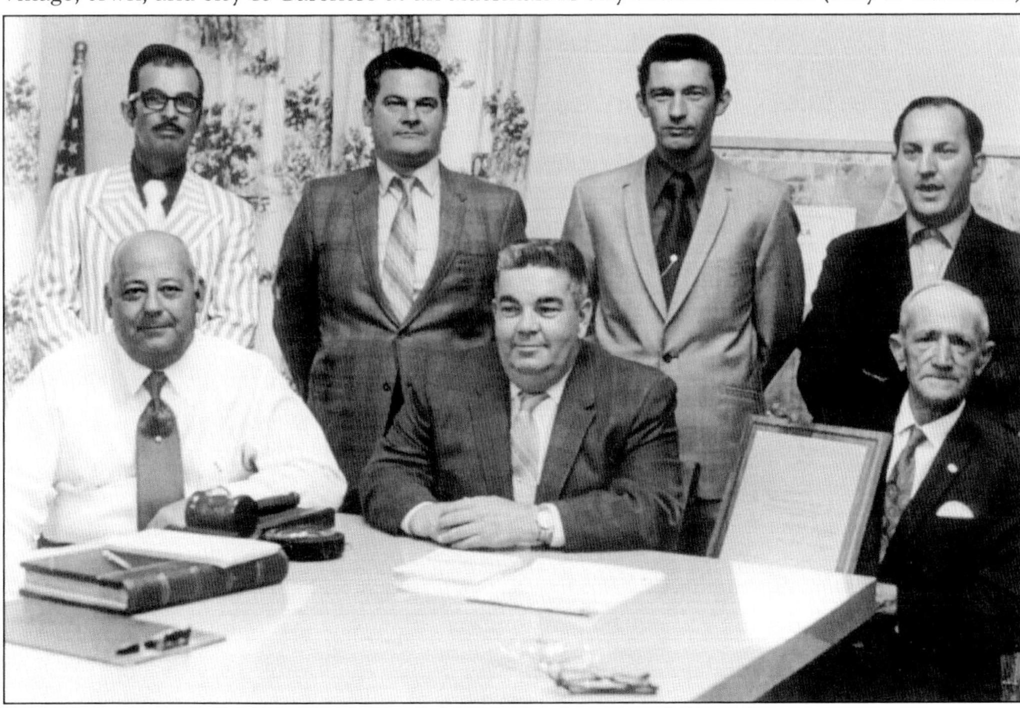

Pictured here are, from left to right, (first row) alderman James C. Angelle, Mayor Robley A. Richard Jr., and alderman John Benoit; (second row) alderman James H. Burleigh, town clerk Carroll E. Guilbeau, alderman Arnold Bernard, and alderman Gerald Arsement. (City of Carencro.)

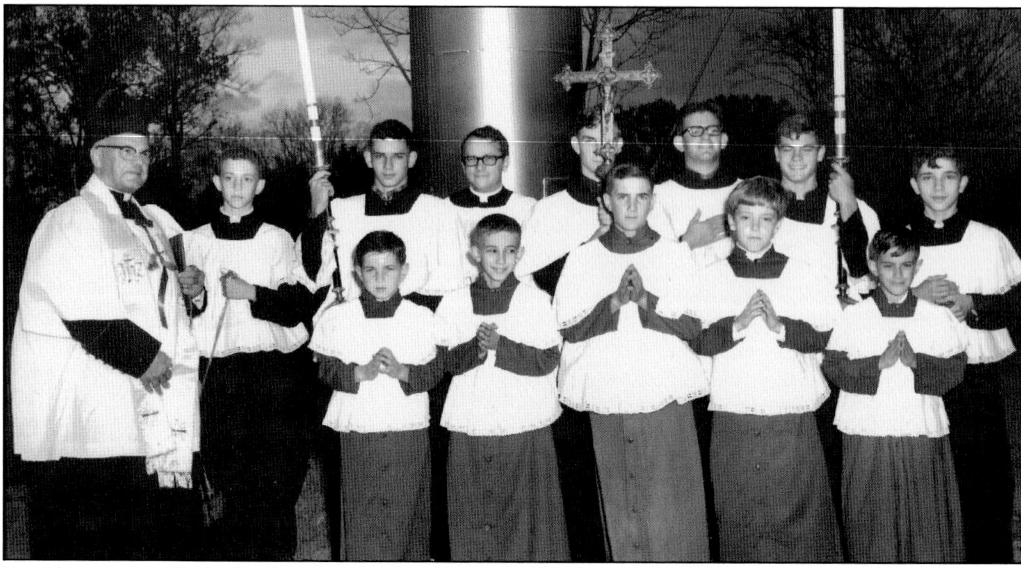

On December 18, 1966, the new water tower was dedicated by Msgr. Auguste Wassler. Among those pictured are Wassler, associate pastor Gayle Nunez, David Brunet, Steve Dupuis, Glenn Brasseaux, Ken Guilbeau, Tony Guidry, Burt Arceneaux, Steven Brunet, Marc Conque, and Matthew Richard. In the mid-1960s, the water plant was renovated. It operated until November 2010, when it was replaced with a modern plant that cost about $4 million. (City of Carencro.)

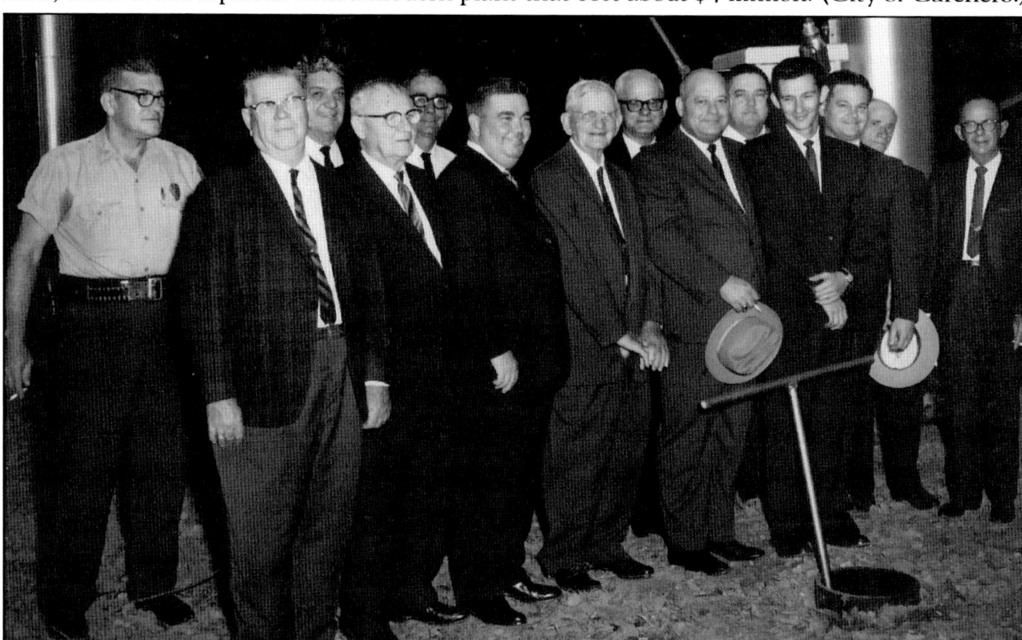

This photograph shows the ribbon-cutting ceremony for the water tower. Mayor A.C. Prejean is pictured here along with aldermen and town officials including town marshal Pierre Pourcio, Burton Andrus, Joseph P. Arceneaux, Lafayette councilman Freddie J. Mouton, fire chief L.F. Babin, councilman Robby Richard Jr., Prejean, treasurer Walter J. Prejean, councilman James C. Angelle, fire chief Gerald Richard, councilman Arnold Bernard, councilman Carroll E. Guilbeau, councilman John B. Benoit, and water superintendent Duchane P. Guidry. (City of Carencro.)

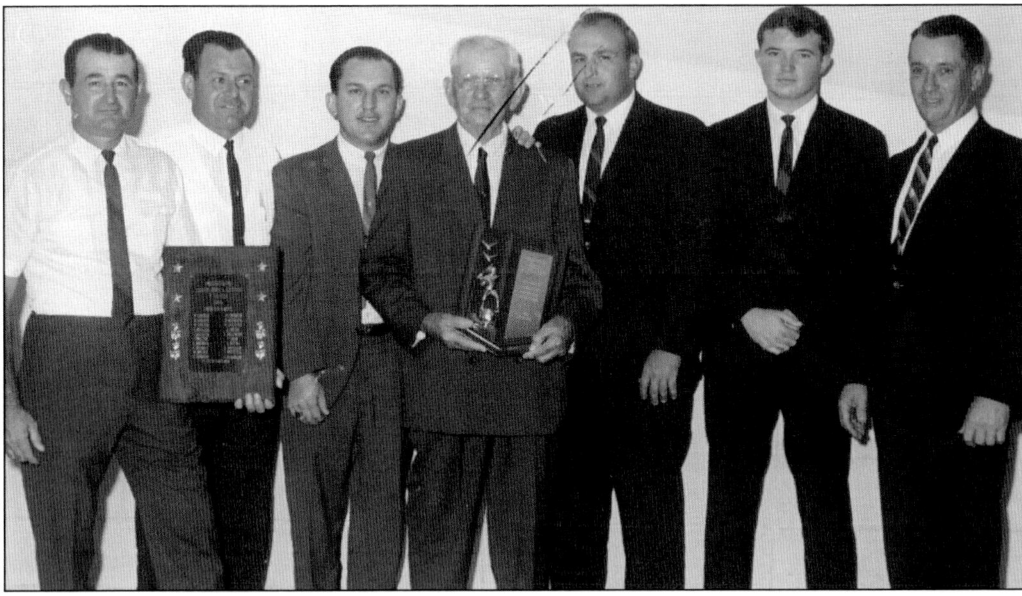

The Carencro Youth Baseball Banquet in 1967 honored leaders who believed in giving back through recreational sports. Current councilman J.L. Richard recently commented: "Looking at the kids enjoying themselves on the field has always been what it is about in Carencro." The coaches pictured here are, from left to right, John Stutes, Jimmie Brasseaux, Gerald Arsement, Mayor Andre "Doc" Prejean, Allen Conque, Ronnie Mott, and Lawrence Lajaunie. (City of Carencro.)

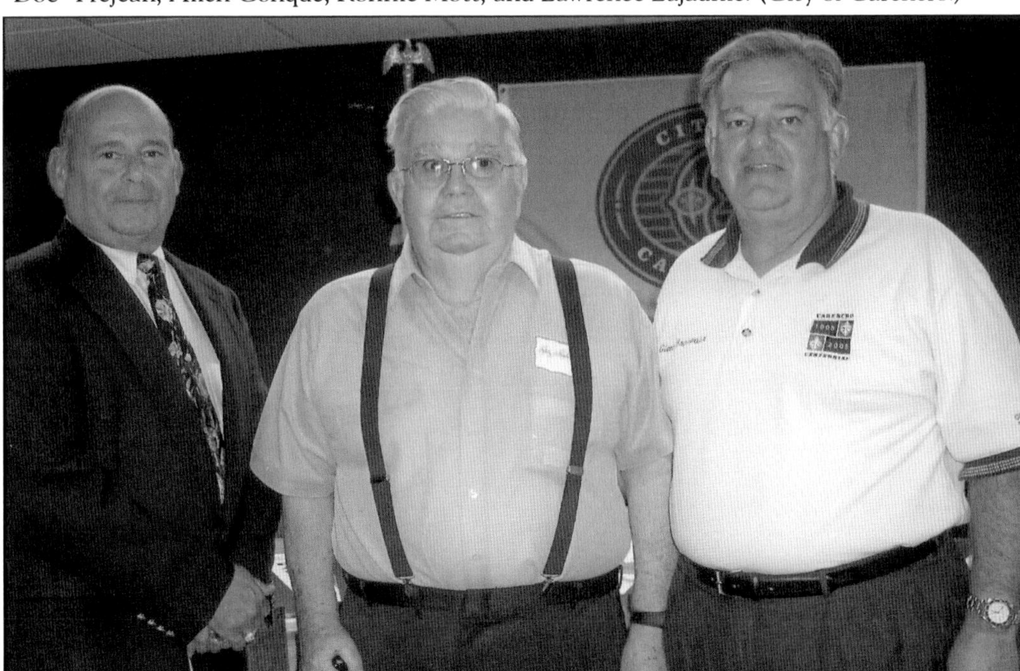

The city of Carencro spent months preparing a centennial celebration for its 100th birthday in 2005. At the celebration, three mayors were present and happy to pose for a group photograph. Pictured here are former mayor Tommy Angelle (left), former mayor Robley Richard (center), and current mayor Glenn Brasseaux. (City of Carencro.)

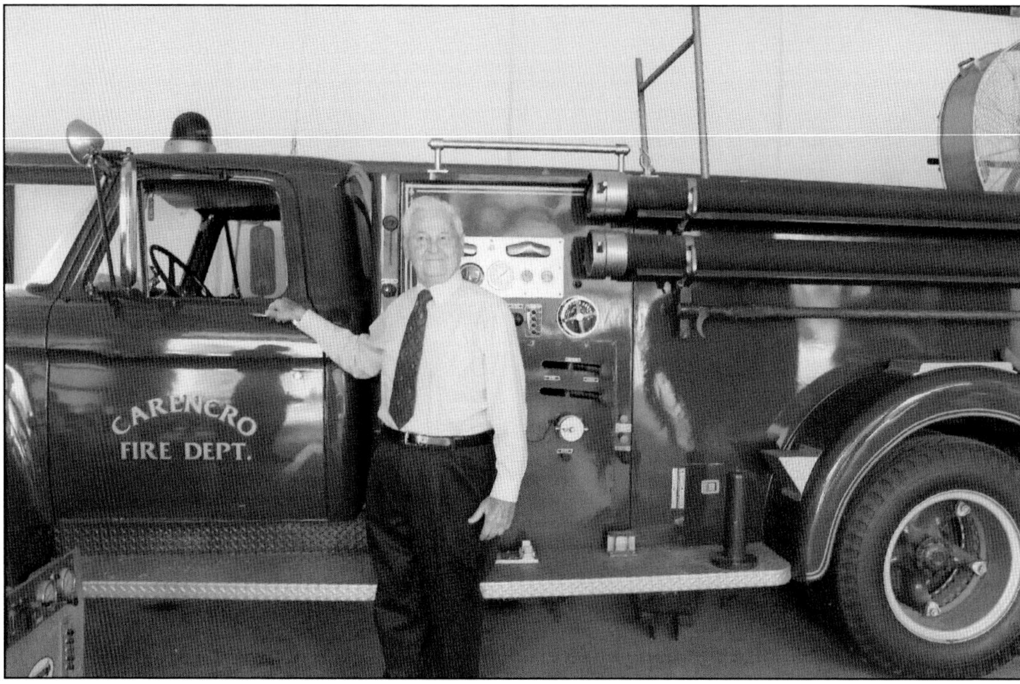

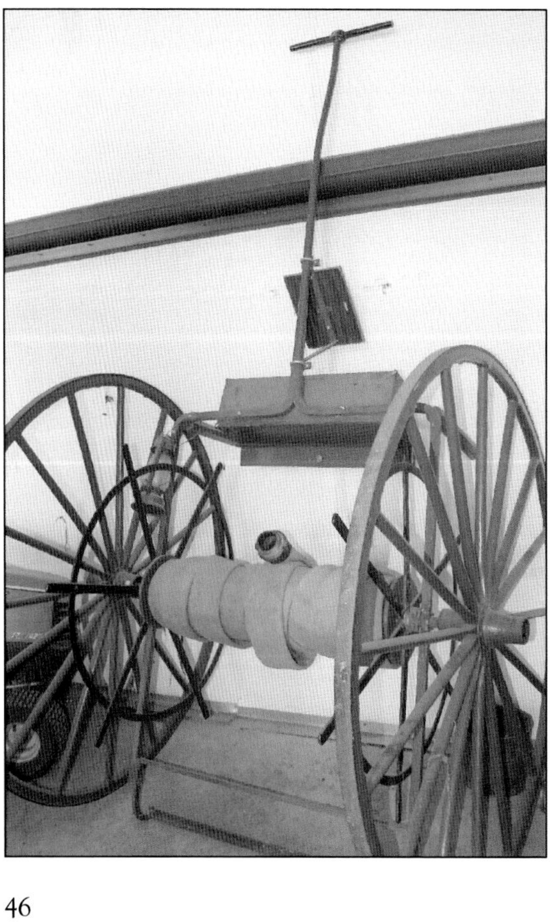

In the early 1900s, the village of Carencro was served by Eagle Fire Company. In the outlying areas, Pelican Fire Department answered calls just over the bridge on North Church Street. Eventually, Eagle Fire Company answered all emergency calls for the community. A bell purchased in 1924 from Lafayette stood on the grounds of St. Peter Roman Catholic Church and was used to alert firemen. Pictured is Carroll E. Guilbeau, who served as president of the Carencro Fire Company from 1948 to 1964.

In the 1940s, the town's Studebaker fire truck was retired, and a stripped Ford chassis was purchased for $500. The truck lacked the necessities to perform as a working fire truck, and firefighters scrambled to find parts that would complete it. A water tank made by a blacksmith and an old World War II water pump were added to the vehicle. In the 1950s, the city built the town hall, fire station, and jail combination on Andre Street. One of several potato kilns on Andre Street served as the garage for the handmade pumper truck. Pictured is the fire hose wheel used prior to a fire truck.

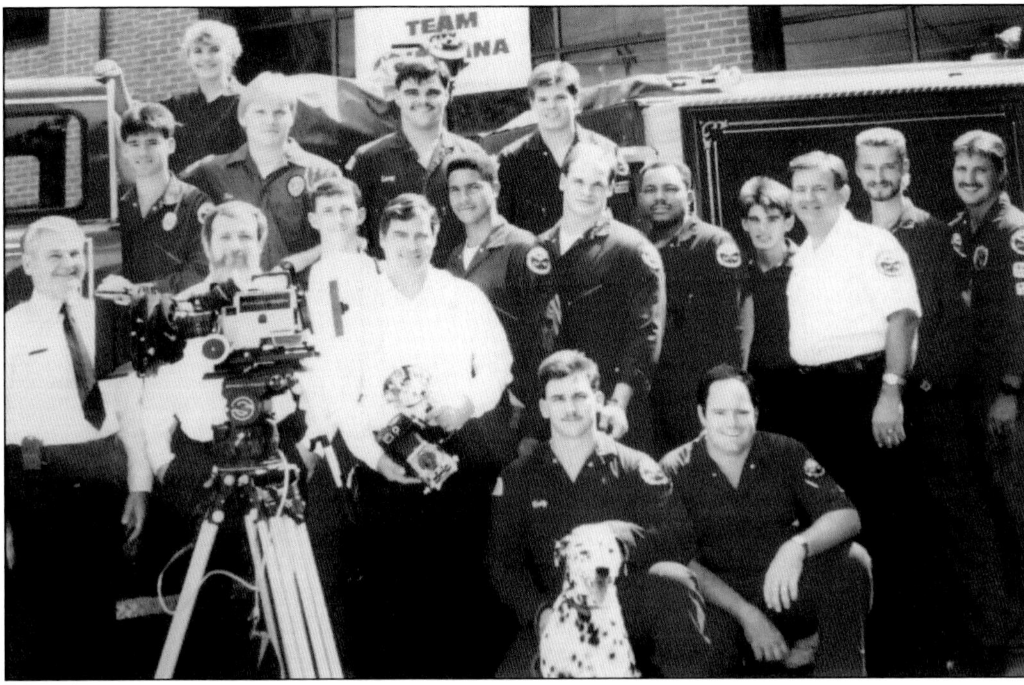

In 1962, the town of Carencro purchased a fire truck for $15,000. The town was bustling with excitement, but there was still much to be done in order to catch up to other fire departments around the state. This 1985 photograph of the Carencro Fire Department was a promotional tool for Gulf State Utilities Company. It was titled "The Energy Team." The fire dog was named Sparky.

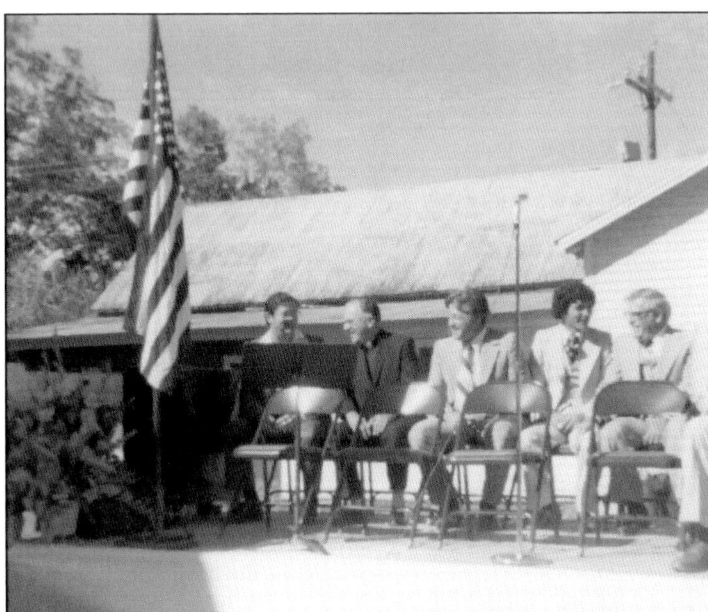

In 1978, the town celebrated the grand opening of the new town hall and fire station on St. Peter Street. Pictured are dignitaries getting ready for their speeches. "I never thought such progress could be made in one area," Carroll Guilbeau said. "Imagine women in the early 1900s outside in their nightgowns directing horse and buggies to the fires. I saw three fire stations built, each showing progression of growth and innovation." (City of Carencro.)

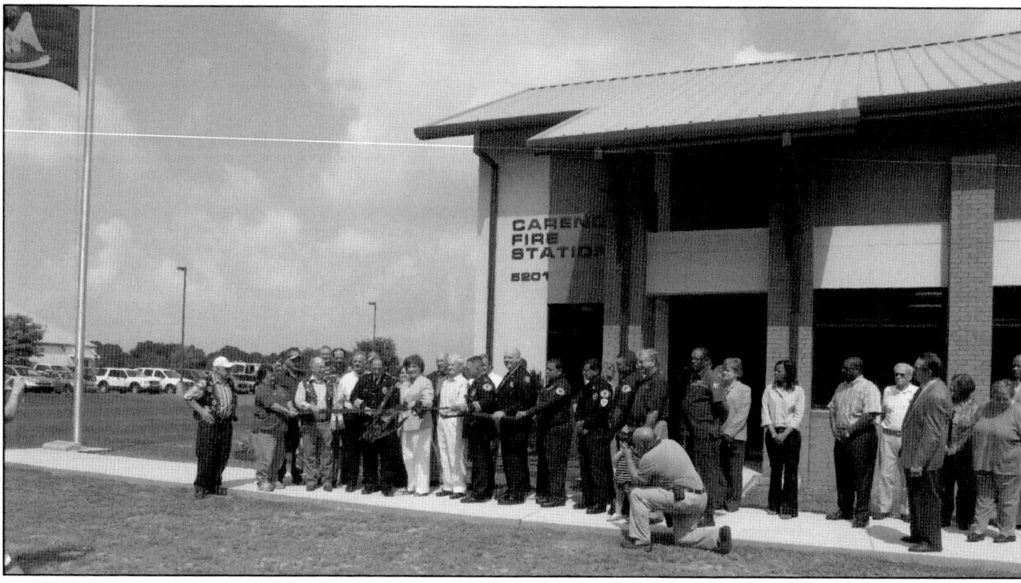

In June 2011, a new fire station on North University Avenue opened to meet the needs of the growing city. Former Louisiana governor Kathleen Blanco—who played a huge part in the city securing the state capital outlay bill grant needed to construct the state-of-the-art facility—was present for the ribbon-cutting ceremony. (Community Chronicles.)

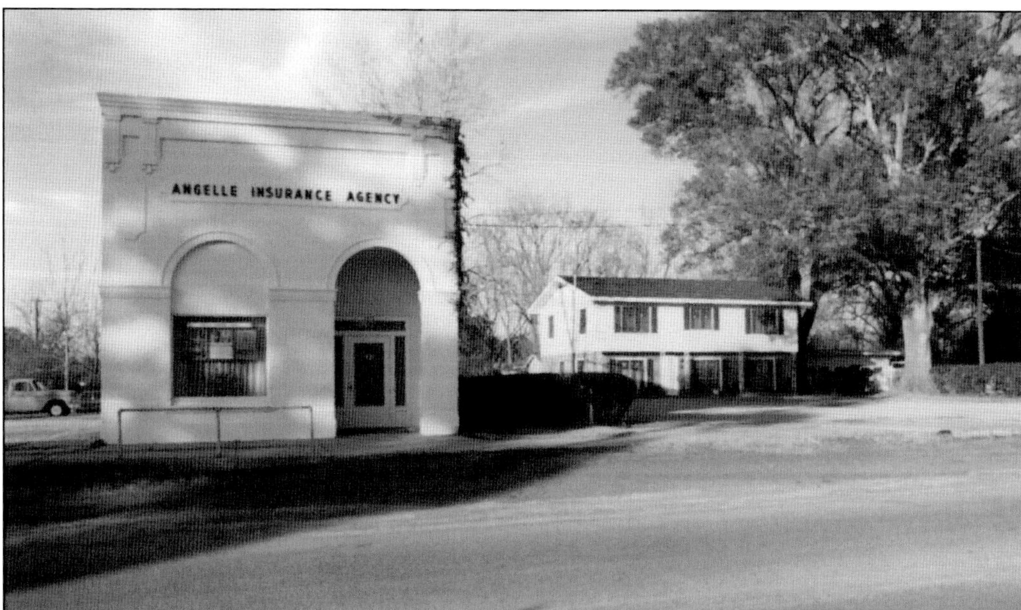

The Bank of Carencro was built in 1906 where it still stands today on St. Peter Street. Odon Guidry was the bank's first president; George Melchoir was the first cashier. The bank was small but mighty in the early 1900s. It grew until the 1920s, when it was taken over by the Lafayette Bank and Trust, which closed its doors in 1932. Eventually, the building became home to Angelle Insurance Agency. Today it is empty, but notice the hitching post for the horses that were once used for travel. (Janet Stemmans.)

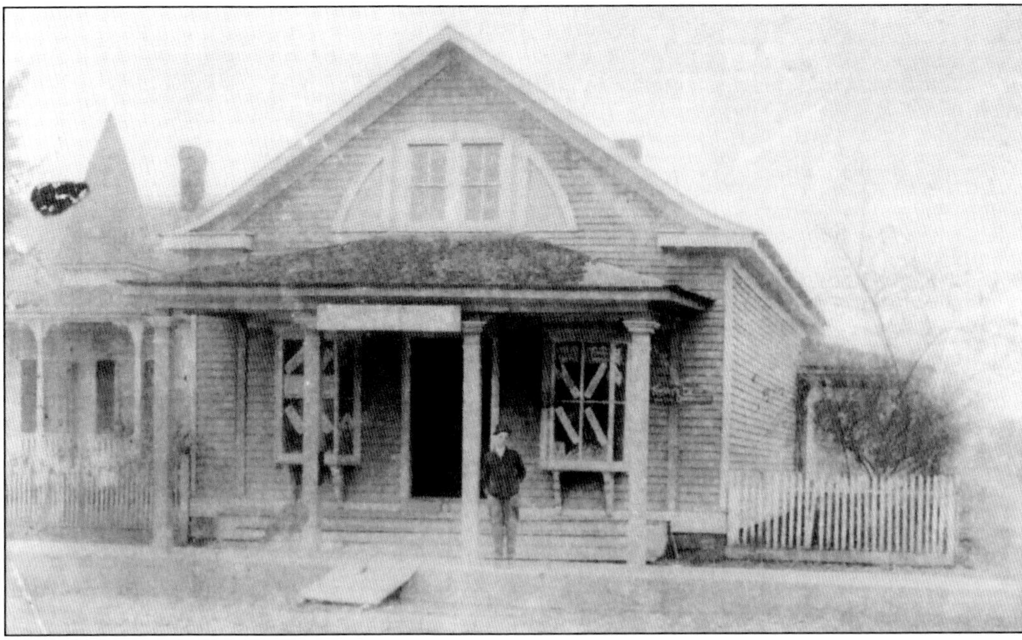

Crescent Pharmacy, owned by Esteve Martin, served the village of Carencro. Martin's pharmacy was divided into two different parts separated by a large mirror. The back of the establishment held all the medicine. In the front, customers could enjoy a fountain soda while waiting on prescriptions. Martin was a pharmacist, a cotton-gin owner, an insurance agent, a race horse breeder, and served as a Louisiana state senator. This photograph was taken around 1915.

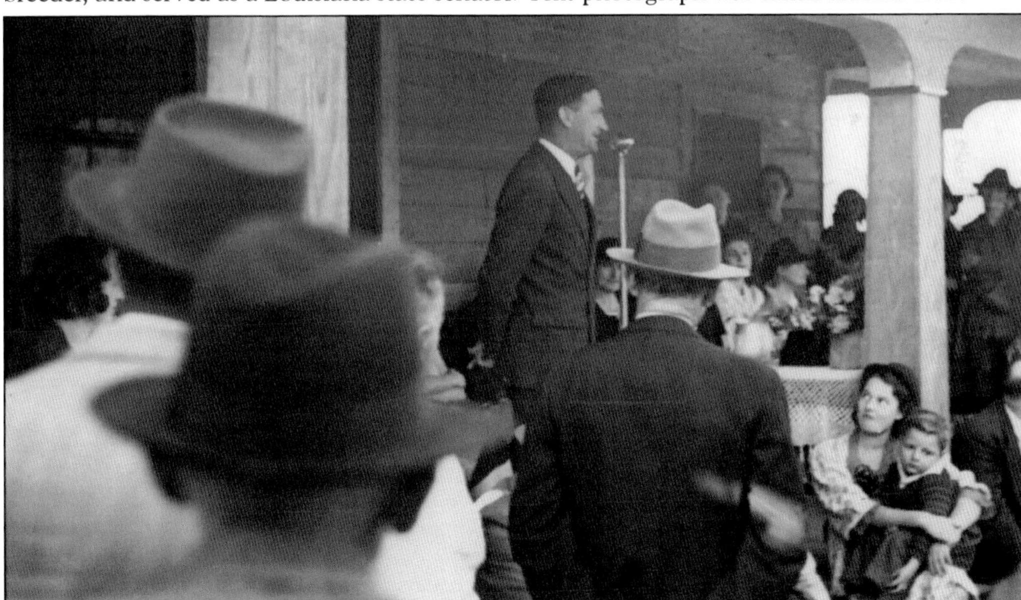

Esteve Martin held political rallies on the steps of the Woodmen of the World building. He once said that the key to gaining a crowd was to talk in hushed tones before a few people. As others got closer to hear what was being said, it would gain the attention of still others. Before you knew it, a large crowd had gathered to hear the speech. By that time, Martin would be shouting, and the excitement could be felt by all. (Catherine Brasseaux.)

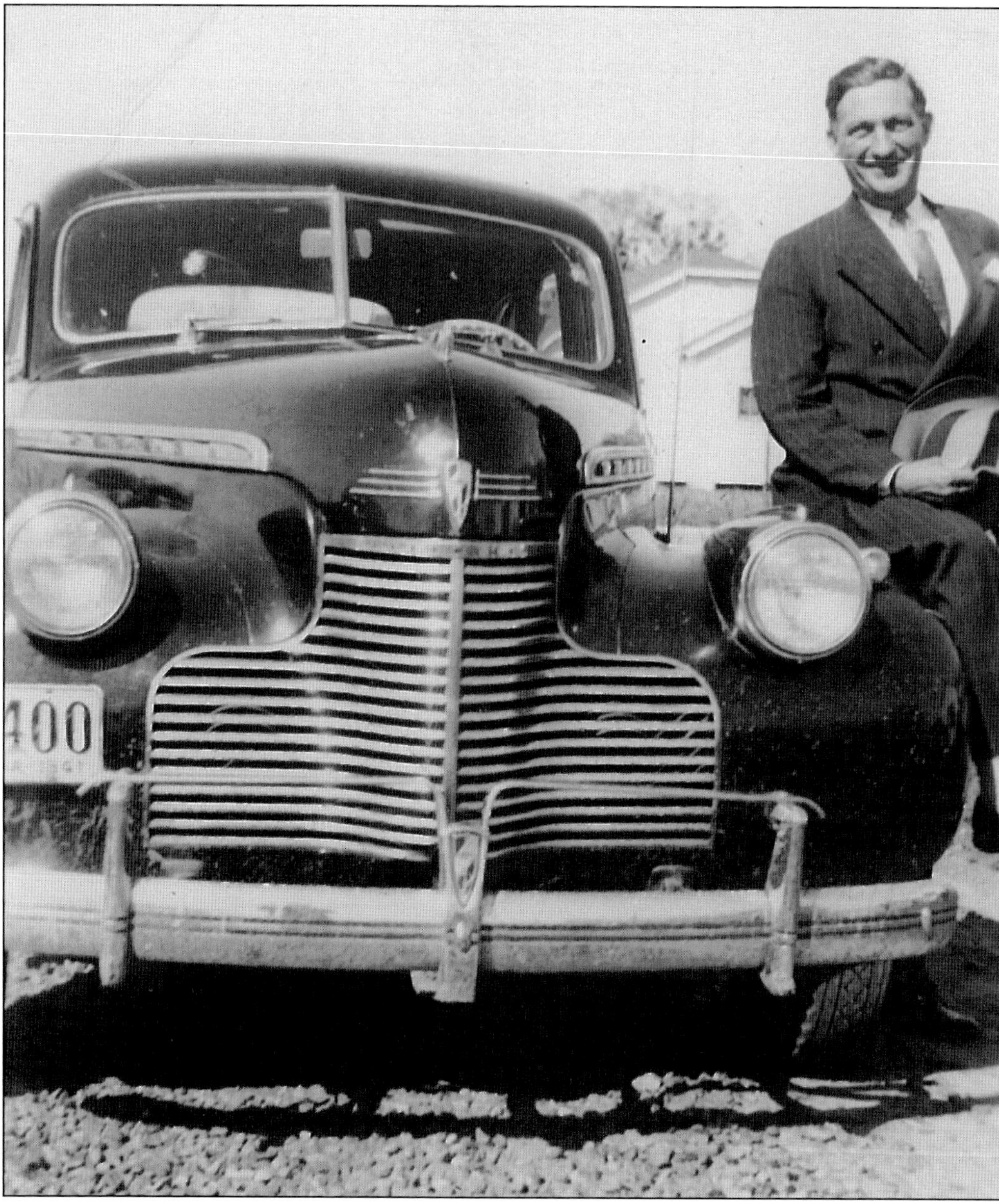

Huey P. Long, former governor of Louisiana, was close friends with state senator Esteve Martin (pictured). Long often visited the Martin home. The two would take the ferry home from Baton Rouge and head to Carencro for some good, home-cooked meals. Catherine Brasseaux and her mother and father (who worked for the Department of Transportation) were on the grounds of the capitol the day that Long was shot. Catherine was later told that her father walked into the capitol while she and her mother waited. Her father was going tell her grandfather, Esteve Martin, that they were heading home early to Carencro. When the shooting occurred, the capitol went under lockdown, and an army of police and emergency officials covered the grounds. It was evening before the family heard that Long had been shot. In Carencro, residents who were not fans of Long held a mock funeral with a procession downtown; this left the mourners of Governor Long very upset. (Catherine Brasseaux.)

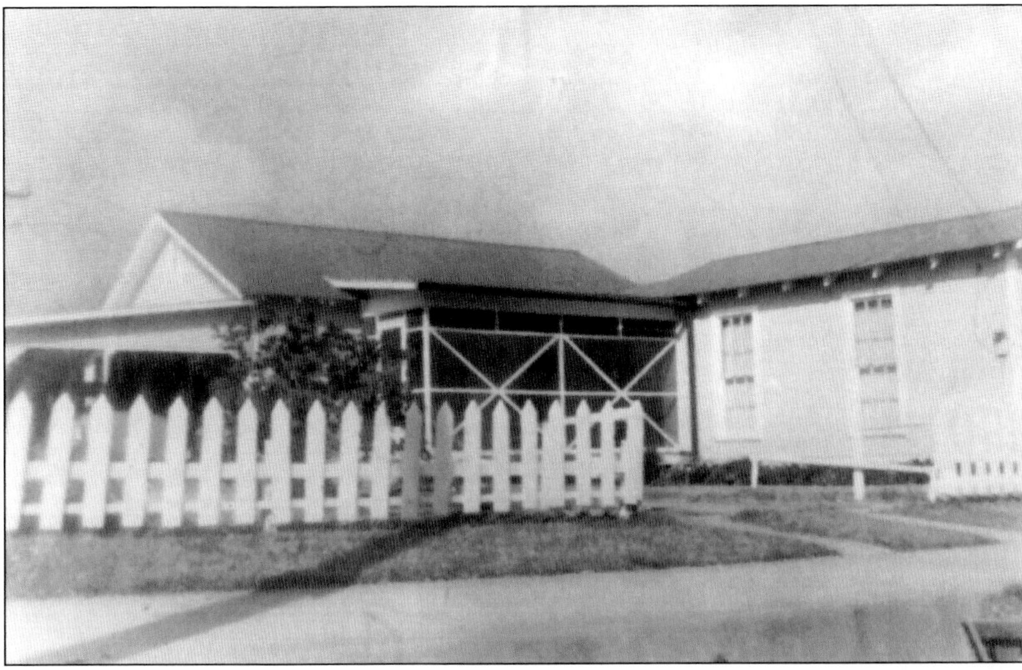

The first Carencro City Hall (pictured) was on Andre Street. The building later became the first utilities office. The new city hall was built on property acquired from Burton Andrus and Warren Arceneaux across the street from St. Peter Roman Catholic Church.

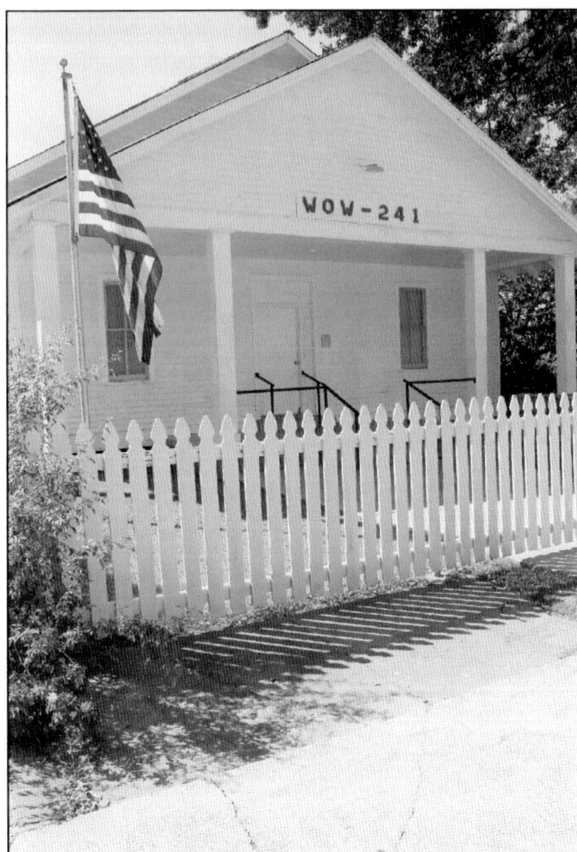

The village of Carencro held its first business meetings at the Woodmen of the World lodge in the early 1900s. In 1947 the village became a town, which brought on one of the first elections for mayor. The town became a city on April 19, 1984. (Community Chronicles.)

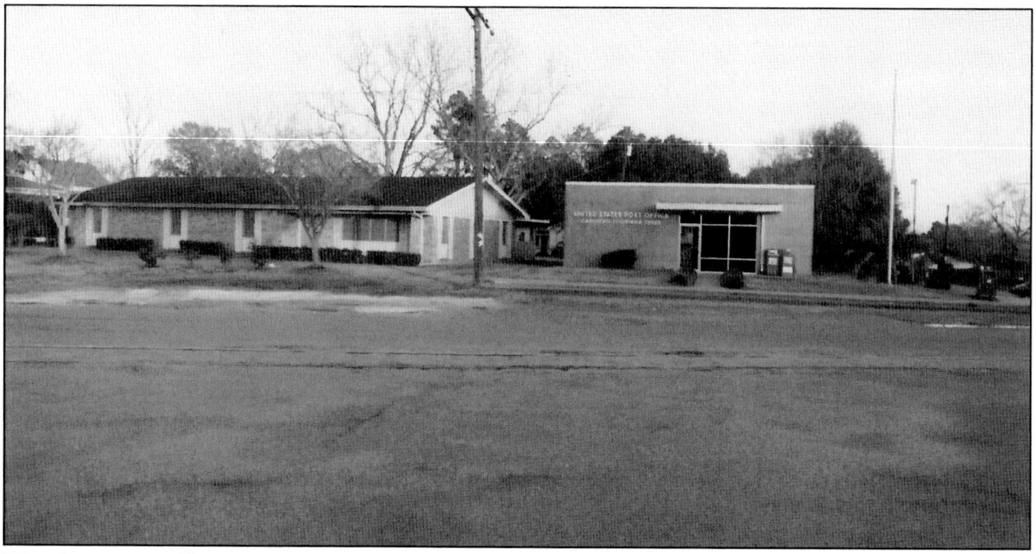

The first post office in Carencro was established on January 1, 1872, with Auguste Melchior serving as postmaster. The original village post office was a yellow building on South Michaud Street that was constructed in 1887. It was connected to another building that served as the home of postmaster Jeanne Crouchet. Crouchet's sister, Laurence, ran a hat shop. This picture shows the second location of Carencro's post office. (Community Chronicles.)

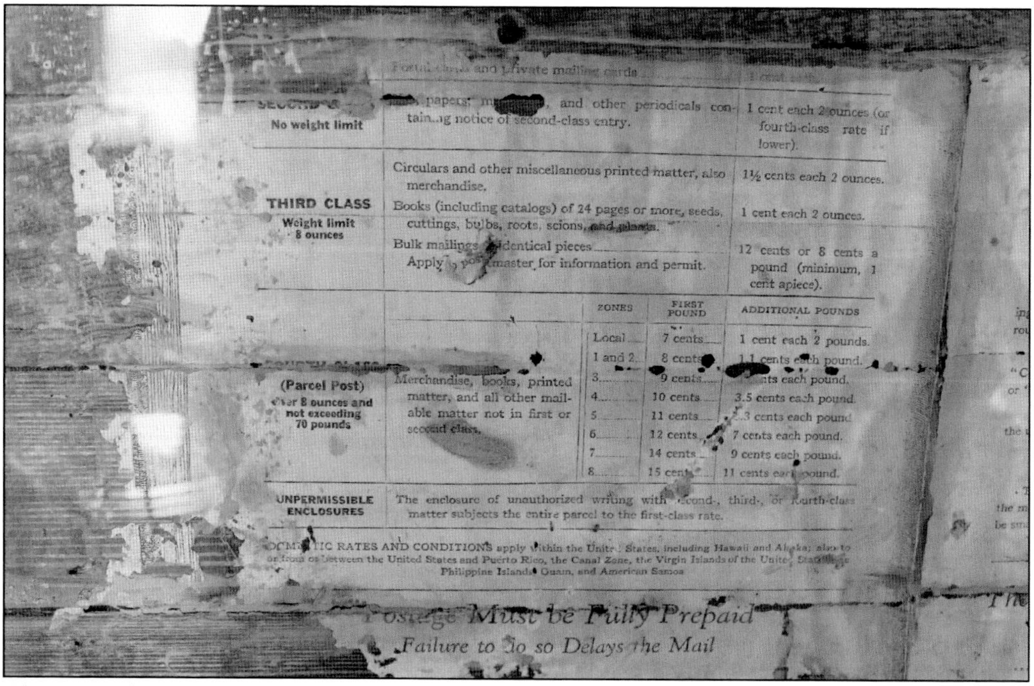

This image shows the prices of postage in the 1900s. At Evangeline Oaks Wellness and Rehabilitation Center, Ozeta Woods spoke of the times that she would walk to the post office and buy stamps for 3¢. (Community Chronicles.)

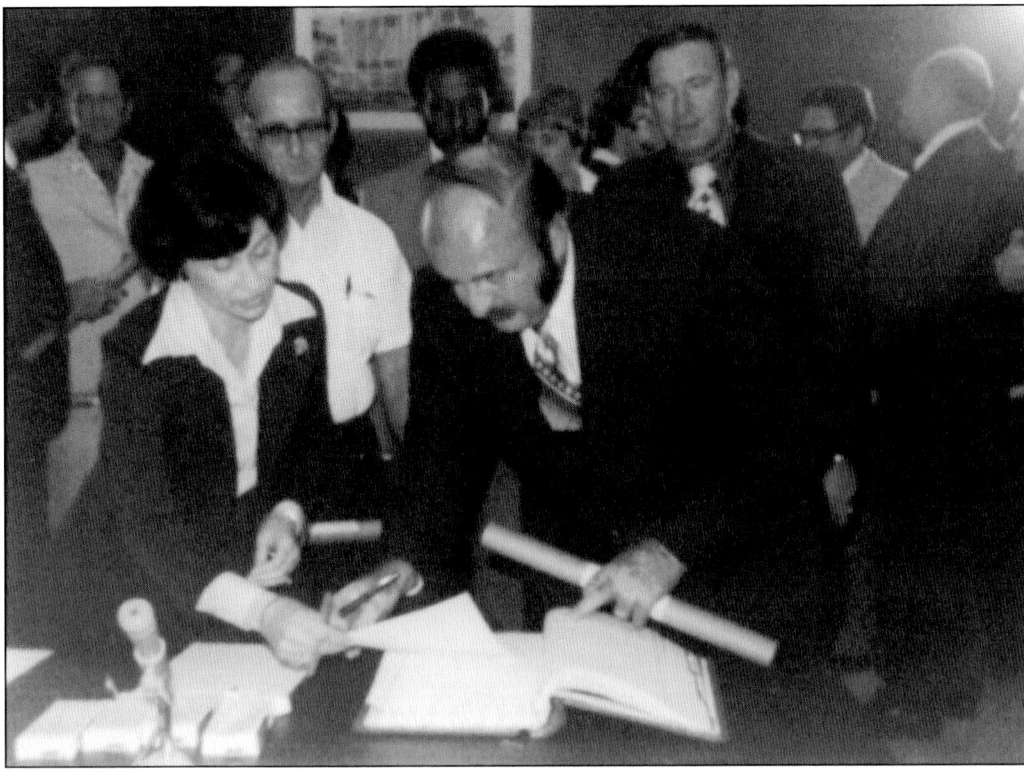

George Allen Conque earned his nickname, "Coach Conque," while coaching students at Carencro High School. Coach Conque ran for a city council seat in 1978. During his years on the council, his popularity was revealed through election results. Mayor Glenn Brasseaux said, "After eight successful elections, Coach Conque either received the most votes or came in second to other candidates. He has influenced so many young people in our community." Conque retired from his seat in December 2010. (Community Chronicles.)

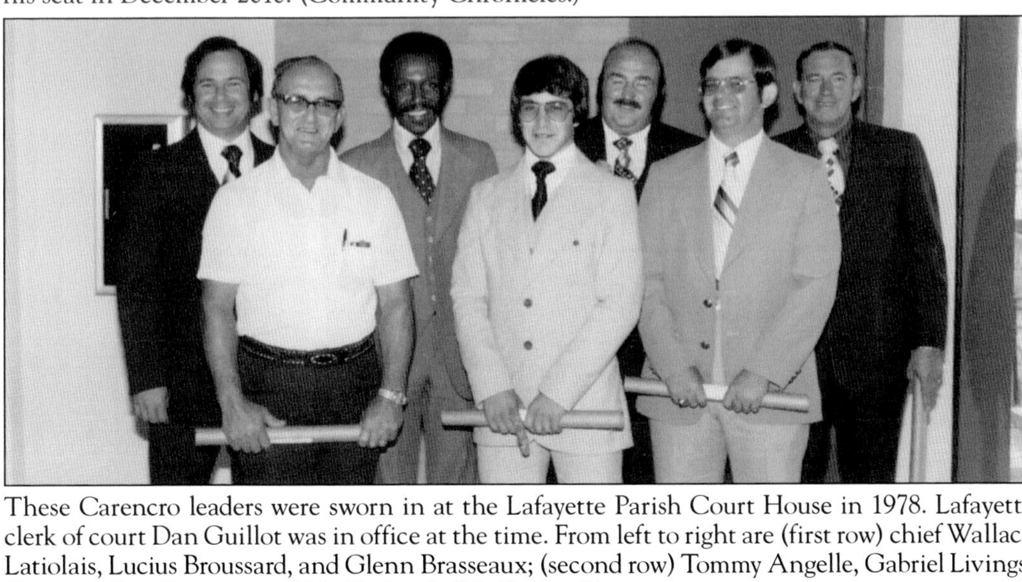

These Carencro leaders were sworn in at the Lafayette Parish Court House in 1978. Lafayette clerk of court Dan Guillot was in office at the time. From left to right are (first row) chief Wallace Latiolais, Lucius Broussard, and Glenn Brasseaux; (second row) Tommy Angelle, Gabriel Livings, George Allen Conque, and J.L. Richard. (J.L. Richard.)

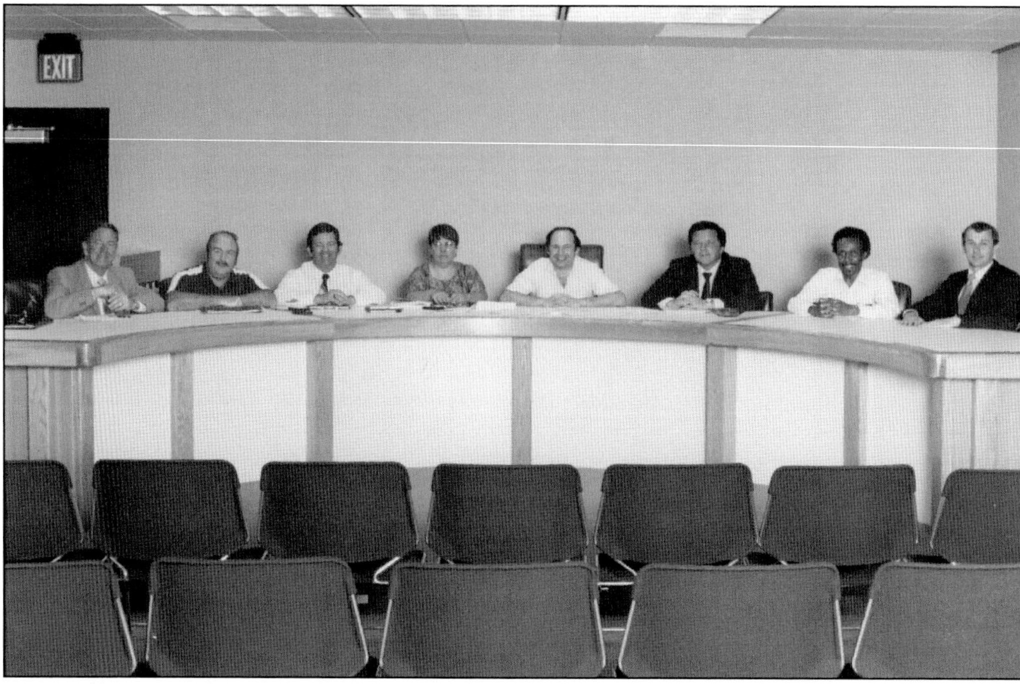

Pictured here are, from left to right, city council members J.L. Richard, George Allen Conque, Glenn Brasseaux, Marie Lemaire (town clerk), Tommy Angelle, Ernie Parker (city attorney), Gabriel Livings, and Lynn Guidry. (J.L. Richard.)

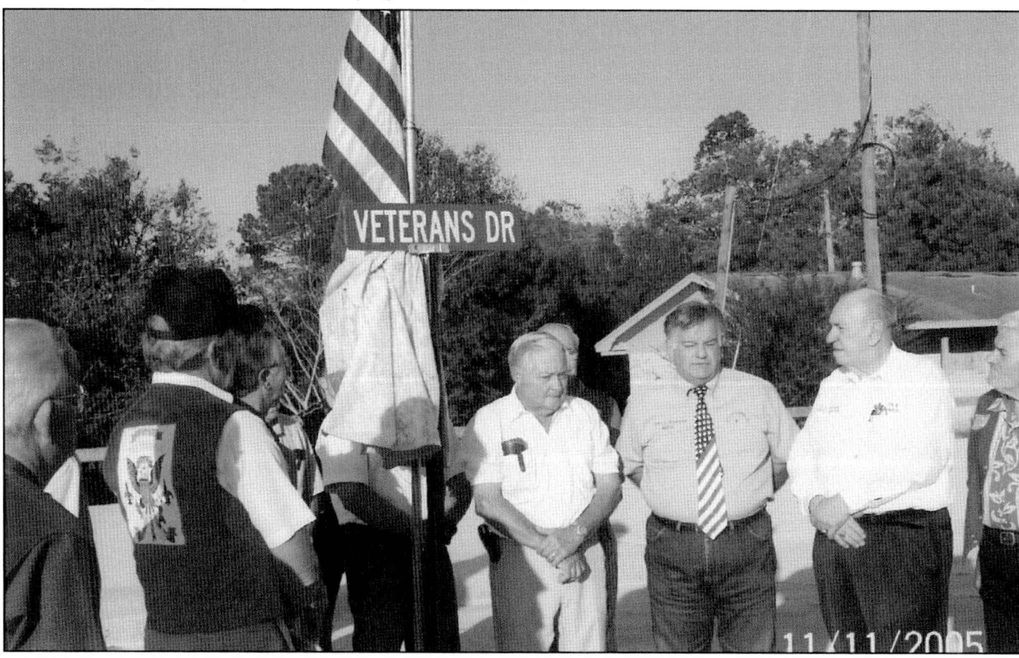

In 2005, Mayor Glenn Brasseaux and the Carencro City Council unveiled Veterans Drive. The event was attended by town residents, Carencro veterans, and city officials—all thrilled to open what would become one of the most traveled roadways in the town in the 21st century. (J.L. Richard.)

Four

Heart of the Community

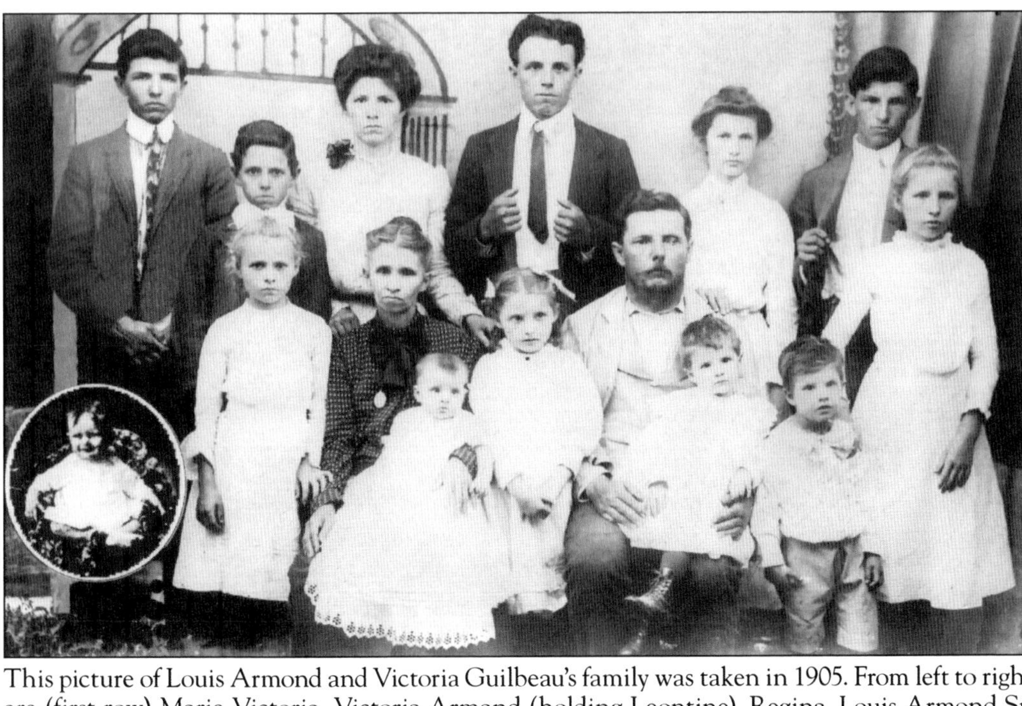

This picture of Louis Armond and Victoria Guilbeau's family was taken in 1905. From left to right are (first row) Marie Victoria, Victoria Armand (holding Leontine), Regina, Louis Armond Sr. (holding Marie Euphraisie), Louis Armond Jr., and Agnes; (second row) Louis Numa, Francois, Aglia, Lucien, Elvie, and Augustine. Cyprien Pierre, who was not yet born when the photograph was taken, is shown in the inset at left. (Clara Baudoin.)

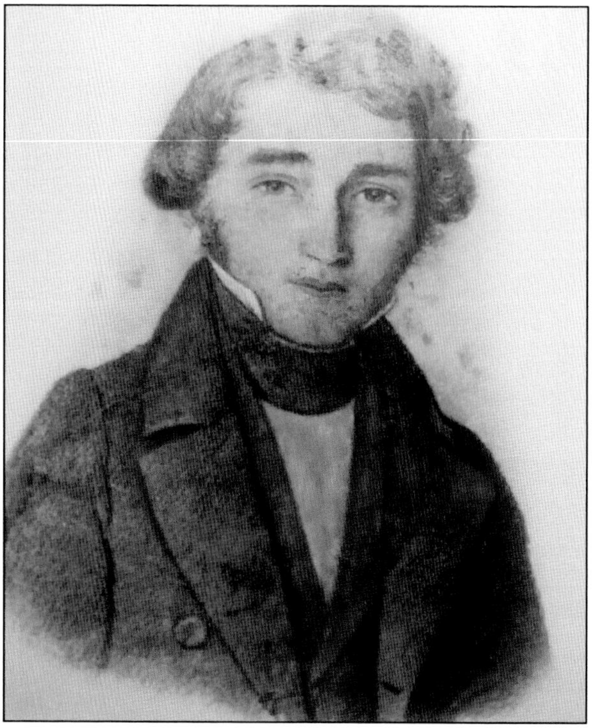

Many accounts list the kingpin of the Arceneaux clan as either Louis Pierre Arceneaux or Pierre Arceneaux. The wealthy cattle rancher is said to have shared his land with his brother and children. While Louis was betrothed to Emmeline Labiche, he made it to the Carencro Prairie before she did. In that time, he met and married Marie Ann Bergeron, and they had five sons and three daughters: Louis, Pierre, Alexandre, Francois, Cyprien Pierre, Catherine, Marie Jeanne, and Francoise. (Carmen Perry.)

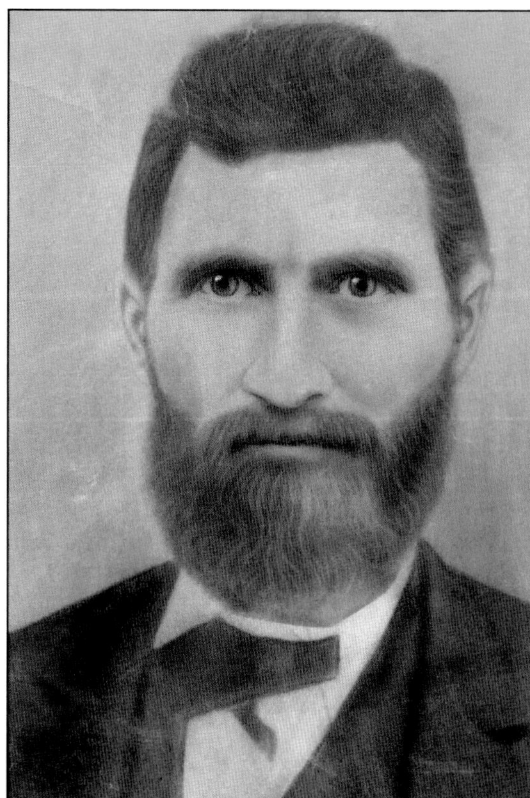

Ovignac Arceneaux was born in 1883 and died in 1894. He was married to Emerante Breaux in 1857. Ovignac and his wife are said to have donated land for the St. Pierre Cemetery. (Janice Martin.)

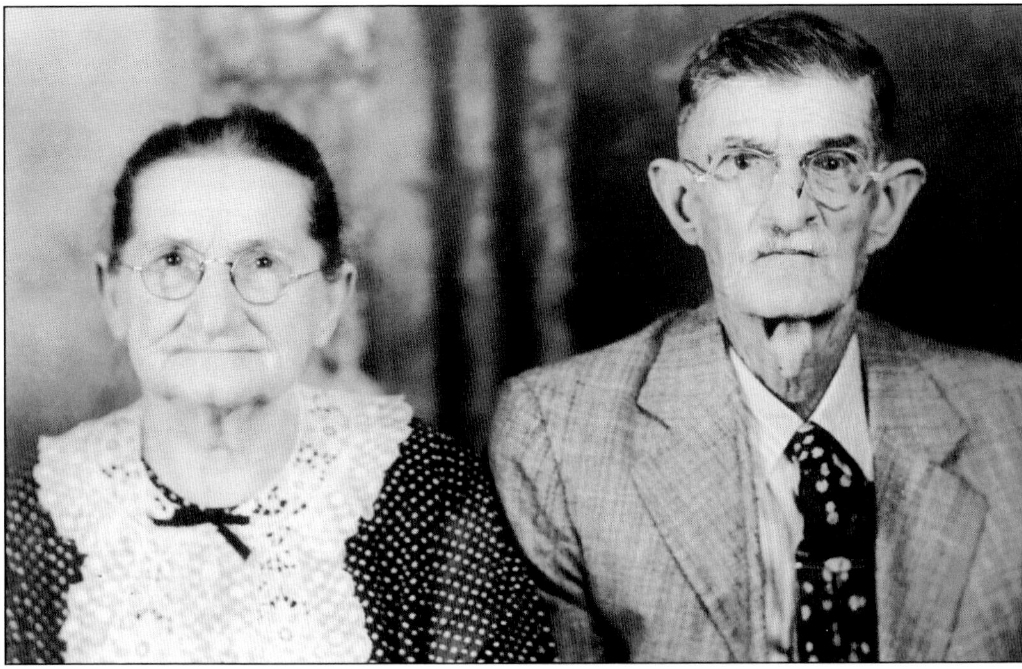

Anna Forrestier was an accomplished weaver. She spun her own thread from cotton on her spinning wheel, then used her homemade loom to weave fabric to make blankets, bedspreads, tablecloths, napkins, rugs, trousers, and more. She did this for many years. Pictured here are Anna Forrestier Benoit and Ophe Benoit. Adolphina Benoit, their daughter, assisted her mother with the weaving. Southwestern Louisiana Industrial Institute, which is now the University of Louisiana at Lafayette, recruited her to do weaving workshops throughout Louisiana and Texas. (Both, Evely Robin.)

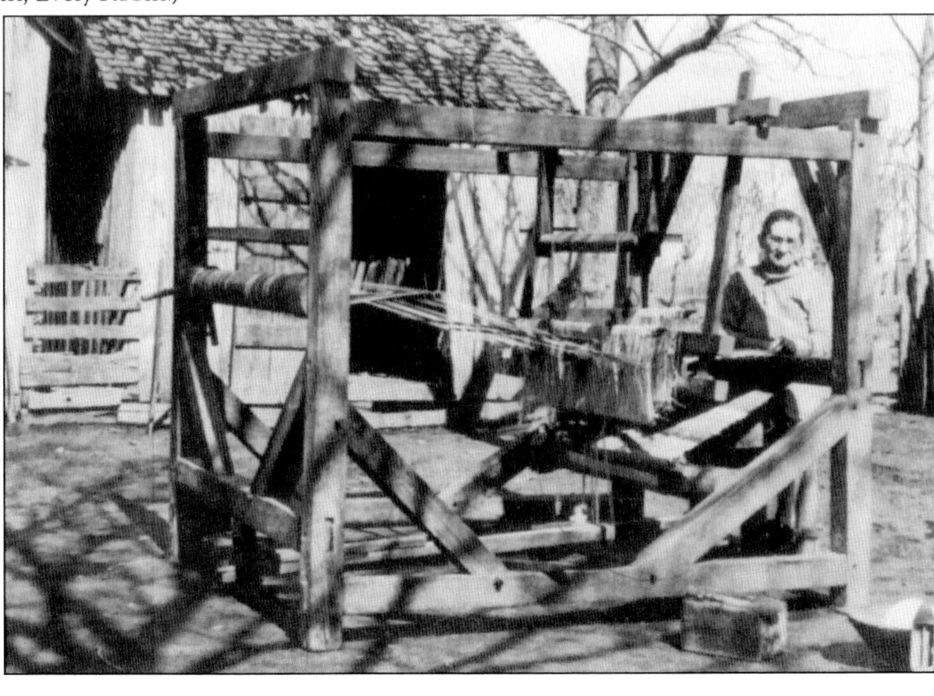

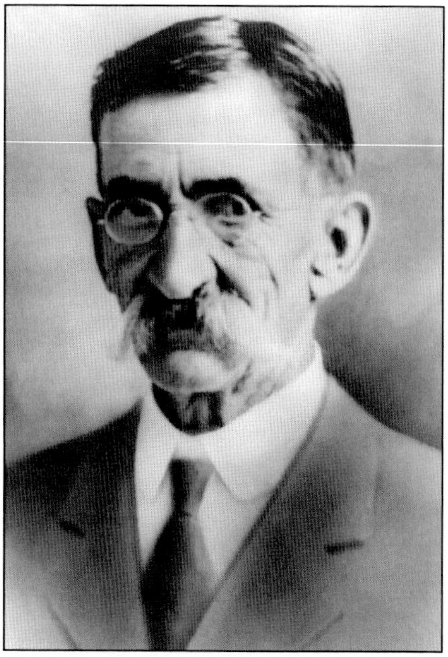

According to Norman Brennan, Dr. Ursin Theomile Prejean was born on September 27, 1855, in St. Landry Parish. He moved to Carencro in 1880 and practiced medicine there for many years. His practice covered St. Landry Parish and a large portion of Lafayette Parish, including Carencro. His home and practice were located on Church Street. He also served in the Civil War under the 18th Louisiana Infantry. (Louis Perret.)

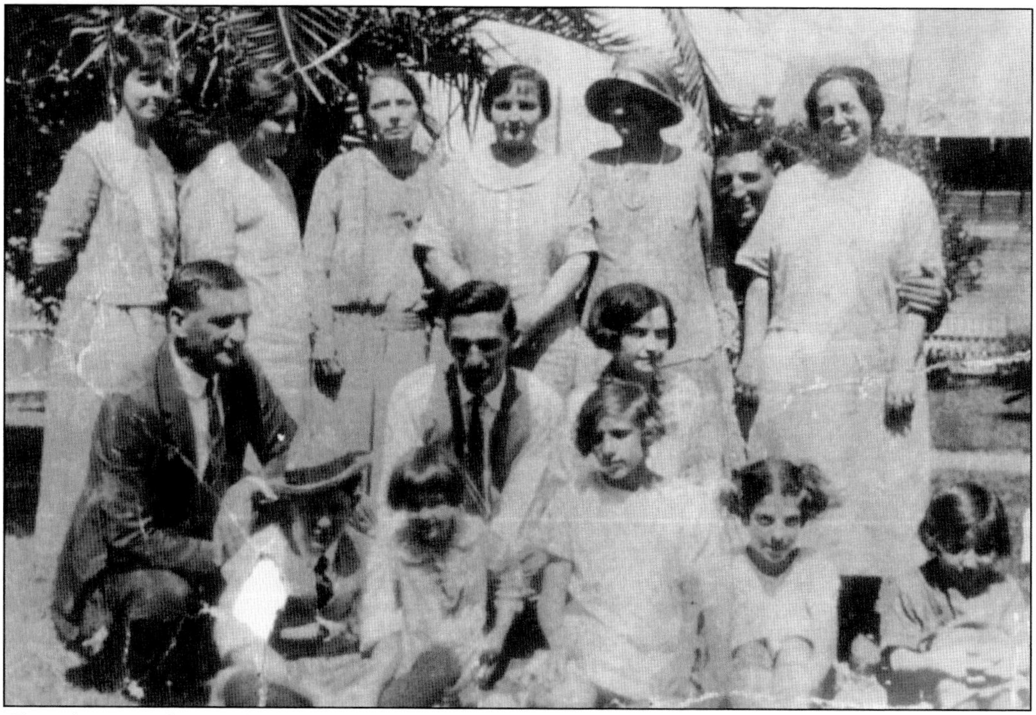

This photograph is of the Martin and Guilbeau families, who had gathered for Elsie Martin's first Communion. Elsie's little sister, Iris, had chicken pox, so only those who previously had the disease could attend. Pictured here are, from left to right, (first row, seated) Eric Guilbeau Jr., Carroll Guilbeau, unidentified, Elsie Martin Arceneaux, and Anna Grace Martin Richard; (second row, kneeling/squatting) Claude Martin, Esteve Martin, and unidentified; (third row) two unidentified, Ethel Broussard Martin, Marie Azelia (Nan) Guidry Guilbeau, Ophelia Martin, George E. Martin (peeking through), and Josianne Guilbeau Martin. (Catherine Arceneaux Brasseaux.)

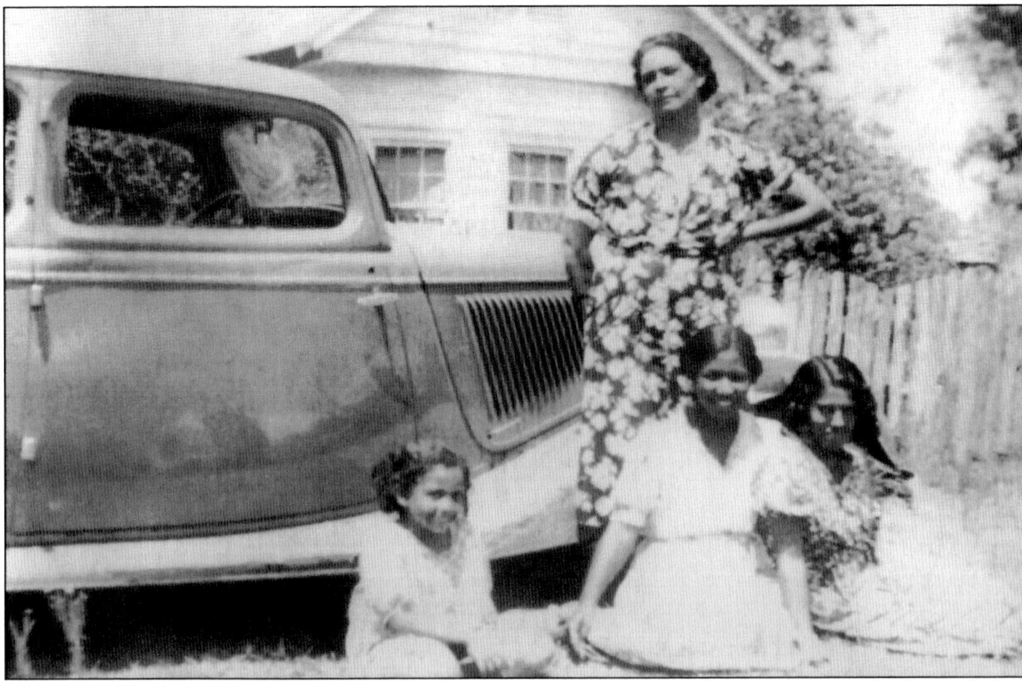

The youngest child in this photograph is Imelda Gordon Oden, and Andrea LeBlanc Gordon is standing. One of the Gordon girls, Christiana Gordon Smith, taught during the school year at St. Elizabeth and attended a normal school in the summer. Smith is now recognized as the first African American to graduate from Southwestern Louisiana Industrial Institute (now known as the University of Louisiana at Lafayette). In 1956, she earned her degree in education. It was said that her degree was inspired by Katherine Drexel. (Lela Gordon Mouton family.)

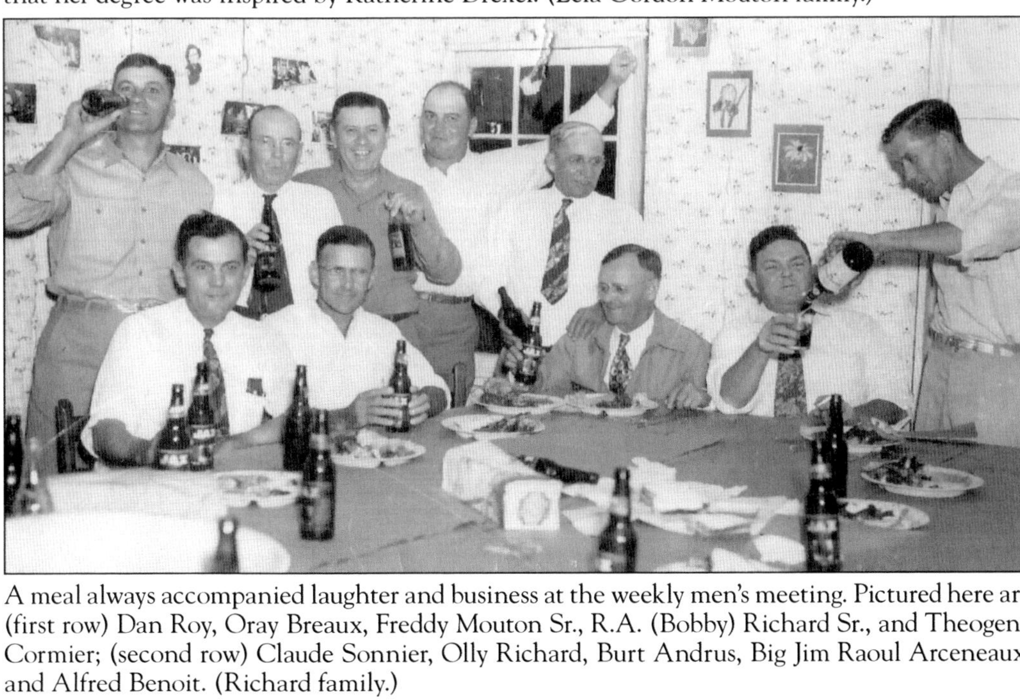

A meal always accompanied laughter and business at the weekly men's meeting. Pictured here are (first row) Dan Roy, Oray Breaux, Freddy Mouton Sr., R.A. (Bobby) Richard Sr., and Theogene Cormier; (second row) Claude Sonnier, Olly Richard, Burt Andrus, Big Jim Raoul Arceneaux, and Alfred Benoit. (Richard family.)

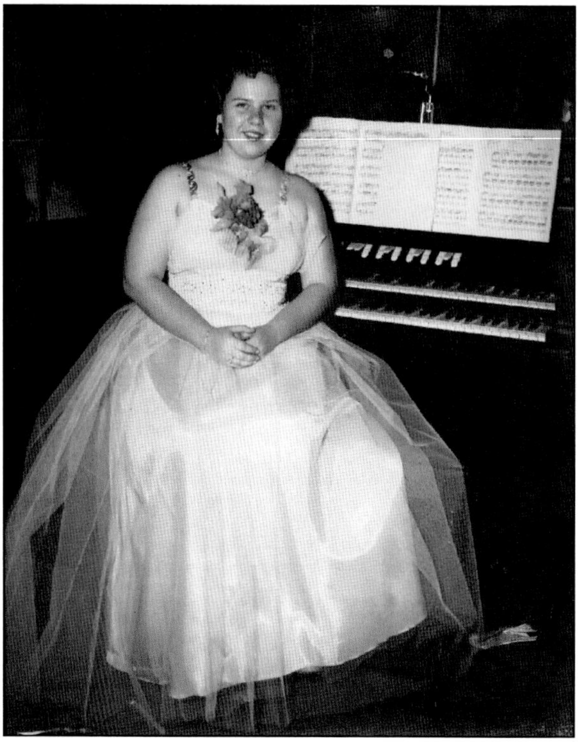

Geraldyne Andrus Arceneaux was born and raised in Carencro. Her father, Burt Andrus, owned a store downtown. She gave back to the community in so many ways, including playing the organ at St. Peter Roman Catholic Church for more than 50 years. At times, she even played in her police chief uniform. She was married to Sosthene Arceneaux and had two children, Burt and Kenny. (Kenny Arceneaux.)

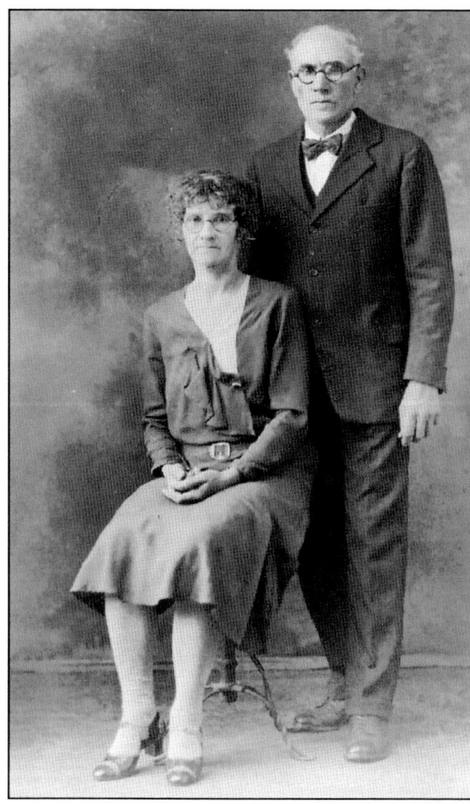

Numa and Philomene Cormier are descendants of Pierre Cormier. Their family donated the land for St. Peter Roman Catholic Church. (Liz Sonnier.)

Five

Learning and Faith

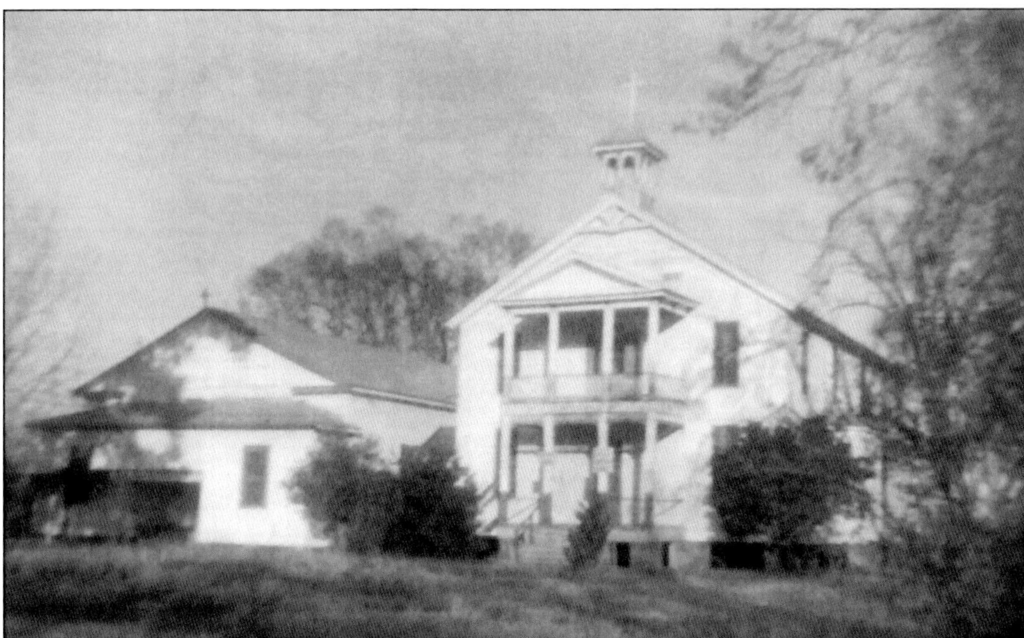

St. Ann Convent was built around 1897. It was located on the corner of Church and St. Ann Streets. The school was run by the Sisters of Mount Carmel. The convent was torn down and replaced by a home for Msgr. Auguste Wassler. Today, the home is used for the residing priest of St. Peter Roman Catholic Church. This picture was taken in 1896.

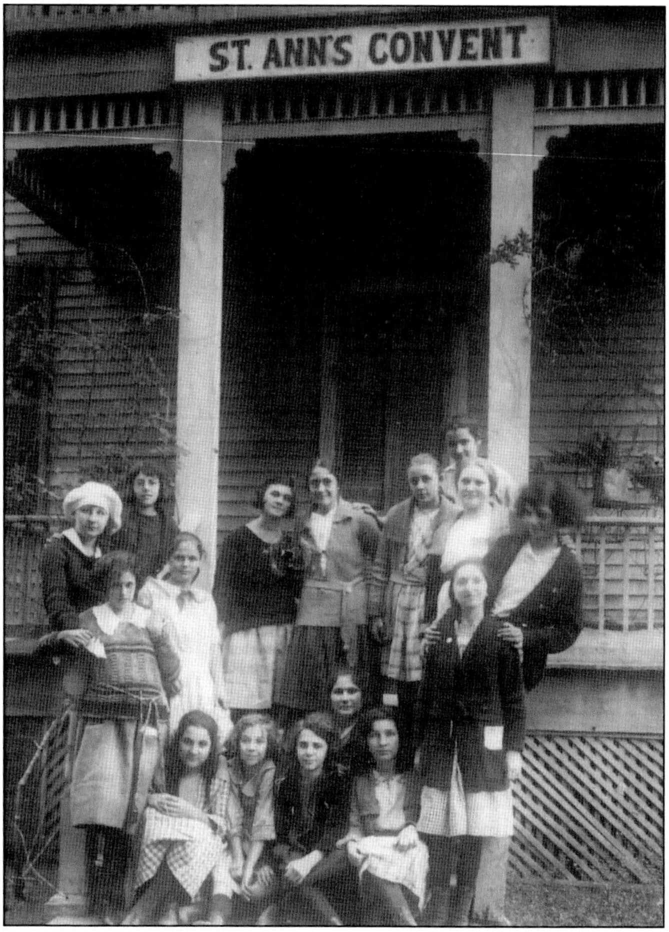

Pictured at left is the St. Ann's Convent class of 1923–1924. Among those pictured are Ida Delhomme, Marie Nine Bechet, Odile Coussan, Judith Miller, Sophie Bernard, Ida Block, Eula Martin, Thelma "Sister" Chachere, Heloise Coussan, Marie Arceneaux, Aurore Arceneaux, Agnes Benoit, Carita Melchoir, and Helen Crouchet. Odile Coussan, one of the young women in the picture, later became Sister Augusta Marie of the Mount Carmel Order. Pictured below is the student body along with the priests and nuns of St. Ann's.

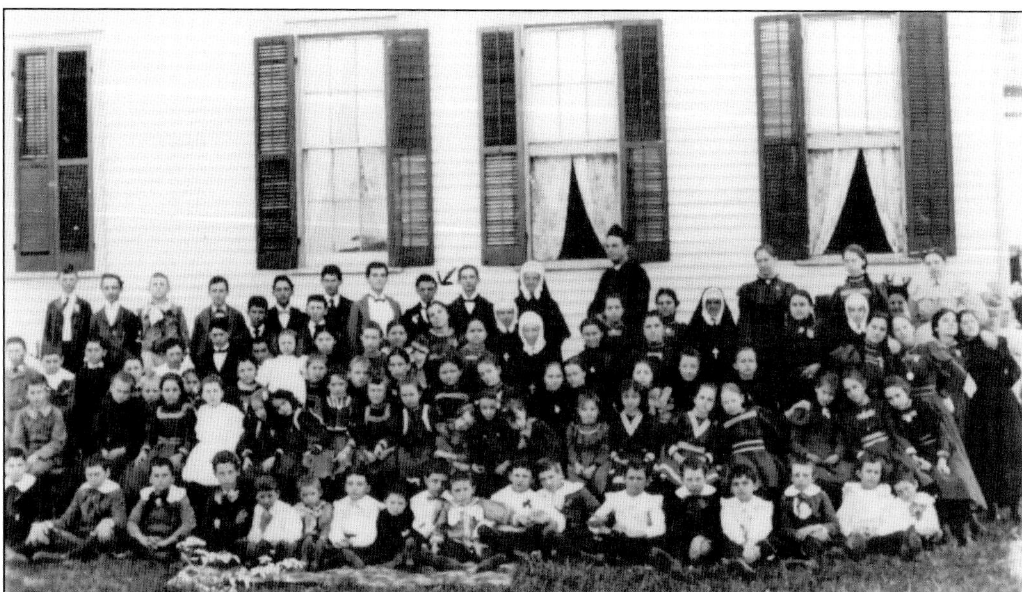

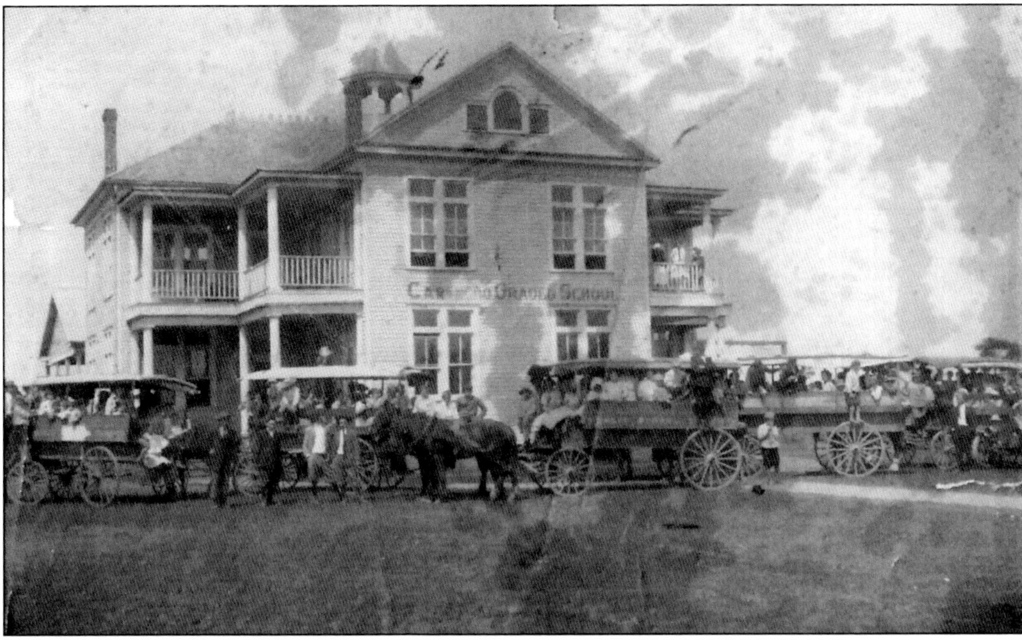

Carencro Graded School eventually became Carencro High School. The school was located in downtown Carencro. The first school "buses" were horse-drawn carriages, as shown here.

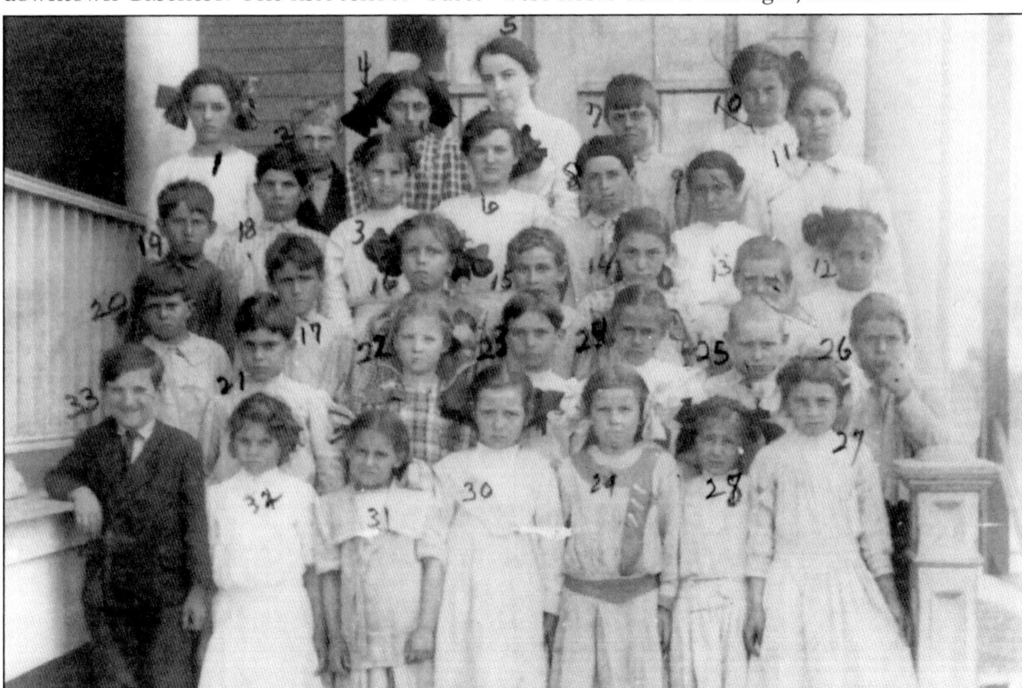

This Carencro Elementary School third-grade class picture was taken in 1911. Among those pictured are Ella Dugas, Ulysee Melancon, Corrine Babineaux, Regina Guilbeau, Cornelia Lane (teacher), Elmire Broussard, Adolph Guilbeau, Leonard Colomb, J. Dupuis, E. Guilbeau, T. Miller, E. Latour, Harris Breaux, R. Richard, Alma Broussard, Corrine Guilbeau, Adam Guilbeau, Gladu Dupuis, Etta Guilbeau, Gladys Bacque, Valsin Richard, and Pete Babineaux. (Louis Perret.)

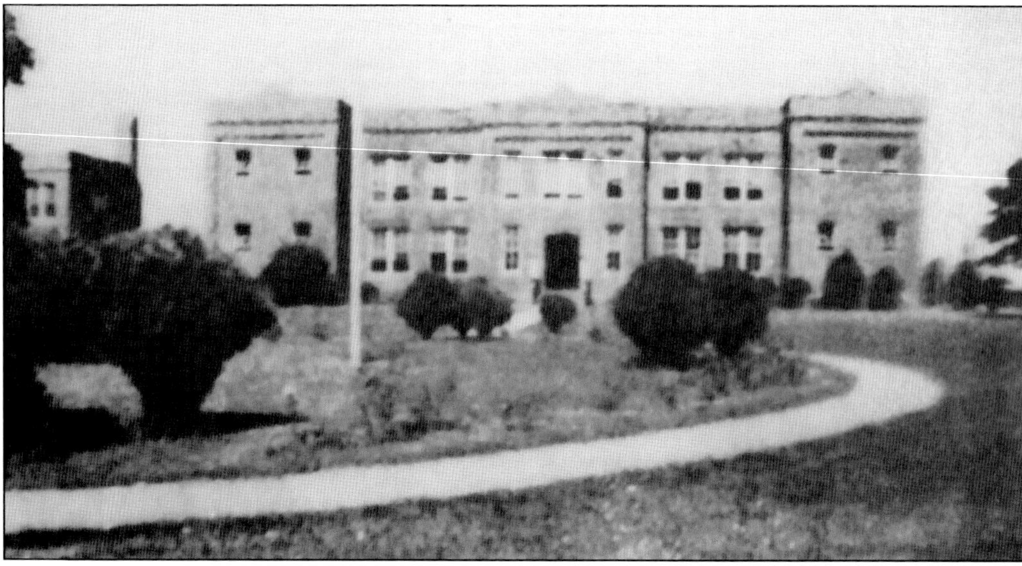

The new Carencro High School had two brick buildings. The front building served elementary school students, and the brick building in the back (pictured) was for high schoolers. Due to a population increase, Carencro High School moved into the new brick building in 1926. These buildings housed both the high school and the elementary school along with an auditorium.

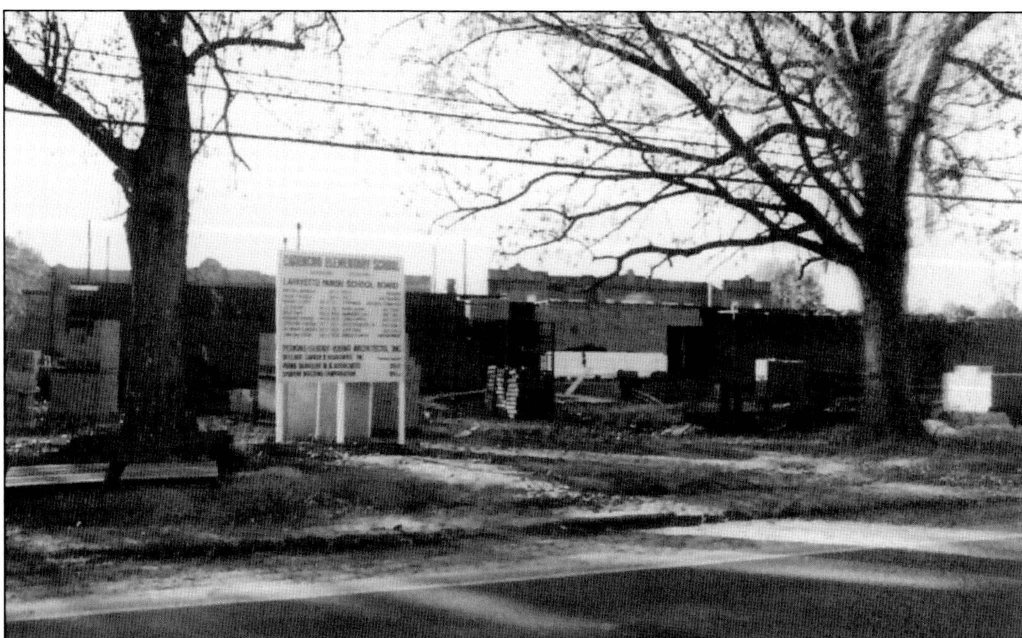

Carencro Elementary School was constructed in 1981. Carencro High School can be seen in the background. Today, the grounds of the former Carencro Elementary School are home to Carencro Middle School.

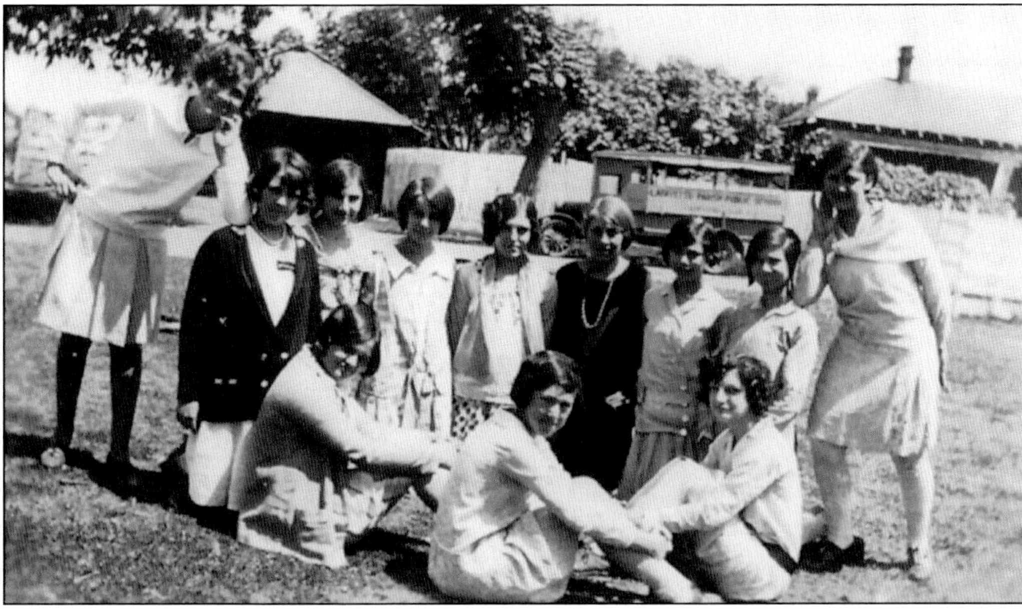

This photograph shows the Carencro High School eighth-grade class of 1927. Notice the Lafayette Public School bus in the background.

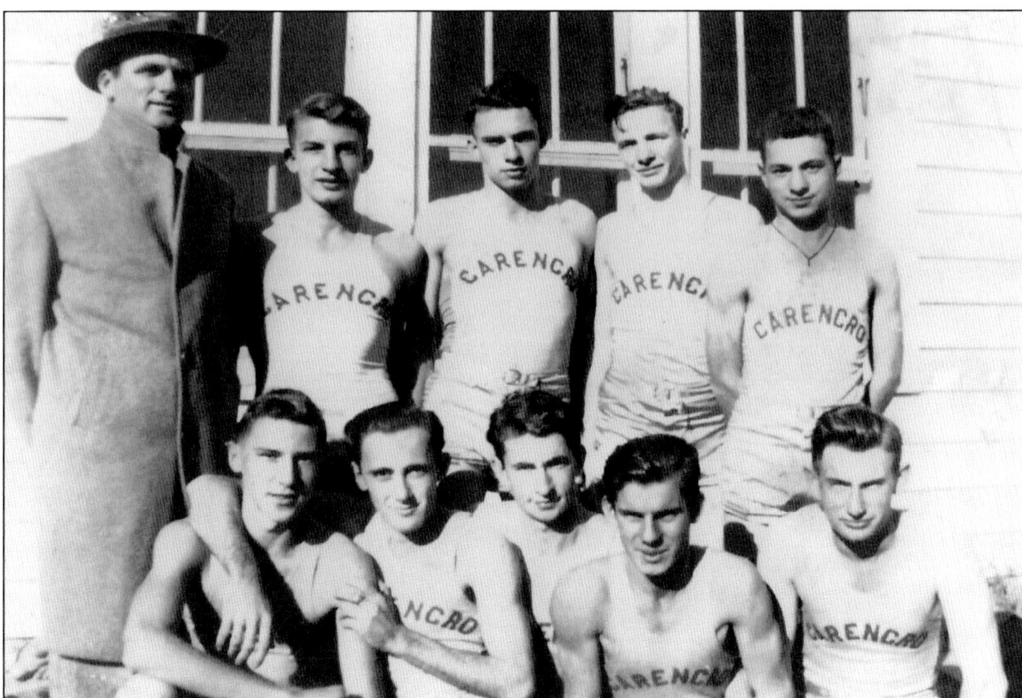

This is the 1947 Carencro High School basketball team. Pictured are, from left to right, (first row) Melvin "Joe" Domingue, Adolph Babineaux, Shelton Sonnier, Dudley Arceneaux, and Alphe "Tee" Guilbeaux; (second row) coach Elmo Authement, Dale Guidry, Edward Cormier, Francis Thibodeaux, and Preston Prejean. (Louis Perret.)

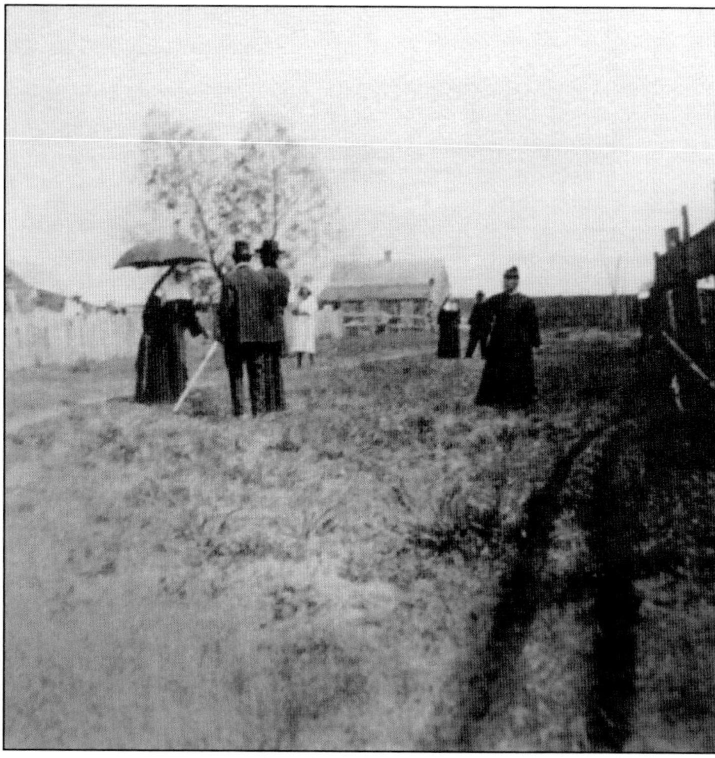

Washington Hayes Gordon and Andrea LeBlanc Gordon firmly believed in education. A piece of the family's land was donated for a two-room schoolhouse funded by Katherine Drexel. Pictured here are Sister Katherine Drexel, Mother Mercedes, the Gordons, and Msgr. Auguste Wassler breaking ground for the new school. (Lela Gordon Mouton family.)

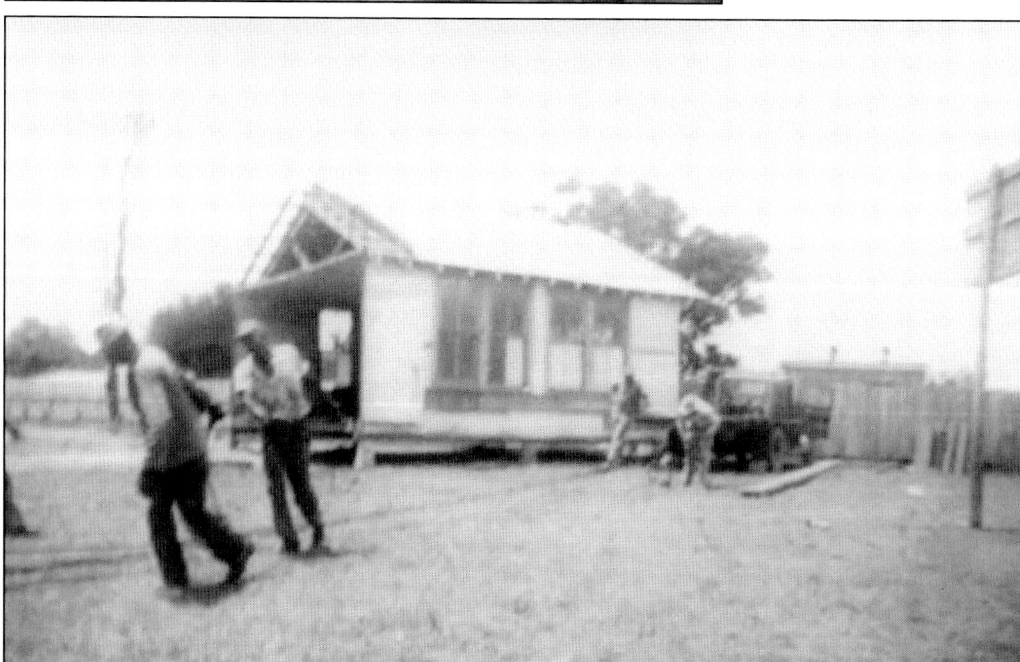

This is the schoolroom from the Sosthene Arceneaux School that was first opened by Katherine Drexel in 1924. The schoolroom was eventually donated to Our Lady of the Assumption School. In the background are the outhouses used by the schoolchildren. (Our Lady of the Assumption School Historic and Preservation Society.)

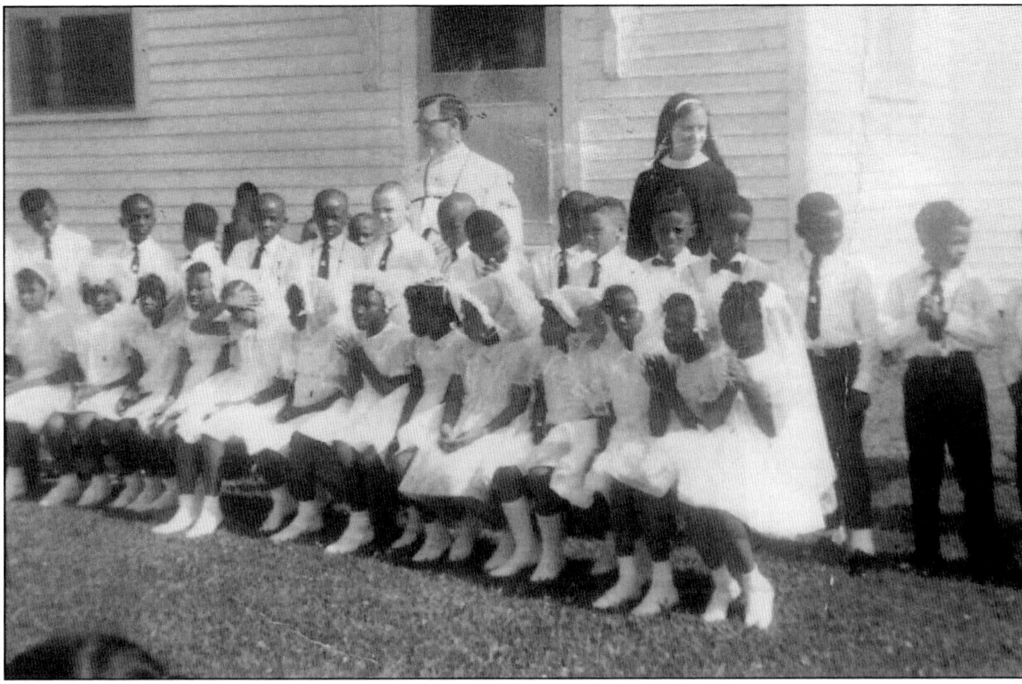

After the death of Katherine Drexel in 1955, all of her schools gradually closed their doors—but someone was looking out for the children of Prairie Basse and the surrounding community, as students were able to attend the first Catholic school for African American children, Our Lady of the Assumption School. (Our Lady of the Assumption School Historic and Preservation Society.)

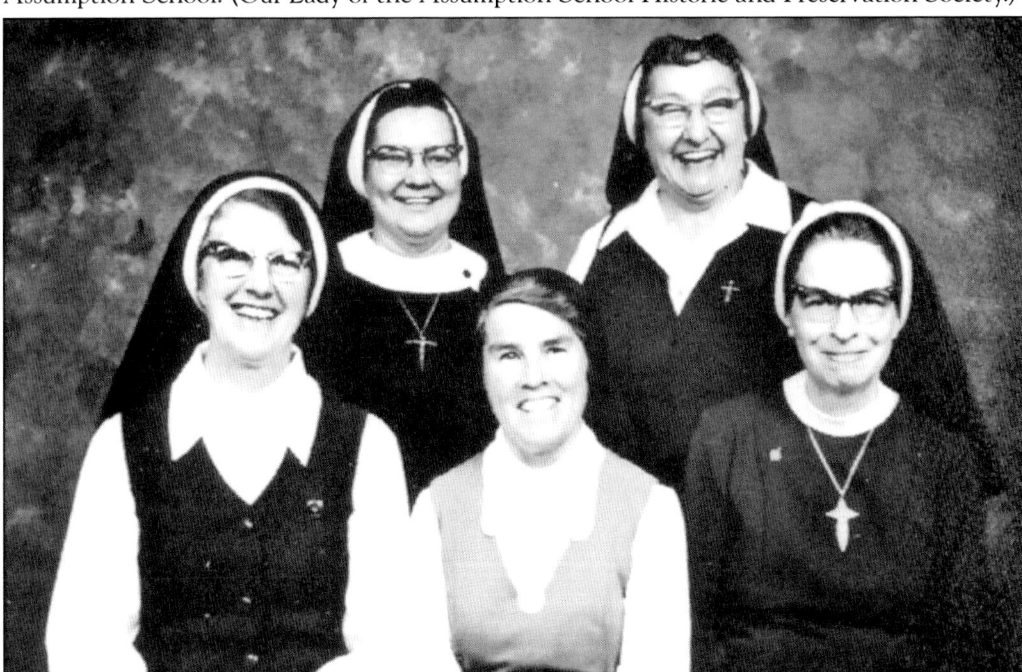

Class at Our Lady of the Assumption School was taught by the nuns pictured here and also by lay teachers. (Our Lady of the Assumption School Historic and Preservation Society.)

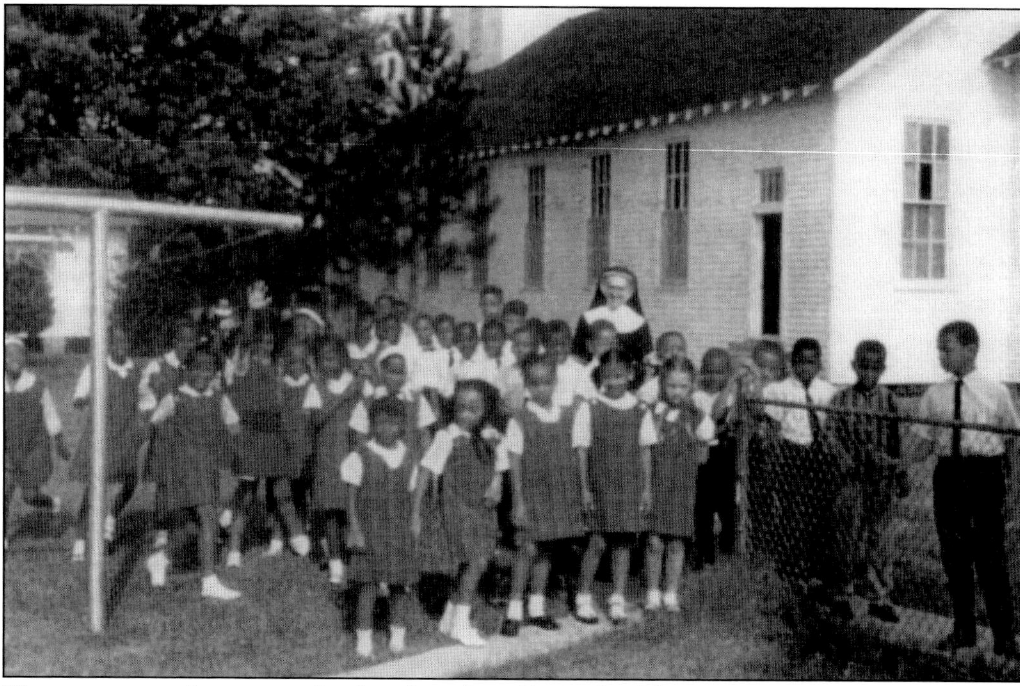

These are young elementary school students from Our Lady of the Assumption School in Carencro. (Our Lady of the Assumption School Historic and Preservation Society.)

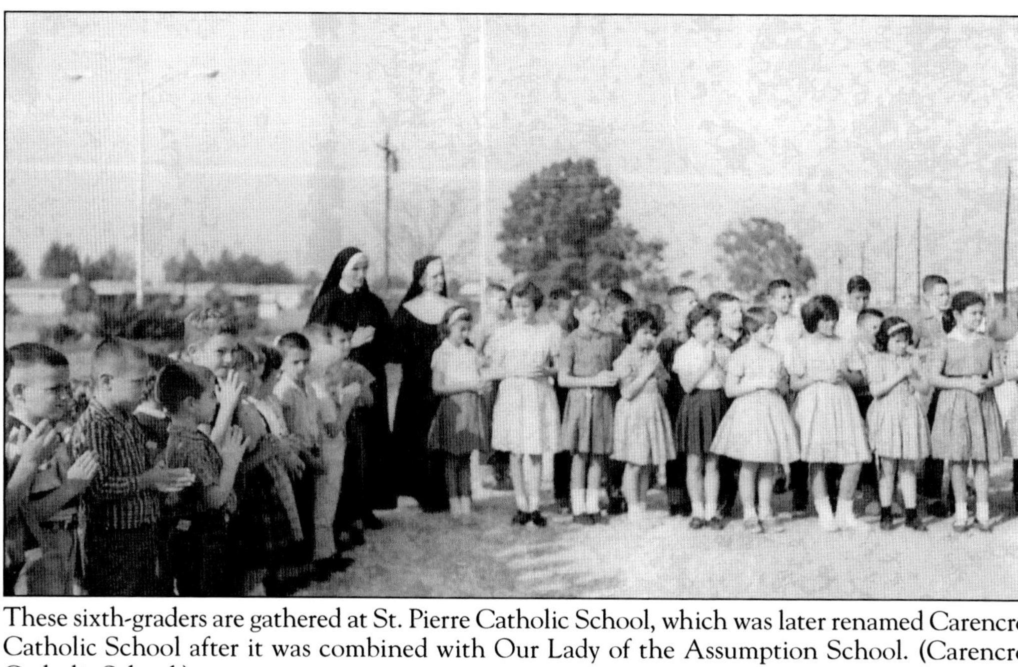

These sixth-graders are gathered at St. Pierre Catholic School, which was later renamed Carencro Catholic School after it was combined with Our Lady of the Assumption School. (Carencro Catholic School.)

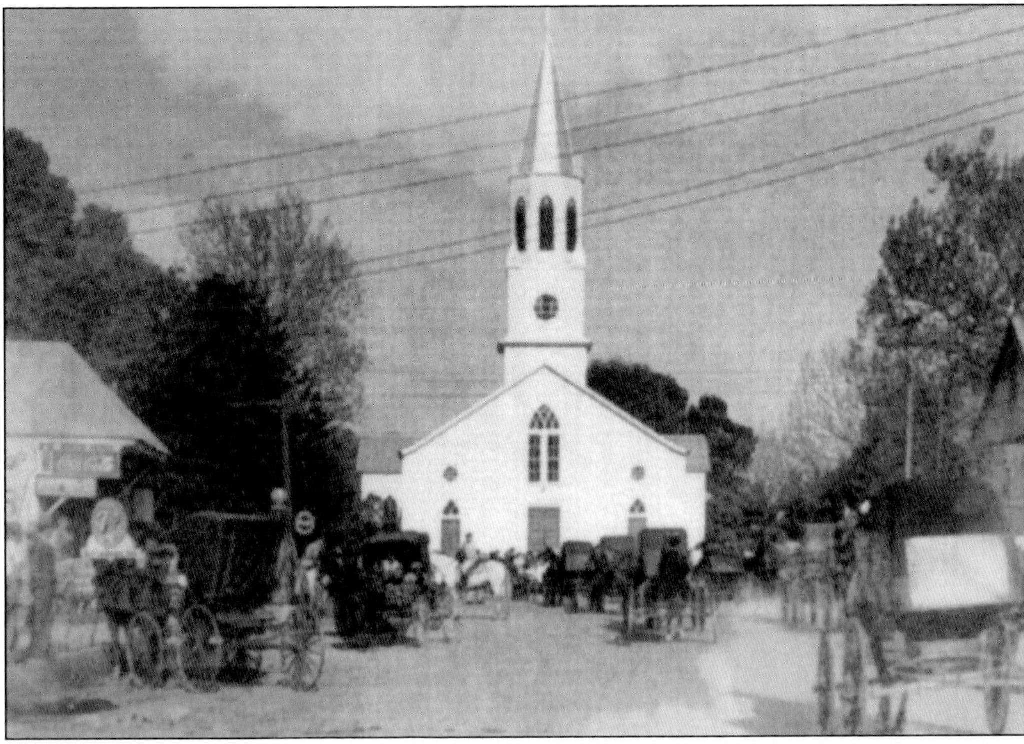

St. Peter Roman Catholic Church was first constructed in 1877. The church was destroyed and rebuilt four times. It was destroyed twice by fire and twice by storms.

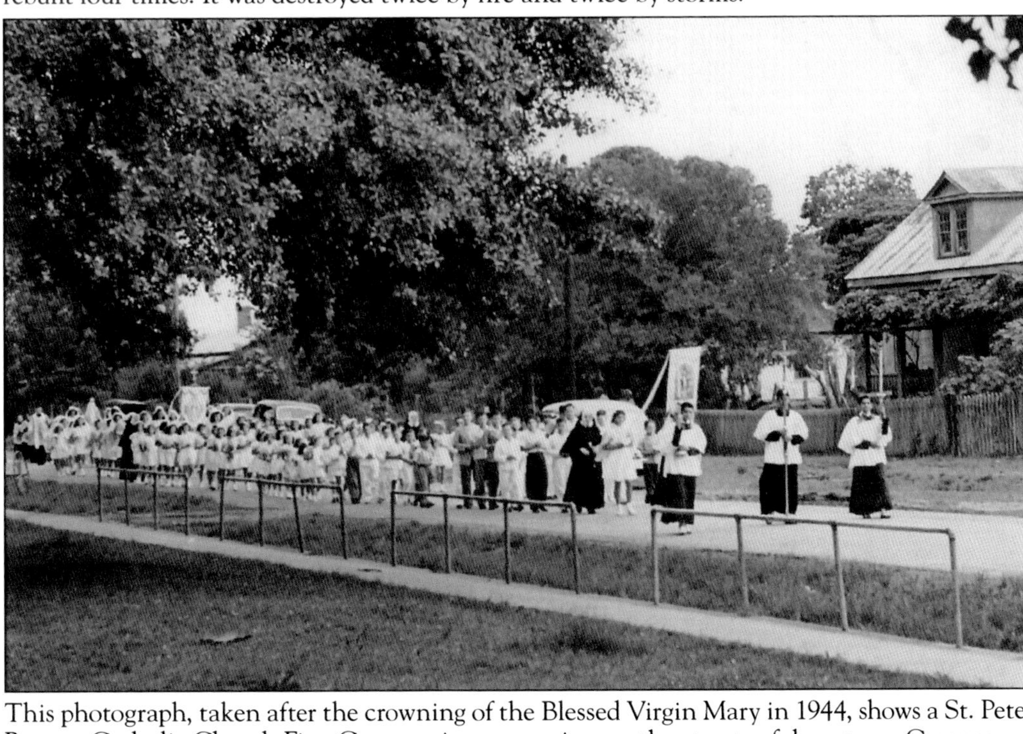

This photograph, taken after the crowning of the Blessed Virgin Mary in 1944, shows a St. Peter Roman Catholic Church First Communion procession on the streets of downtown Carencro.

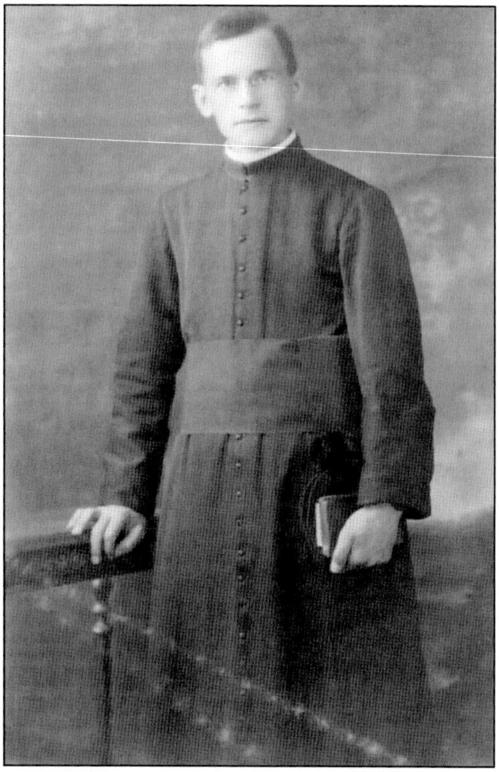

Msgr. Auguste Wassler worked for many years to redo the interior of St. Peter Roman Catholic Church. From the altar that was hand-carved in Belgium to the sparkling stained-glass windows designed in Colmar, France, Monsignor Wassler desired a place of beauty where many generations could worship for years to come. The pews, designed with the crests of families who worshipped in the parish, were installed by Monsignor Wassler in 1966. Today, the church stands as a testament to his dream for St. Peter Roman Catholic Church.

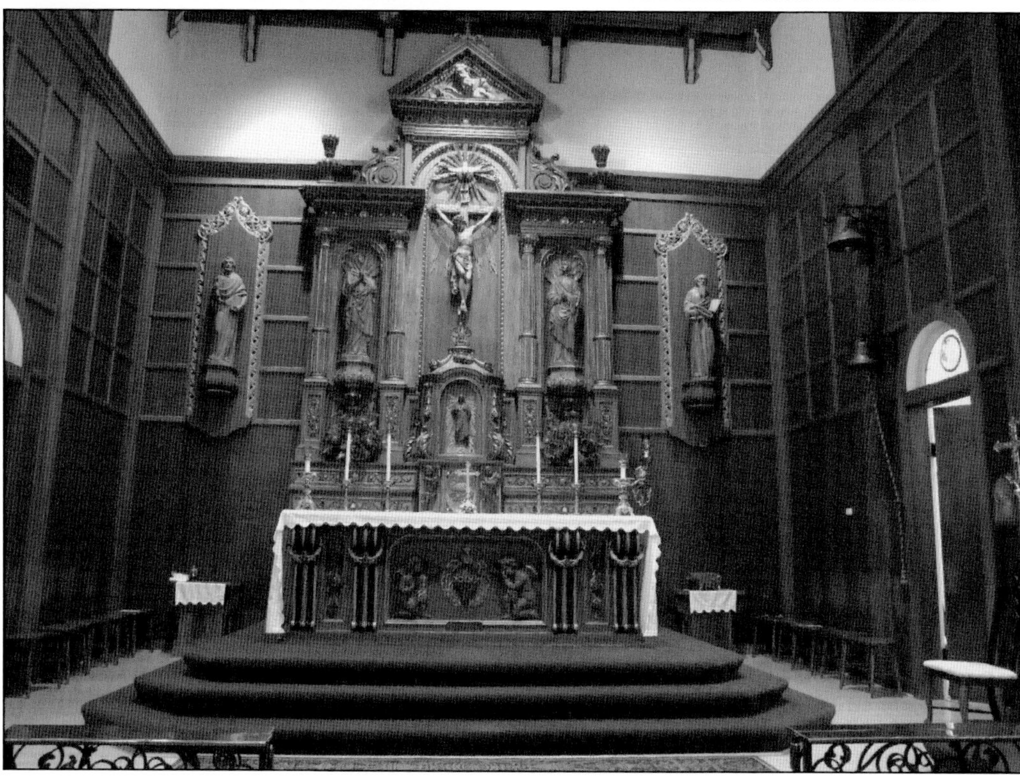

St. Peter Roman Catholic Church is seen here with a brick facade. The church celebrated 140 years of service in May 2014. It was created by Archbishop Napoleon Joseph Perche of the Roman Catholic Archdiocese of New Orleans. Rev. A.J.M. Guillot was appointed the first pastor of the parish. Fourteen pastors have served St. Peter since its establishment in 1874. Fr. Mark Ledoux is now the pastor, and Fr. Andre Metrejean is the associate pastor.

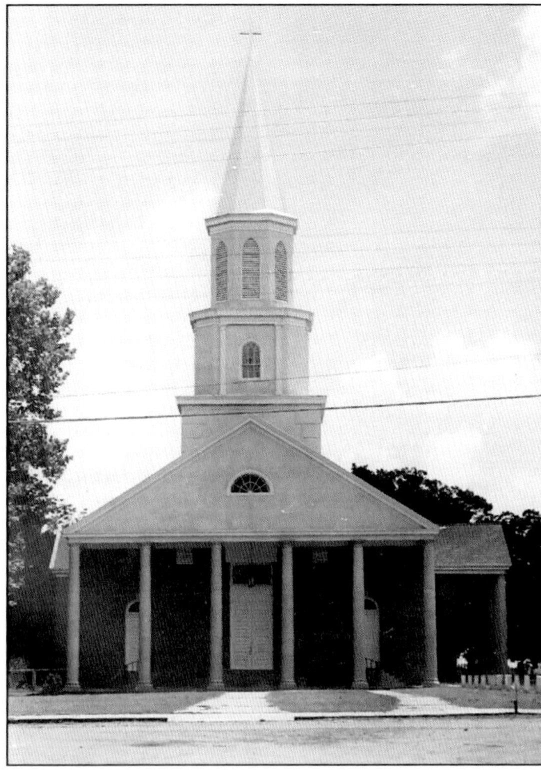

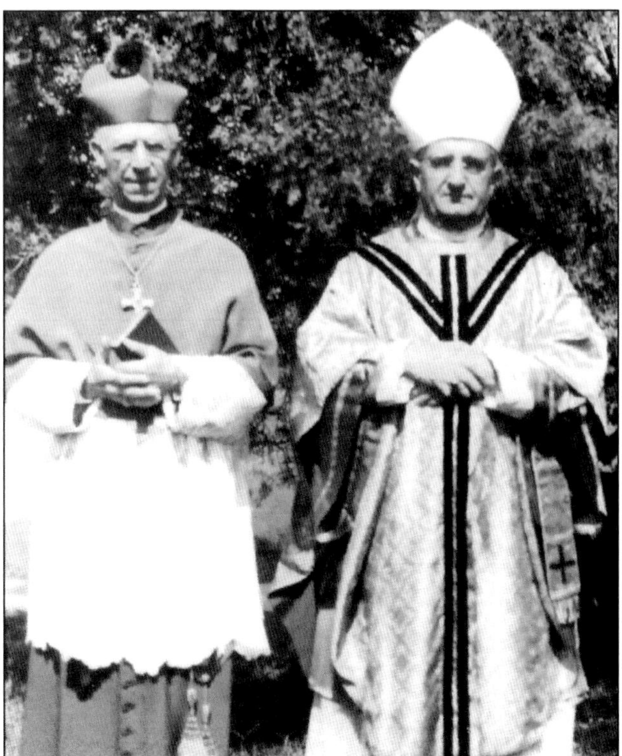

Bishop Jules B. Jeanmard (left) lived with his parents in Carencro for many years. He was installed as the first bishop of Lafayette in 1918 and established a number of separate African American churches and also, with assistance from Mother Katherine Drexel, a number of schools for African American children. Jeanmard is pictured with the first chancellor of Lafayette, Msgr. John Vigliero.

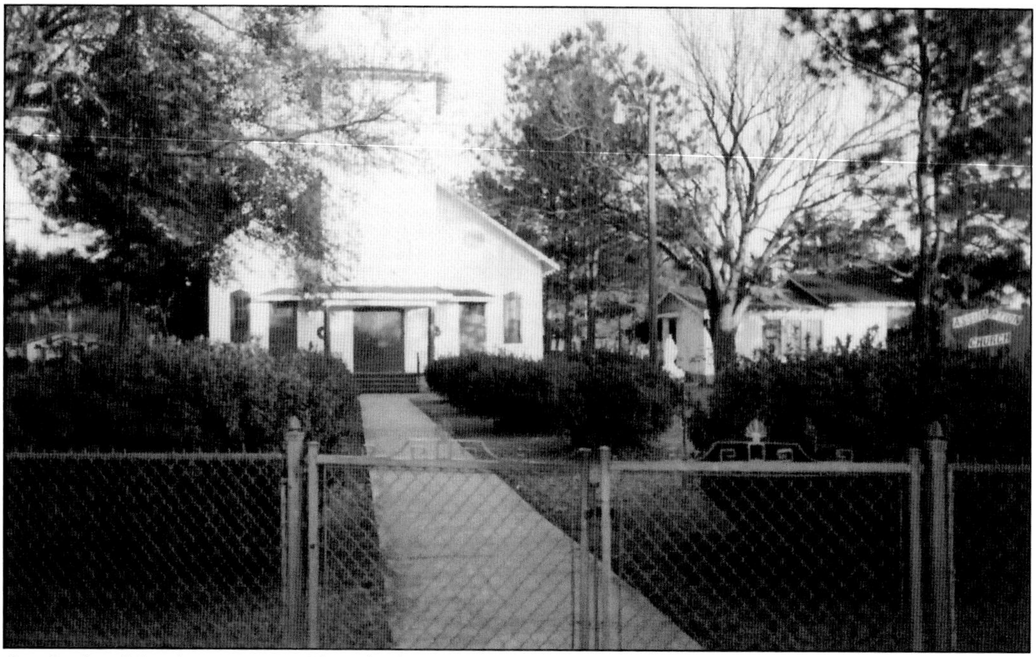

Our Lady of the Assumption Church's history dates to 1925, when Bishop Jules Jeanmard established and personally oversaw the building of a Catholic church to serve the African American community of Carencro. The first pastor, Rev. Joseph Dolan, supervised the purchase of land on Michaud Street to build the first church structure in 1926. (Our Lady of the Assumption School Historic and Preservation Society.)

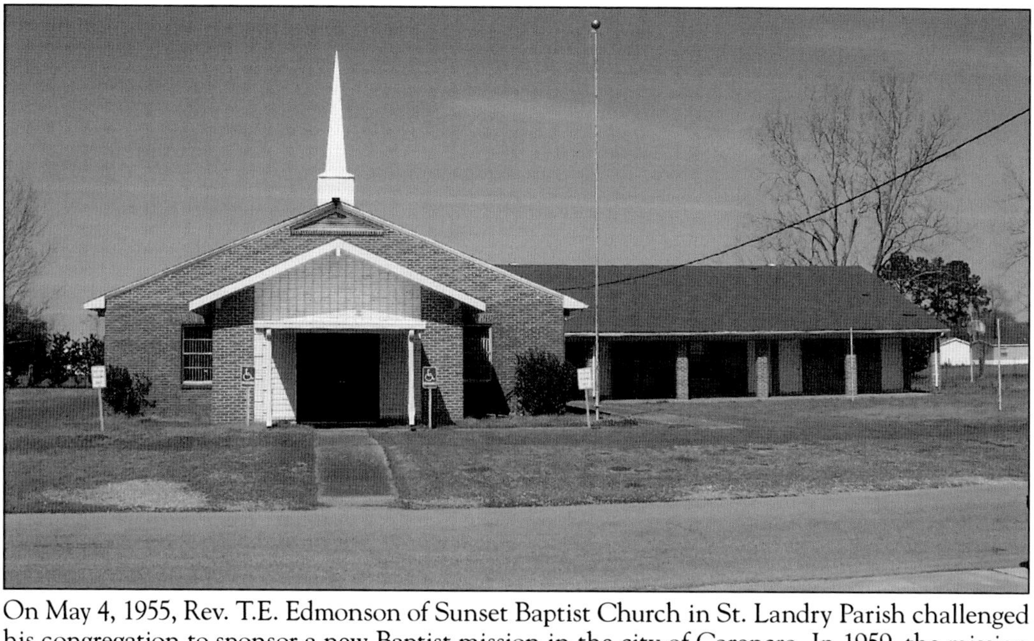

On May 4, 1955, Rev. T.E. Edmonson of Sunset Baptist Church in St. Landry Parish challenged his congregation to sponsor a new Baptist mission in the city of Carencro. In 1959, the mission voted to elect a building committee and purchased property to build a church. Today, the church sits at 242 St. Pierre Boulevard. (First Baptist Church of Carencro.)

Six

Homes with History

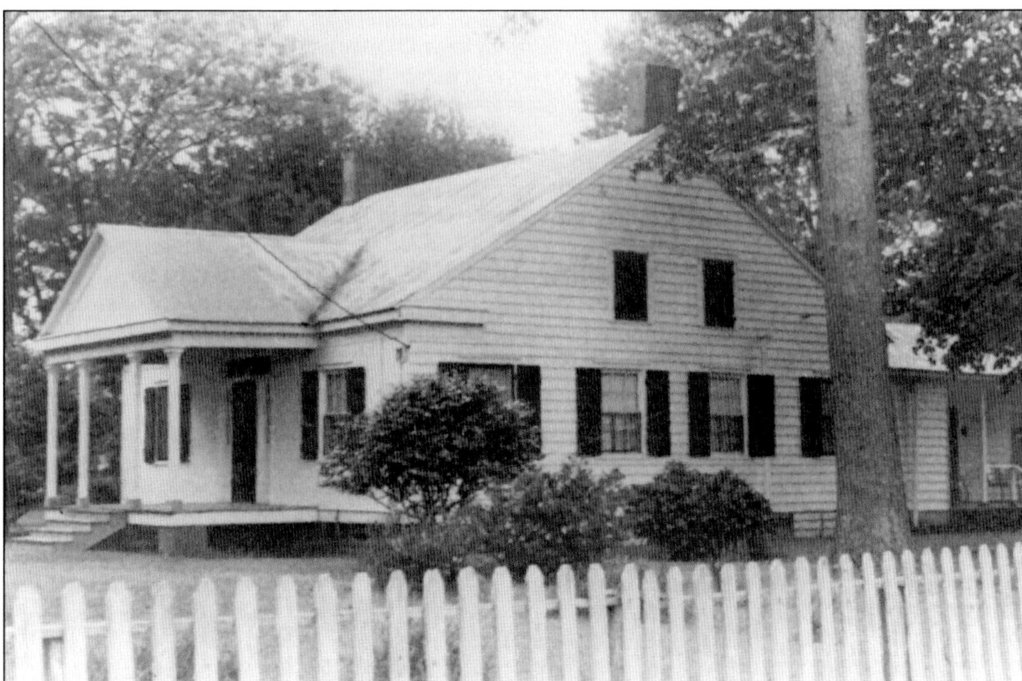

Louis Pierre Arceneaux had his home built along the bluffs in Beau Bassin around 1765. A successful rancher, Arceneaux had land spread over eight tracts of 324 arpents. He constructed two homes next to each other in similar styles. He and his wife, Marie Ann Bergeron, raised their children on the land. Arceneaux was reputedly the source for the character Gabriel in Henry Wadsworth Longfellow's poem *Evangeline*.

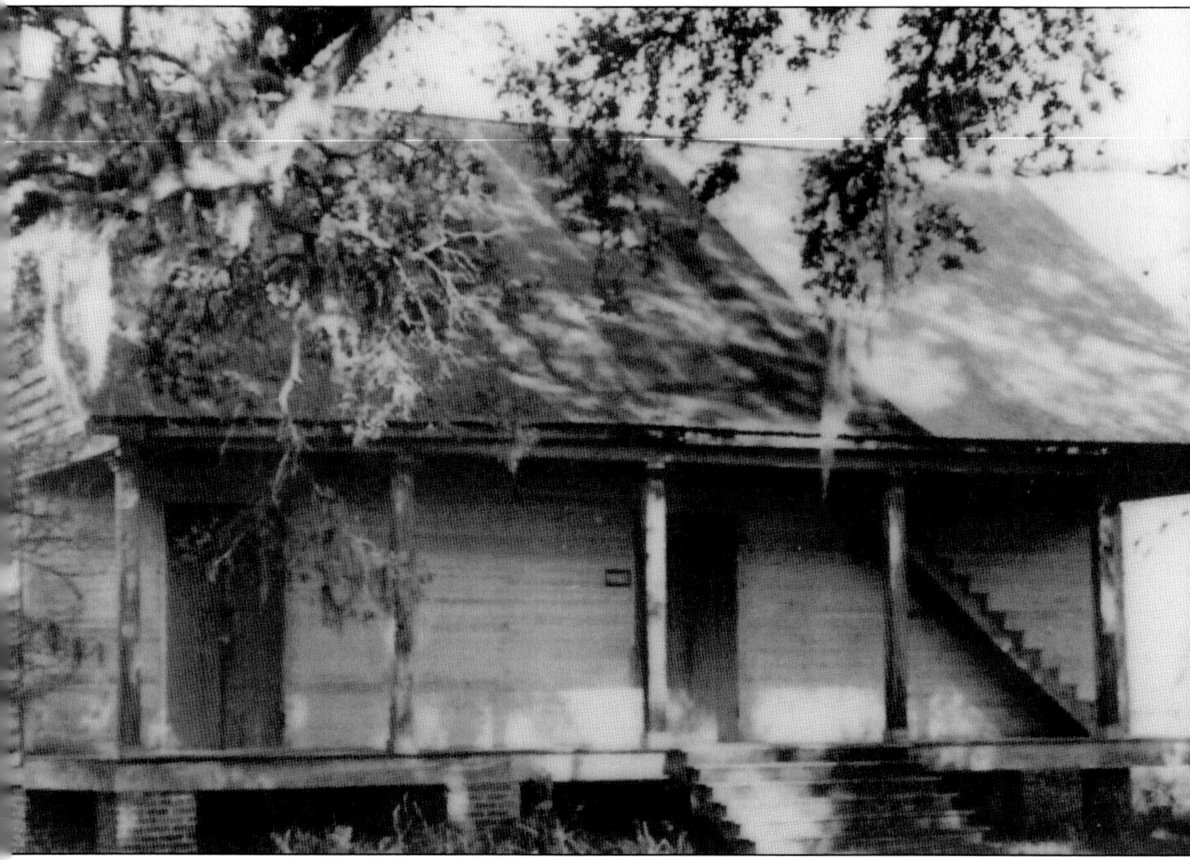

In the 18th and 19th centuries, it was common for a family's land to hold more than one home. When a child left home, they would build their own home on their parents' property, which is what happened on the Arceneaux land. One of the homes from Louis Pierre Arceneaux's property on Beau Bassin now sits in historic Vermilionville. The other home was moved closer to Carencro and is located on Louis Arceneaux Road. Carmen Perry stated, "Never has a home been loved or filled with love like this one. The house when moved from Beau Bassin was done so with oxen and logs. For holidays prior to selling in 2014, family would still gather to celebrate."

The walls in the Louis Arceneaux home show a mixture of colombage and bousillage. These materials could be found in many homes in the Carencro Prairie. In fact, the walls of the Arceneaux home are still filled with the mixture of clay and grass. Reportedly, children would gather for school in the attic. (Community Chronicles.)

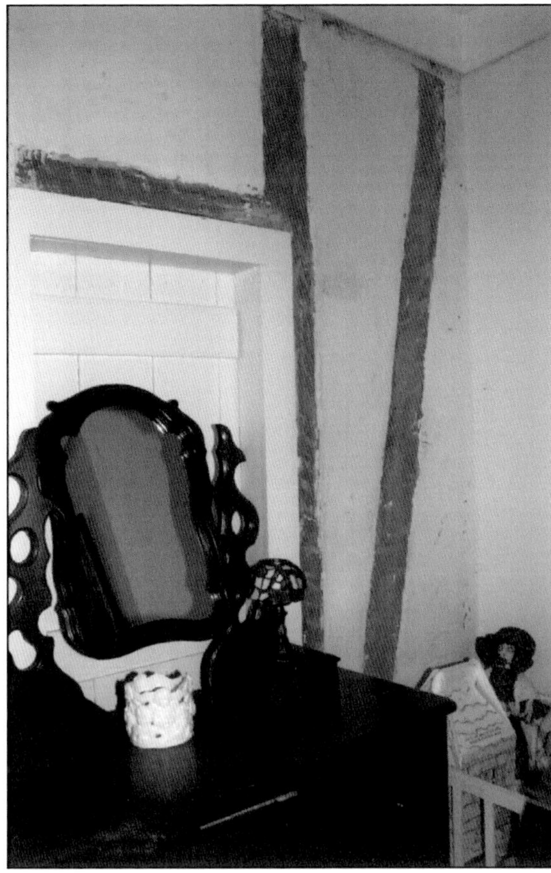

The Alexandre Latiolais House is a one-and-a-half-story gable structure. The first construction on the home occurred in 1790. The completed home had four rooms, a front and rear gallery, and attic space. Around 1827, the earlier structure was enlarged. The new look was known as Federal style. The beautiful home stands on Butcher Switch surrounded by historic oaks.

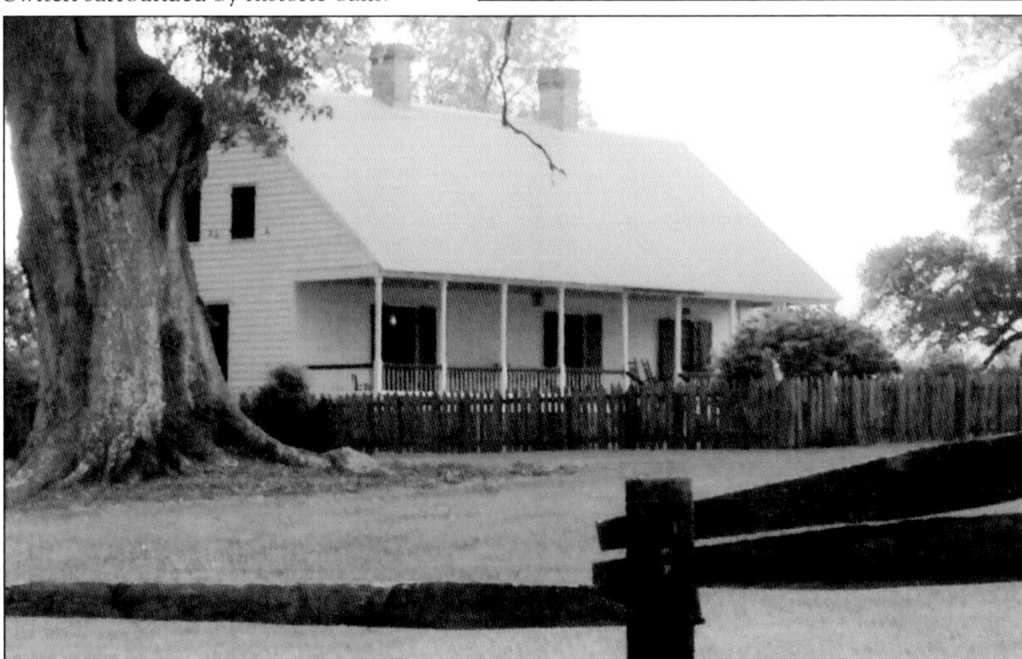

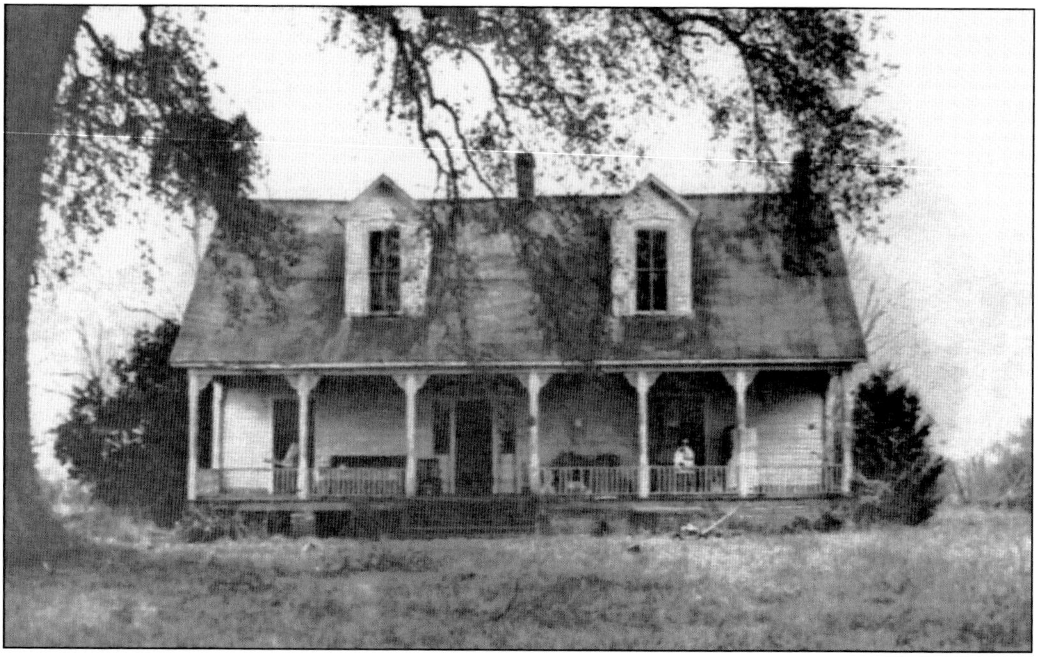

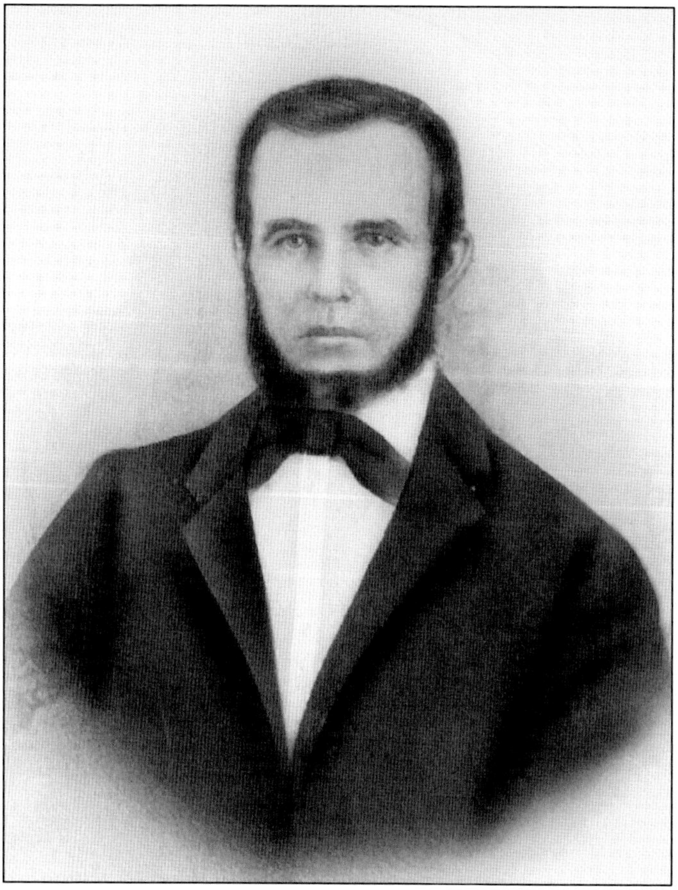

Romain Francez was born in France on March 2, 1817. Dr. Francez's family came to the United States, and Francez himself settled in St. Pierre on what is now known as Rue Des Etoiles on the outskirts of Carencro. The home was built prior to the Civil War. Dr. Francez treated many Carencro Prairie people during the yellow fever epidemic in 1858.

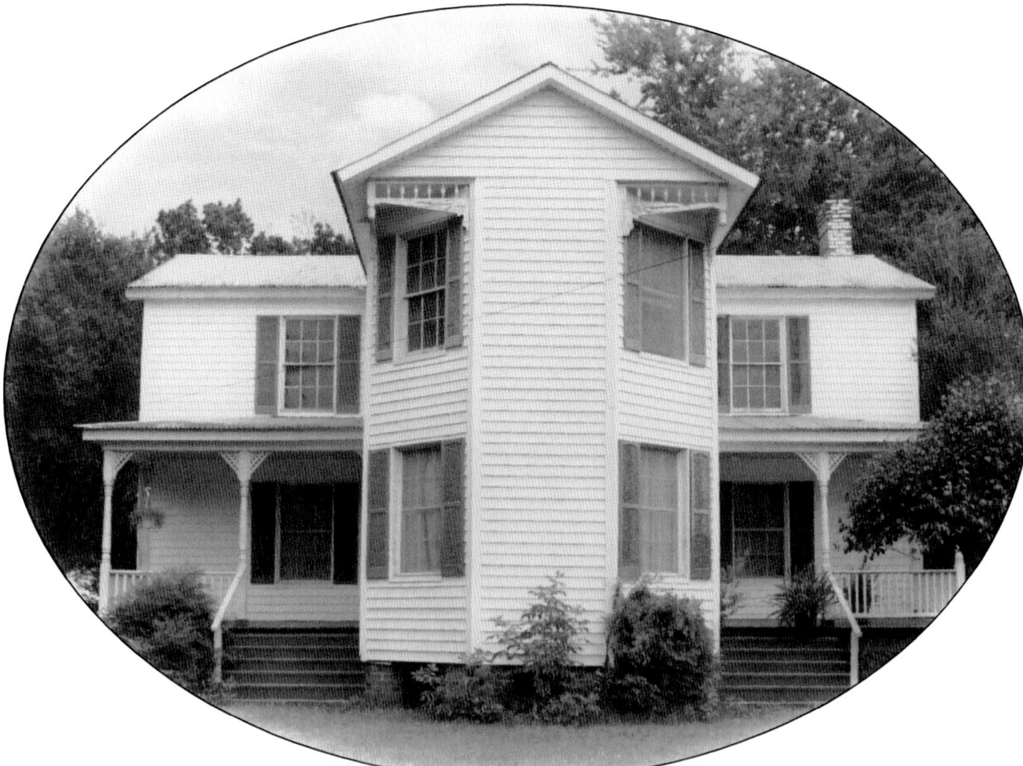

This large, white Victorian-style home is located on Theo Street. Fifty arpents were purchased by Edouard Hector Magnon from the Pierre Cormier family on January 20, 1872. On March 31, 1885, Oscar S. Lyon negotiated the acquisition of the western 20 arpents. On December 12, 1888, the Lafayette Building Association accepted two acres as collateral and built the home in 1889. The two-story framed house has 3,000 square feet, with four fireplaces and two wide porches. In 1899, Bishop Jules Jeanmard Jr. lived in the home. Bishop Jeanmard's family remained in the residence until 1918, when Theo Joseph Breaux purchased the property and home. (Landry Studios.)

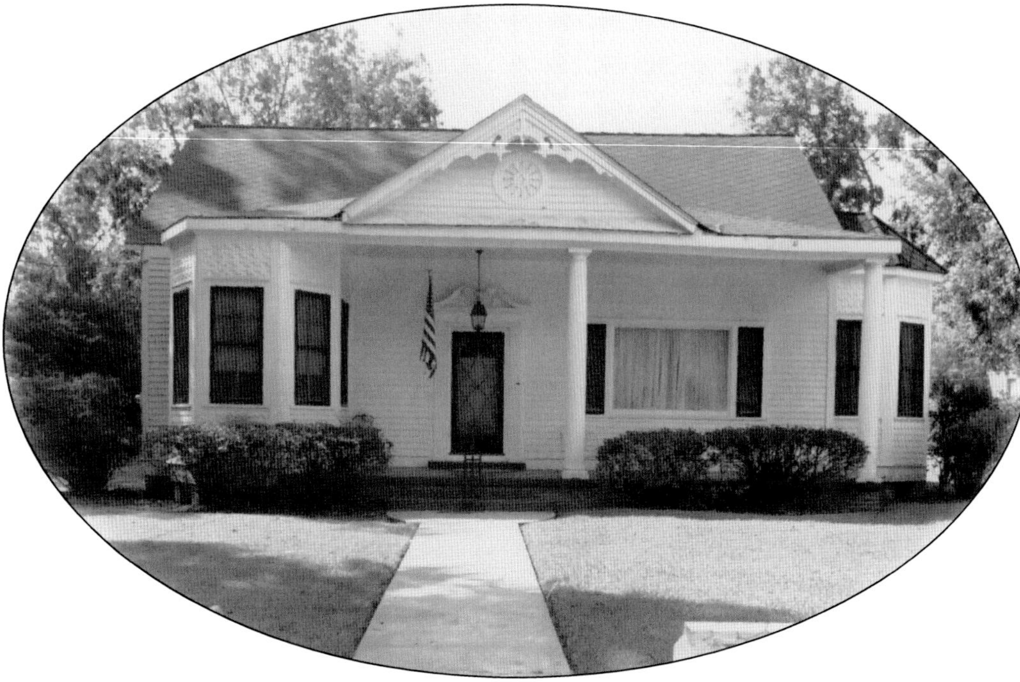

The home of Cecile Francez Guilbeau remained in the family for 112 years. Family member Carroll Guilbeau said, "At one time, my grandmother and her two daughters, Elsie and Iris, all lived in the home with their families. A home occupied by more than one family was not uncommon, especially when an elderly person in the family could not care for themselves any longer."

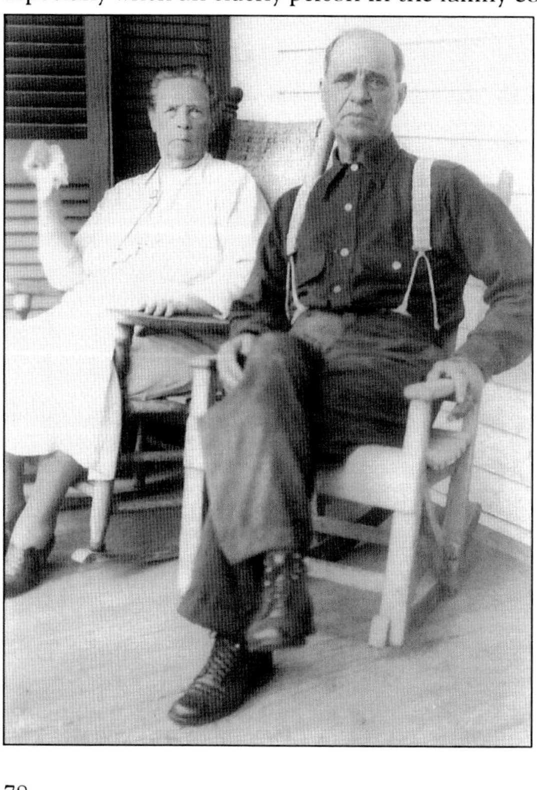

Ernest Francez and Cecile Francez Guilbeau were brother and sister. They could both be found on Cecile's porch on the corner of North University Avenue and St. Peter Street talking politics. While the buildings on the side of the home have since been rebuilt to house other things, the home still stands as a beacon of the past.

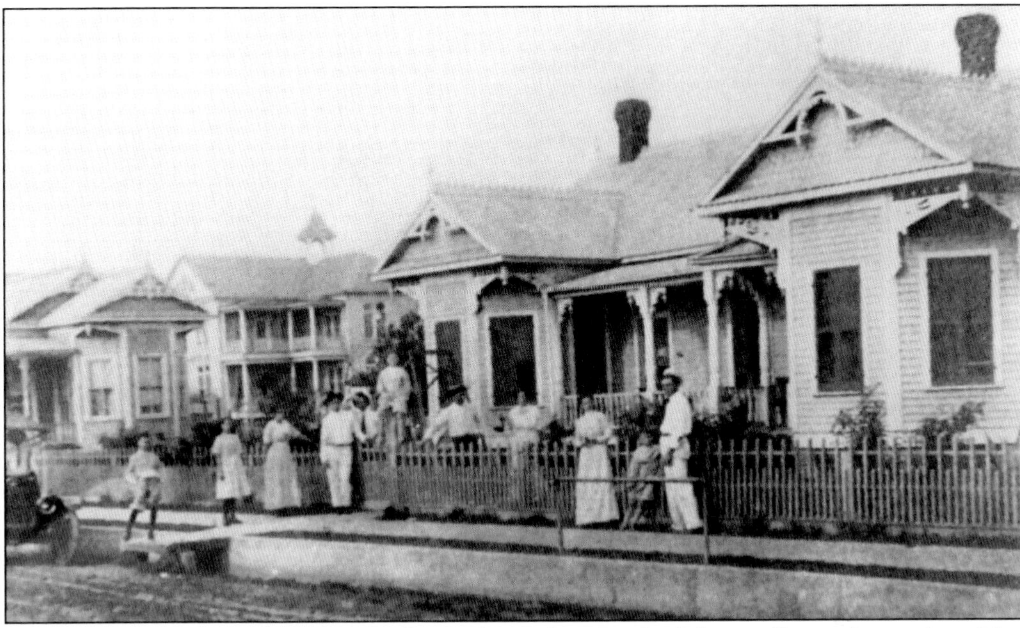

The home of Simonette Breaux was located near Joe Guidroz's home. Breaux's grandson Marc Breaux was a choreographer who left the Carencro Prairie to make a name for himself in movies such as *Mary Poppins*, *The Sound of Music*, and other classics. During the war, in the 1940s, the home had four families living in it. This home was torn down, and a gas station was built in its place. Carencro Automotive currently sits in this location. (St. Pierre Genealogical Society)

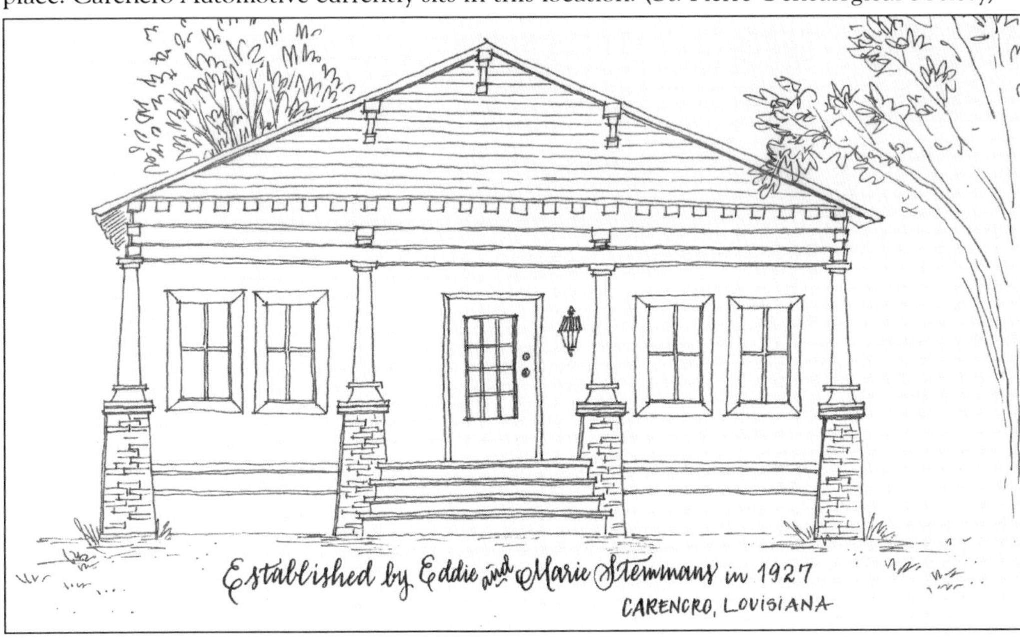

A home built in the mid-1920s has been the foundation for a strong family for decades. Don Stemmans and Judith Stemmans Gary grew up in the home, which cost their parents a total of $500. Their parents loved the community of St. Pierre. Eddie Stemmans, Don and Judith's father, was a blacksmith in the St. Pierre area. He learned the trade from his father, Joseph Stemmans. The historic home now houses Nanny's Candy Company & Fricassee Café. (Community Chronicles.)

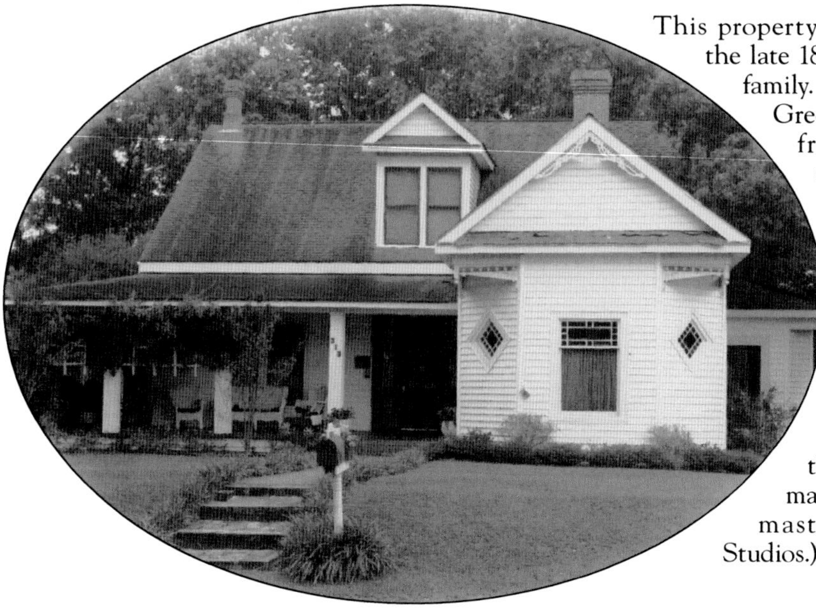

This property was purchased in the late 1800s by the Estilette family. Darcus Dimmitry, of Greek descent, traveled from New Orleans and acquired the property. He began constructing the A-frame home, made of full-inch red cypress, in 1894, and it was completed in 1896. The Bechets purchased the home in 1904 and made it into a Victorian masterpiece. (Landry Studios.)

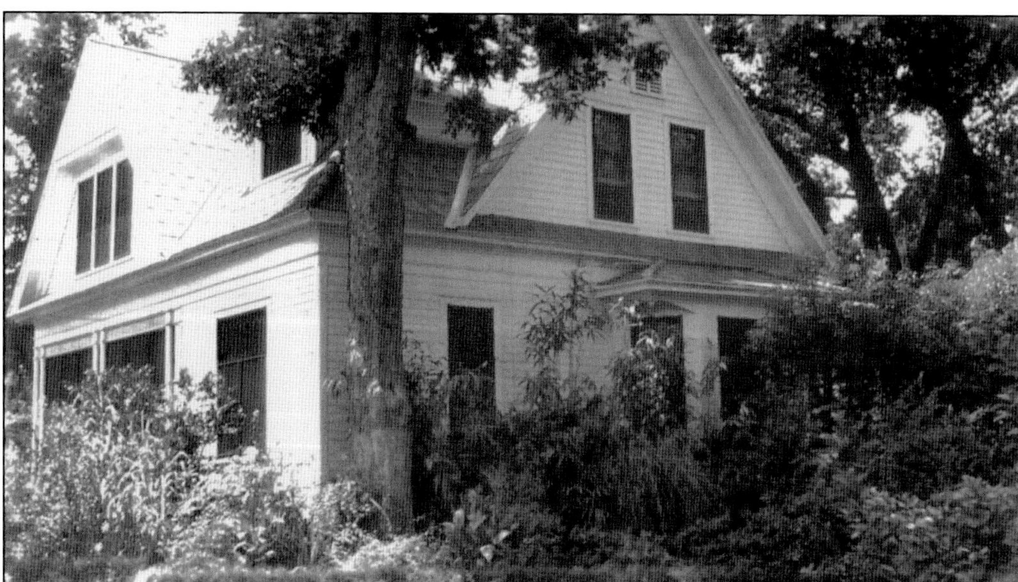

Paul André Bechet was born in the Bechet House the year that his father and mother, Alvin Charles and Sarah White Brown Bechet, began to call it their home. As a little boy, Paul found all the secret hiding places. One daughter, Lucile Maroney, tells of a time when a rope was discovered behind the front room's wall: "An old aunt and I were working on some necessary renovations when we discovered a rope hanging from the rafters in the attic. My aunt said 'That is how your father disappeared when we played *cache-cache* (hide and seek) all those years.' He would hide in the attic and jump onto the rope to remain hidden. His secret was never revealed until the rope was found."

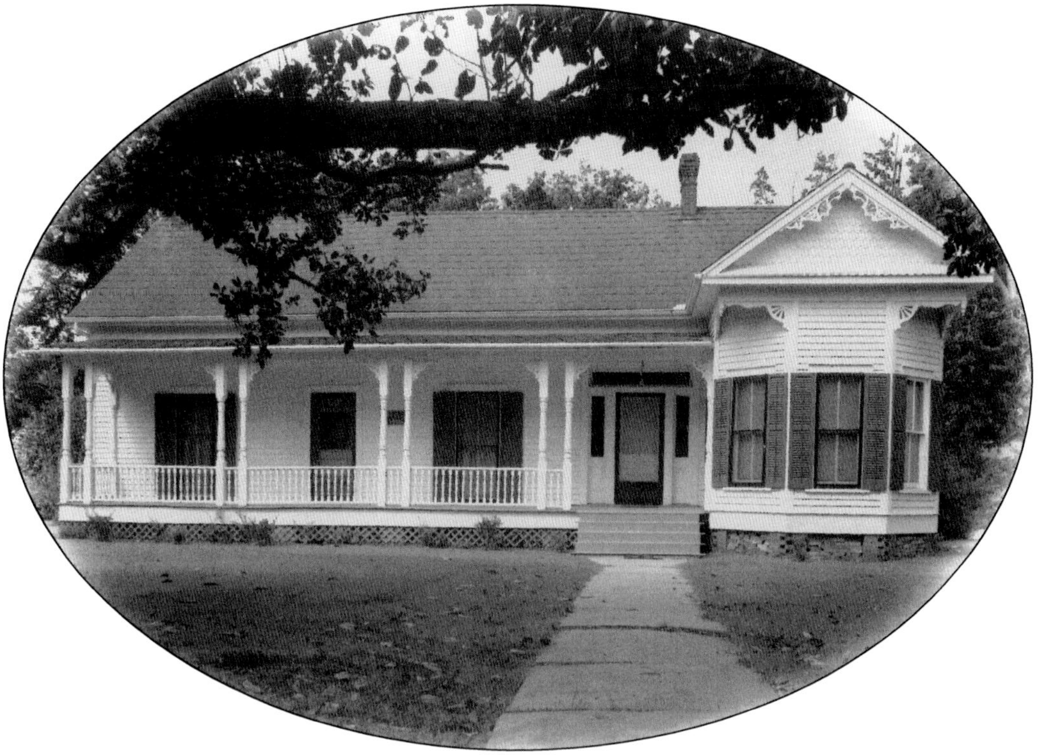

Dr. Eric Edor Guilbeau Sr. and his wife, Azelia Marie Guidry Guilbeau, raised five children in this home. The Guilbeaus had three sons fighting in World War II. Azelia Guilbeau received a letter from her son, Eric, which read: "Mr. Ben our neighbor must be having trouble getting gas for his car." The Guilbeaus were dumbfounded, as there was no Mr. Ben in the Carencro area, much less a neighbor. Days later, Eric's father heard on the radio that a major attack had happened near Gaza. The family figured out that Eric was trying to tell them—through a secret code—of his location, which was near Benghazi. Letters like this were common; it was not surprising to discover a letter had been opened and was full of holes, which meant that it had been censored. (Landry Studios.)

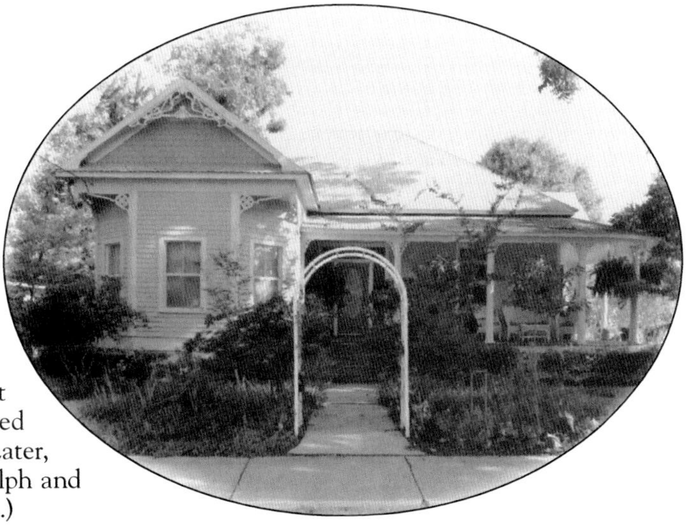

This home, located on Michaud Street, was built in 1913. It was first owned by the John Breaux family, who also owned and operated L.L. Breaux Meat Market. It was previously owned by Jules and Daisy Guilbeau. Later, the home was purchased by Ralph and Mable Prejean. (Landry Studios.)

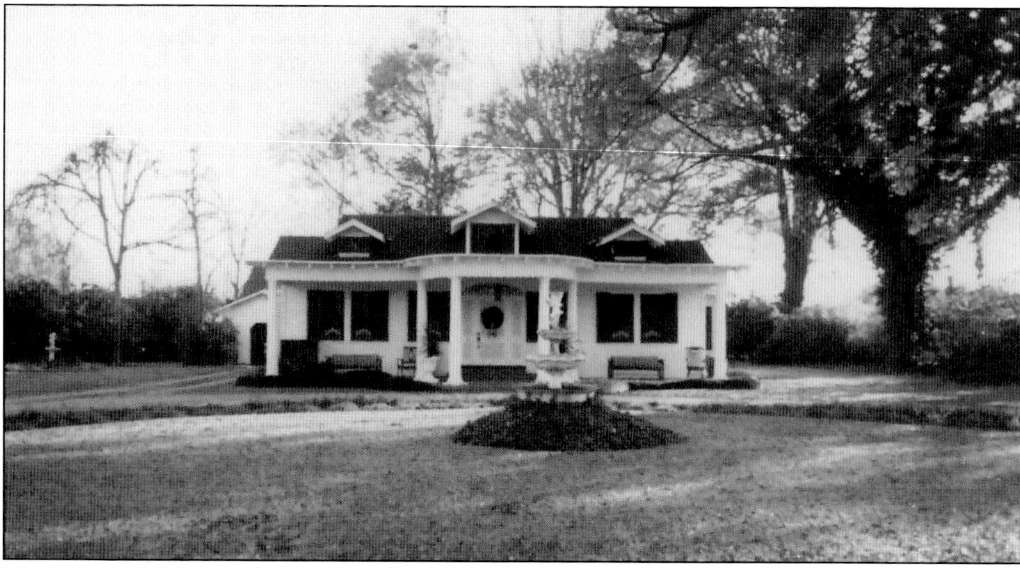

The home of C.J. and Anna Grace Richard was built just before World War II began. As C.J. went off to serve in the Navy, Anna Grace took her newborn son, Charles, and stayed with her parents. The home would not be occupied by the Richards until the war ended.

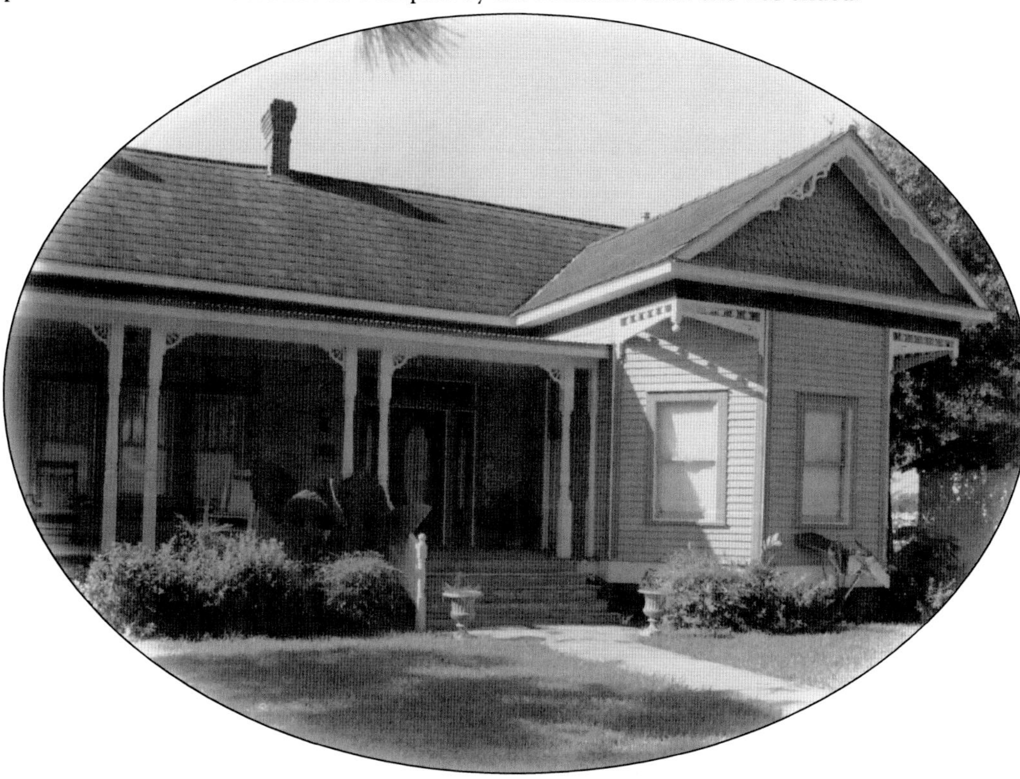

This home was built in 1889. Originally known as the Odon Guidry Home, the William Guidry Home was next door to the family's general store downtown. The general store that the family once owned was in the building that is most well known for being the location of Edward Miller's Miller Haberdashery Store. (Landry Studios.)

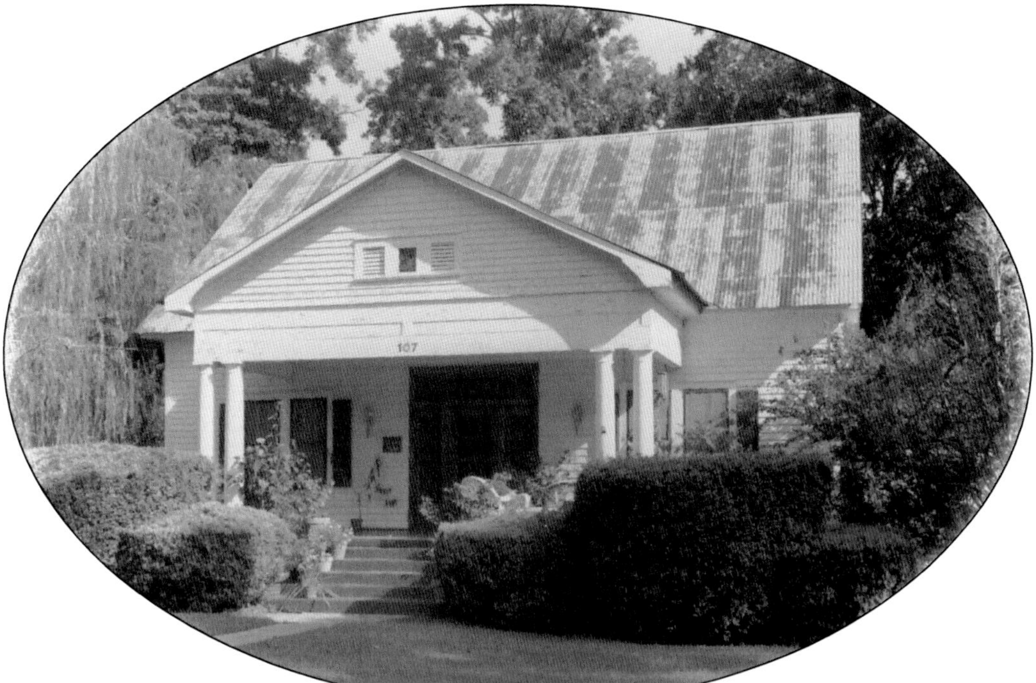

This home was the residence of Freddy and Polly Mouton. The Mouton family raised their entire family downtown. They were neighbors to Dr. Andre Prejean. (Landry Studios.)

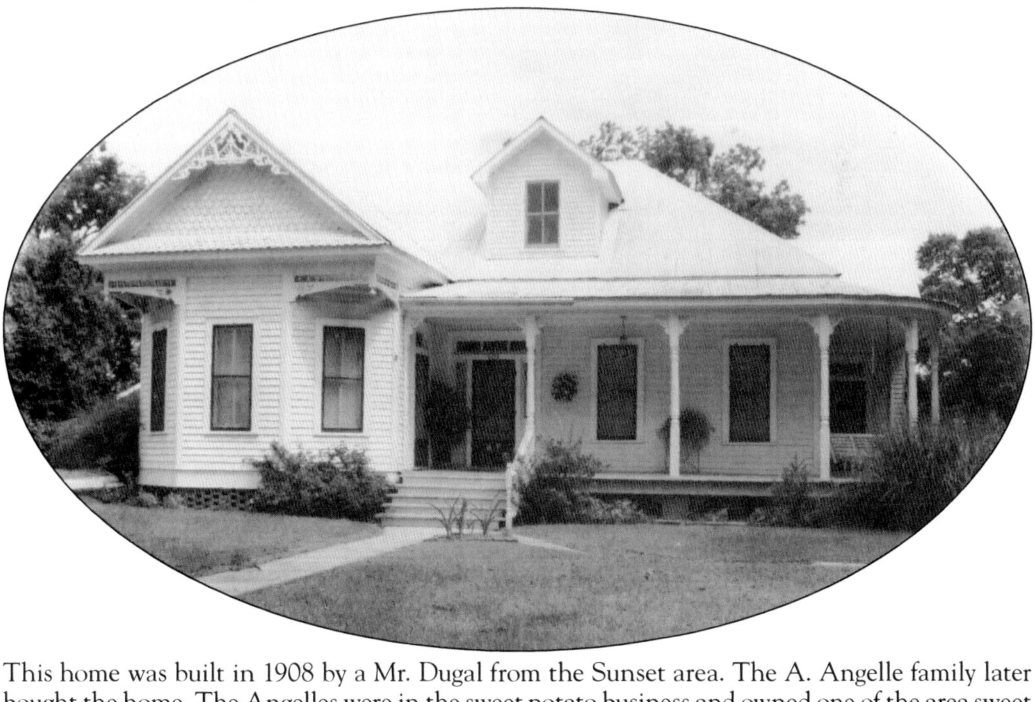

This home was built in 1908 by a Mr. Dugal from the Sunset area. The A. Angelle family later bought the home. The Angelles were in the sweet potato business and owned one of the area sweet potato kilns. A. Angelle's son James inherited the home. His son, Tommy, eventually became one of Carencro's mayors. (Landry Studios.)

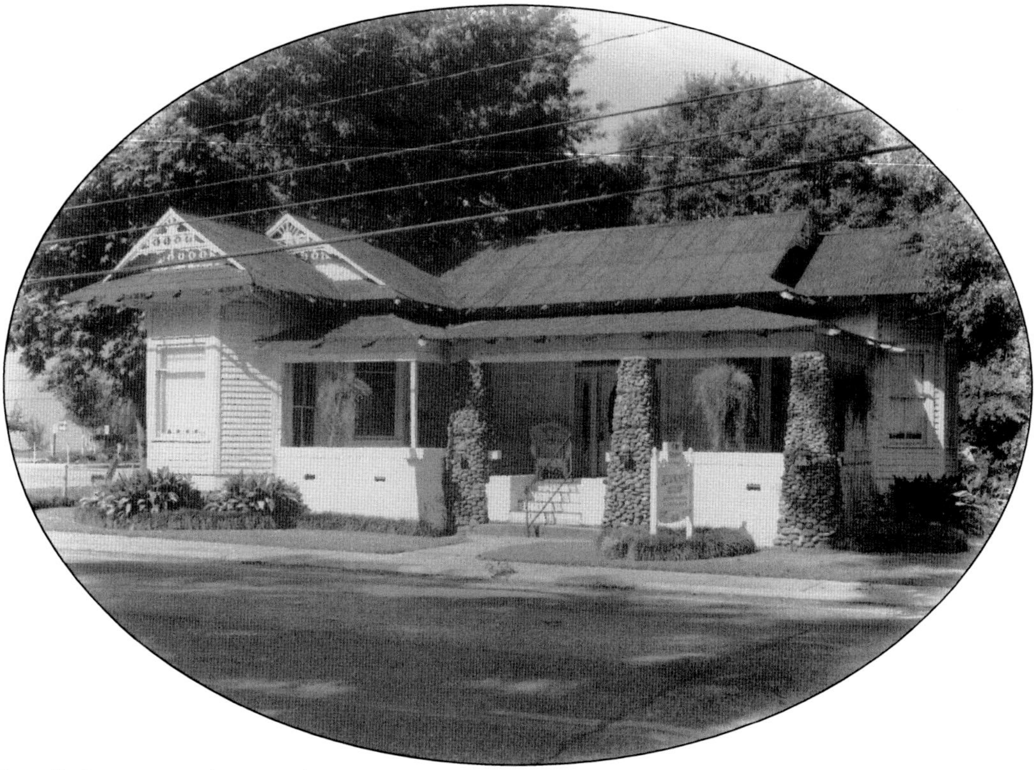

Lucille Breaux Guidroz was the original owner of this home built in 1910. The stones used to build the columns were imported from Arkansas. The home was a residence as well as a hat shop. Louis Brasseaux bought it in 1940 and opened a gas station next door. The language spoken within many of these homes was Cajun French, which was spoken by many in the Carencro Prairie. The language still lives in the city of Carencro. It was common for members of the older generation to never speak a word of English—many of their conversations had to be interpreted when they encountered someone who did not speak their language. (Landry Studios.)

Seven

Good Times

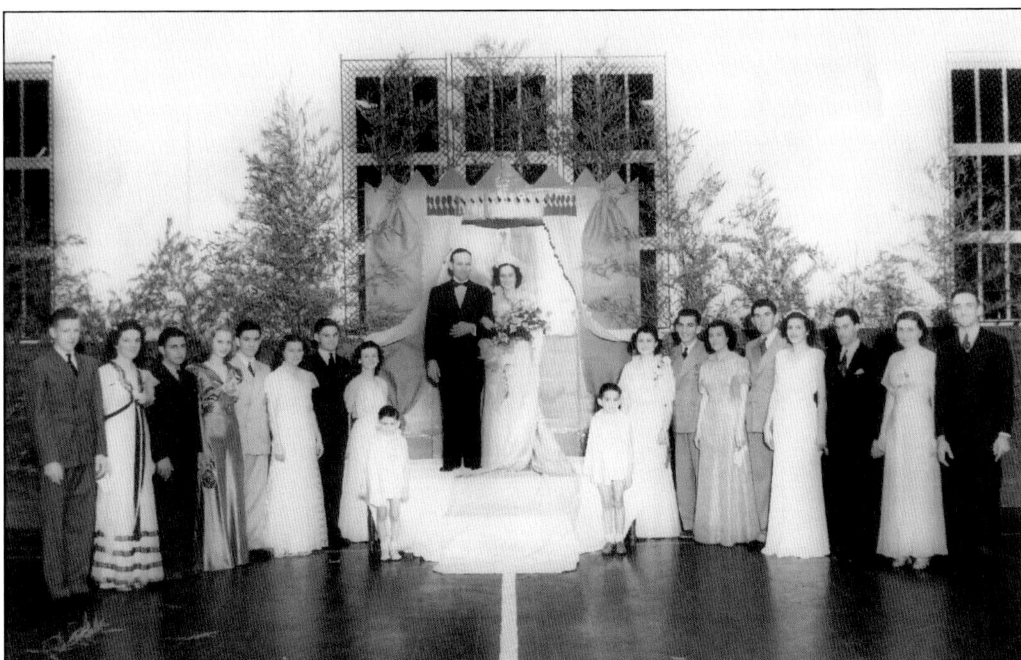

The first Carnival season in Carencro happened in 1938. Carnivals and parades have always been a way to celebrate Mardi Gras. Parades were also popular during the Christmas season. Among those pictured here are King LL "Lolly" Breaux (mayor), Queen Iris Martin Pressler, and pages Jimmie Brasseaux and Harry LeBlanc. Attendees include, from left to right, Stanford Prejean, Cenna Lee Dugas, Lester (Theo) Breaux, Lou Conques, Robby Richard Sr., Gracie Hebert, Carroll Guilbeau, Dorothy Hebert, Louelle Breaux, A.J. Dugas, Ameliee Coussan, Numa Martin, Hazel Prejean, Alfred Benoit, Emma Lou Prejean, and Felix Martin Jr. (Catherine Brasseaux.)

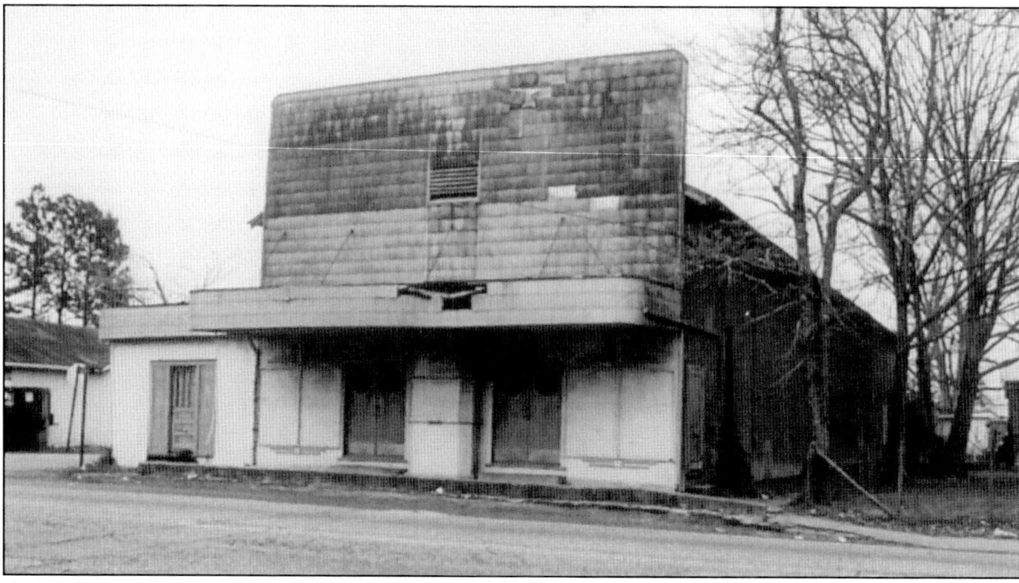

According to Carol Prejean, the Tip Top Theater was enjoyed by many during the 20th century. Westerns would play on the big screen while moviegoers sat on the edge of their seats. One elderly farmer took his wife to the Tip Top Theater one evening, and when a train came on the screen and looked like it was heading into the audience, he threw down his wife and said, "get down, Marie!"

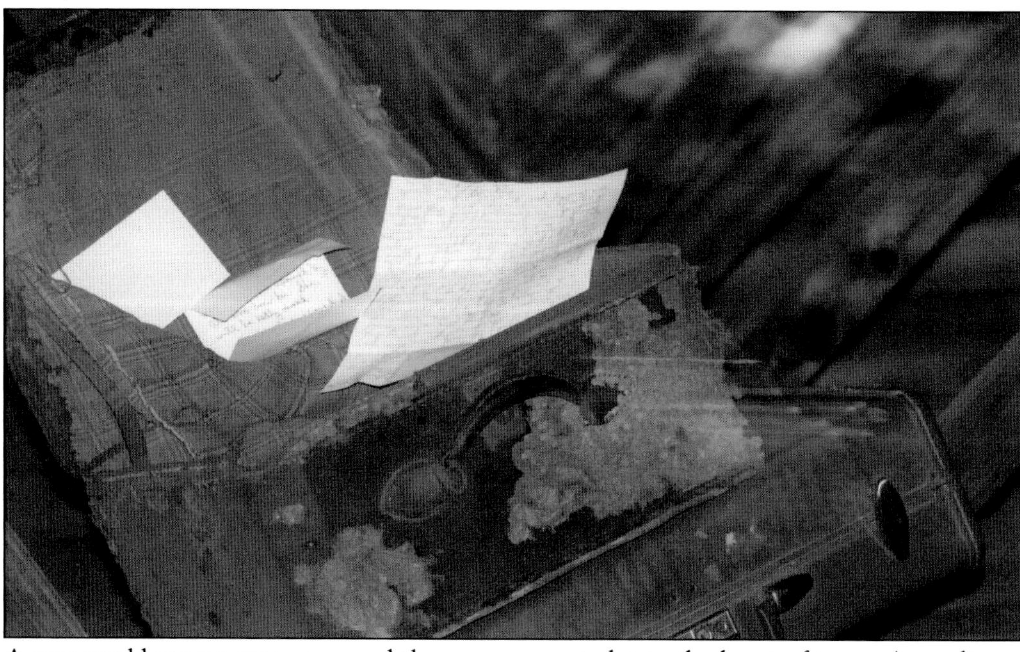

A tent would appear every now and then on an empty lot in the heart of town. According to Carroll Guilbeau, the villagers knew that once the tent arrived, a movie would be shown in the near future. Before the movie would begin, live performers would entertain the crowd with a skit. A story of one of these performers who entertained prior to the movie states that she fell in love with a Carencro resident—love letters written by the couple were discovered in the attic of Kim Guidry's historic home downtown. (Kim Guidry.)

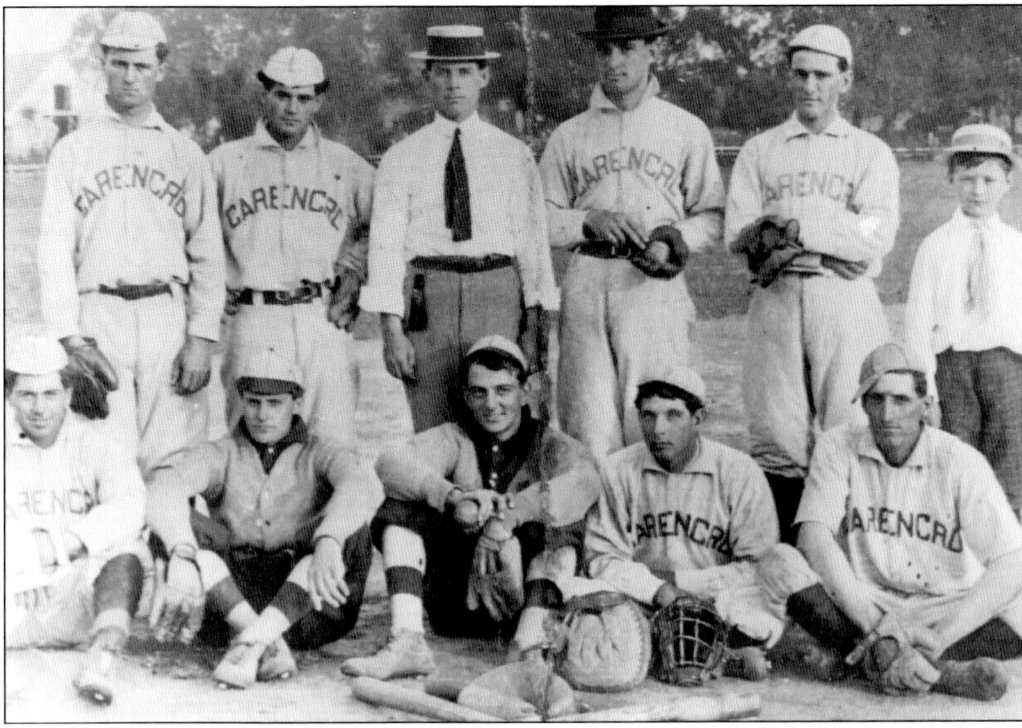

Carencro had a baseball team that was owned by Dr. E.E. Guilbeaux in 1911. Pictured here are, from left to right, (first row) Bayou Guidry, Husville Melancon, Albert Boudreaux, Linex Francez, and Ben Broussard; (second row) Aristide Domingue, Kossut Benoit, Dr. E.E. Guilbeaux, Simon Prejean, Rosemond Breaux, and bat boy Elmer Brown. (Louis Perret.)

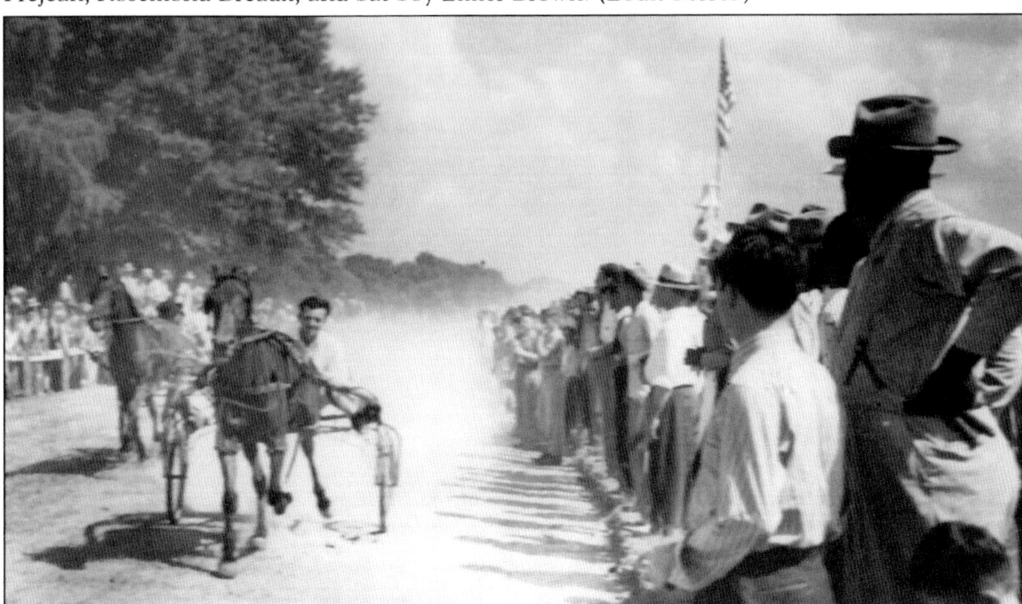

Racing has been a favorite pastime for Carencro residents since the first bush tracks were constructed in the late 1930s. (Louis Perret.)

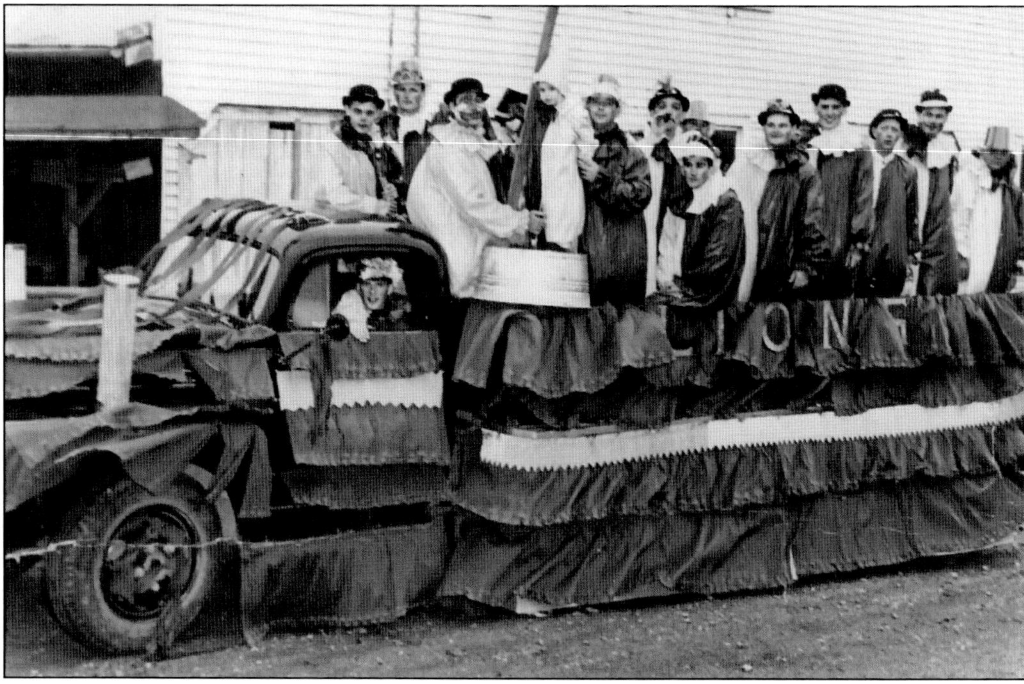

The Carencro Lions Club hosts the Carencro Children's Christmas Parade. Paul Pressler is the driver of the truck in this Christmas parade hosted by the Carencro War Veterans. The riders are, in unknown order, Norwood Guidry, Elmo Authement, Wallace Broussard, Tommy Angelle (baby), Dick Angelle, Joe Arceneaux, Carroll Guilbeau, William Broussard, Pat Duhon, Mickey Delana, Jules Dupuis, and Billy Breaux (seated). (Louis Perret.)

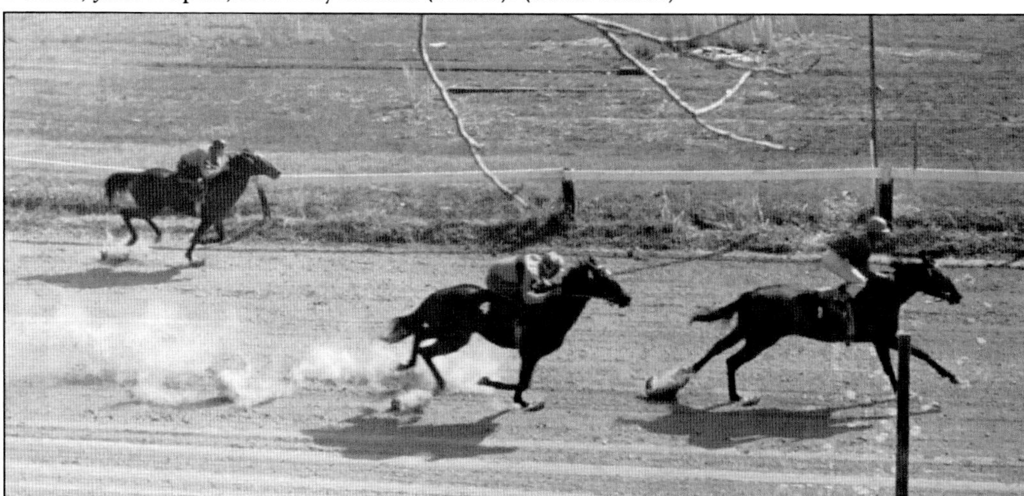

The horse-racing track was constructed in 1957 after Gilbert Borel Jr. leased some of his father's land to Albert LeBlanc. The land was formerly a sugar plantation. After the passing of Gilbert Borel Sr., Lester Breaux, June Angelle, and Heath Begnaud transformed the land to provide another pleasure for the community: Carencro Raceways. This track sat on the eastern boundary of the land where Melancon Funeral Home now resides. The dry goods store on the property was reopened as a restaurant and bar for the crowds. A movie called *Casey's Shadow* was even filmed at Carencro Raceways. (Don Stemmans.)

Bob Lily was instrumental in seeing that members of all races were included in the game of baseball. After suffering from polio, Lily was disabled, but this did not stop him from walking over 15 miles to sign up one of his teams to play ball in the city of Lafayette. Lily is in awe of how beautiful the baseball field looks today. He said, "I always knew that every child was a blessing from God. On my team, it didn't matter if you were black or white. My players walked away knowing that you can make it if you try." (Alfred Sinegal.)

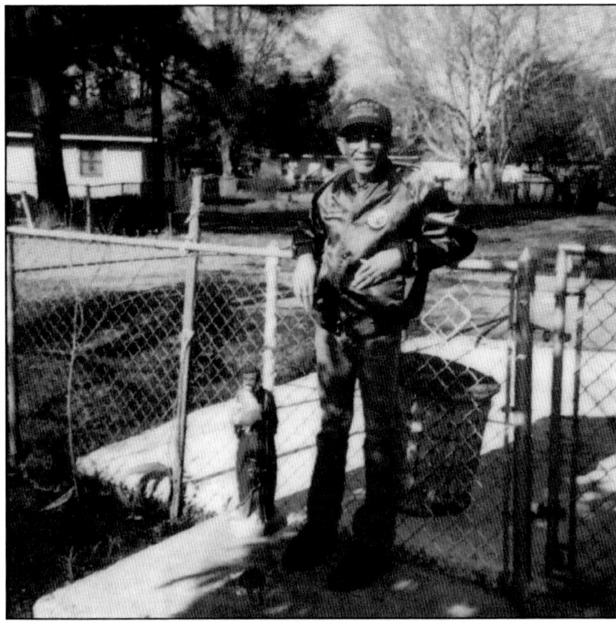

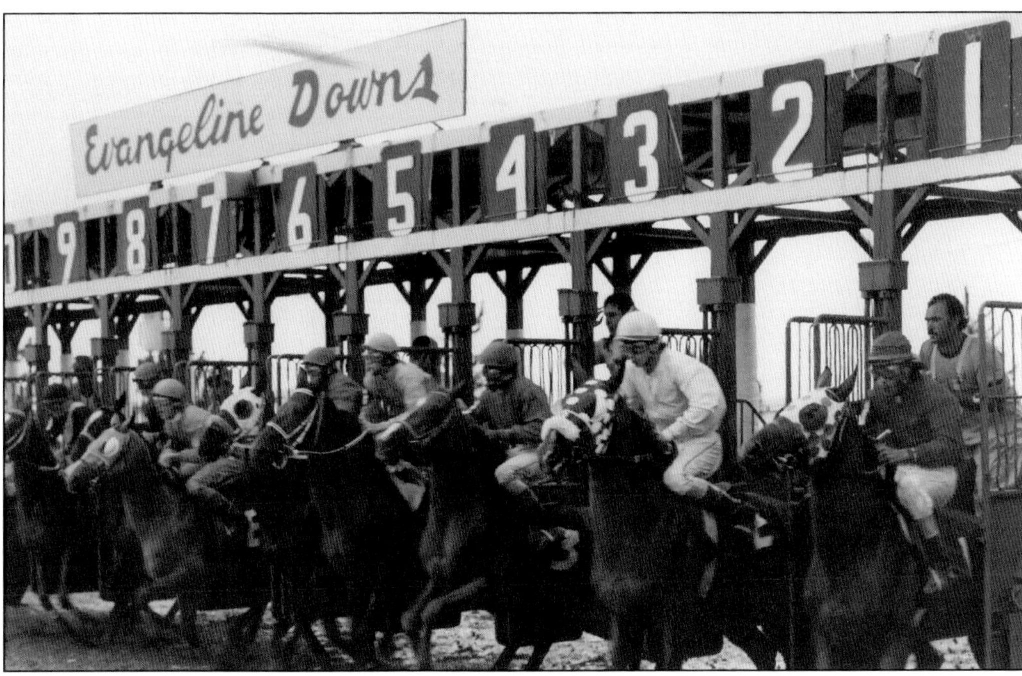

Evangeline Downs opened the race track in Carencro on April 28, 1966. The track produced many of the world's best jockeys, including Robby Albarado, Ronald Ardoin, Calvin Borel, Kent Desormeaux, Mark Guidry, Curt Bourque, and Kenneth Robinson. (Ned Guiterrez.)

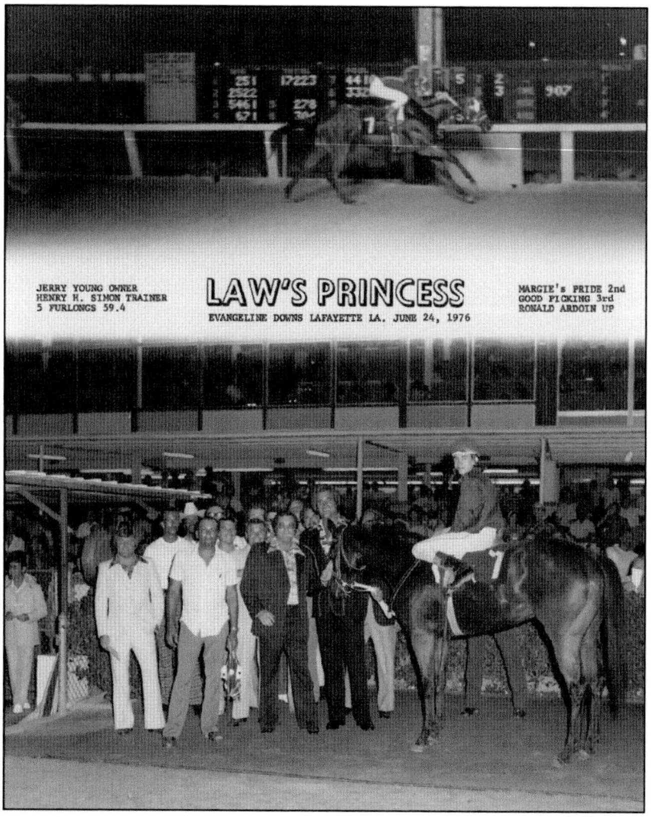

Ronald Ardoin was born and raised in Carencro. He is known as one of the most successful Thoroughbred jockeys from the South. Over his career as a jockey, which began at the bush tracks in Carencro, Ardoin had 5,226 wins. He retired from racing after an accident in 2014. (Ardoin family.)

This picture shows many of Carencro's prominent businessmen and city officials toasting with Santa Claus prior to a Christmas parade. Among those pictured are Tommy Angelle, Lynn Guidry, Allen "Coach" Conque, fire chief Carroll E. Guilbeau, Joseph "Joe" Arceneaux, and J.L. Richard. (Glenn Brasseaux.)

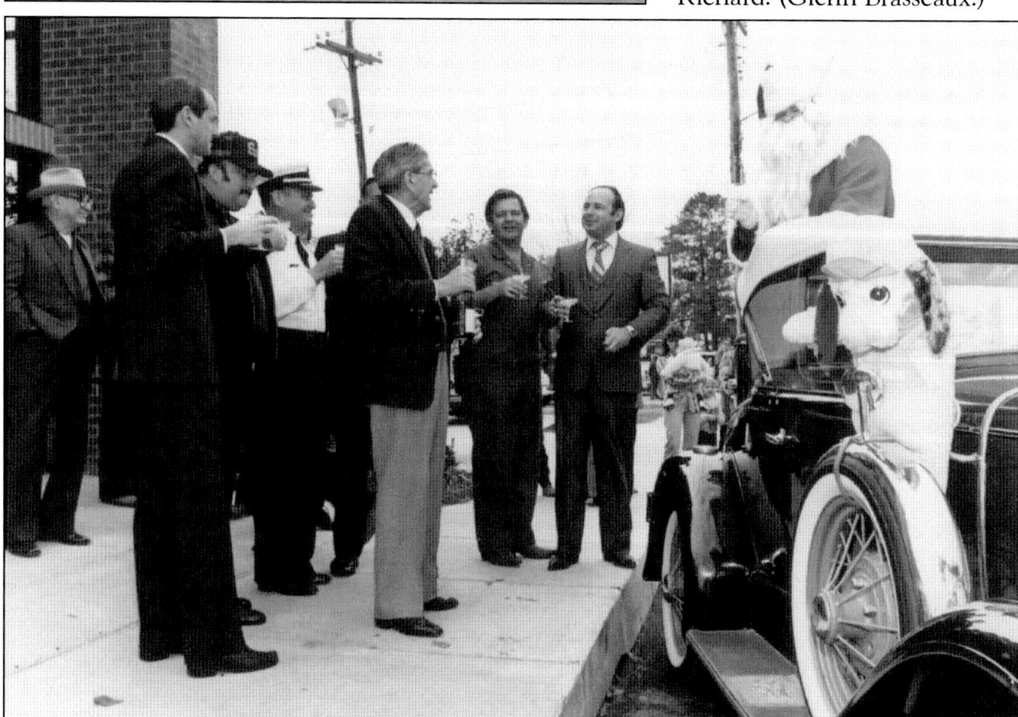

Kenneth Courville was born on June 7, 1948, and passed away on June 20, 2013. Courville was a well-known vocalist from Carencro who recorded three gospel albums. He was the drummer for Lil Kenny and the Heart Breakers for over 20 years and was one of the original founders of the band GTO and D Street Brass. He played Cajun music in his and his son's band Matthew Courville and the Cypress Knees. (Courville family.)

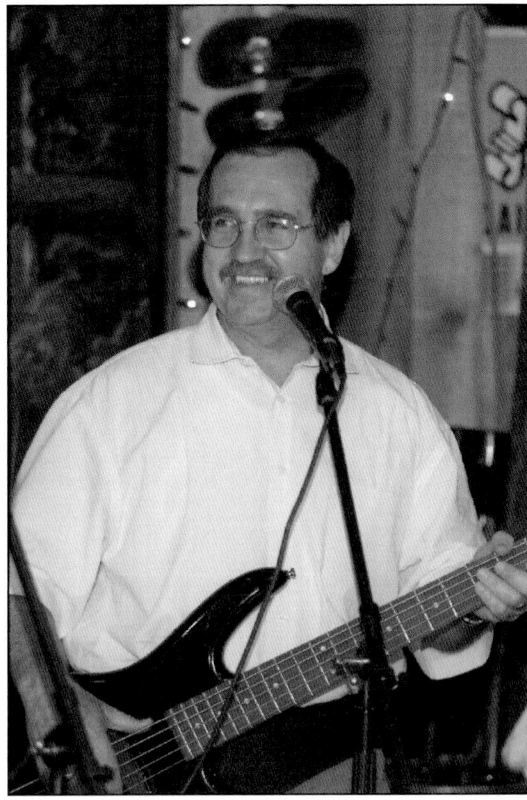

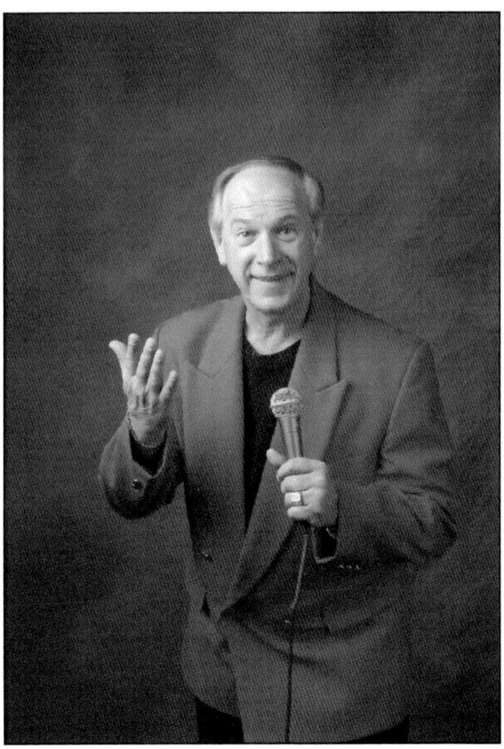

Murray Conque hails from Carencro. For over 30 years, he has entertained audiences at banquets and conventions across the country—from Las Vegas to Quebec. He has recorded five humor albums and is the coauthor of two popular books, *Cajun Humor* and *Cajun Spices for the Mind*. (Kenny Champagne.)

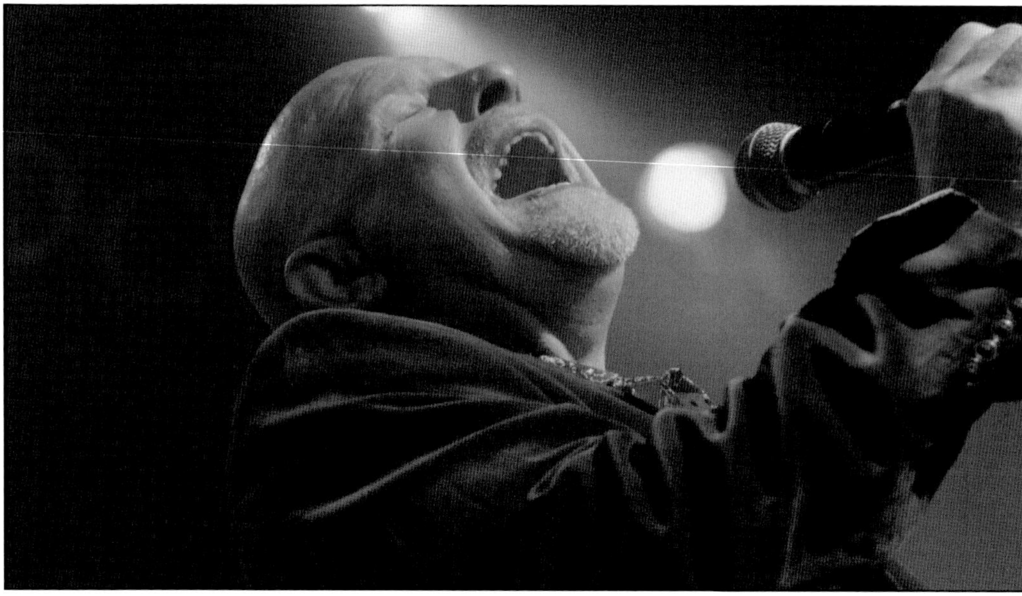

Gregg Martinez, born and raised on a farm near Carencro, began a lifelong singing career in the choir at St. Peter Roman Catholic Church. He has recorded 10 solo albums and has performed all over the United States and around the world. He was the last of the great legendary vocalists of the Boogie Kings and wrote the title song for their last album, *Never Go Away,* in 2007. He is a member of the Louisiana Music Hall of Fame. He is still very active with his current group, Gregg Martinez and the Delta Kings. (Gregg Martinez.)

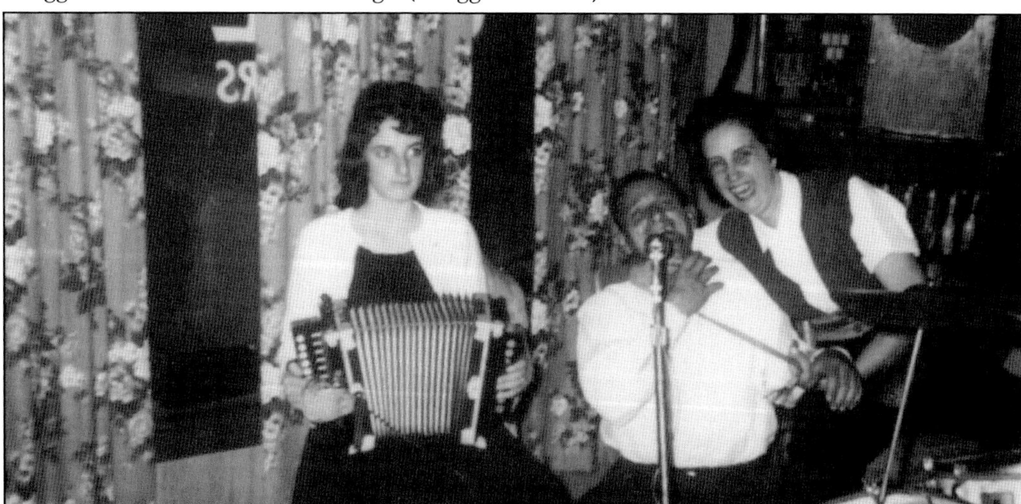

Carencro resident Sheryl Cormier (left) began playing music at age seven, when she stole her father's beloved accordion. As Cormier's father left home for the fields one day, the little girl watched until his profile disappeared across the field. She recalled, "I wanted to play his forbidden musical instrument. For a farmer, the accordion was a prized and costly possession, and the children weren't allowed to touch it. I quickly taught myself to play the Cajun music that I often heard my father and his band play." Last year, Cormier's lifelong talent earned her a spot in the Cajun Music Hall of Fame. Cormier can be found on stage with her husband, Russell, her son, and the rest of her band, Sheryl Cormier and The Cajun Sound. (Cormier family.)

Ray Landry has lived near the Carencro and North Lafayette boundary line since age 19. He is a leader in Cajun music and has been recording for years with his band Ray Landry and the Basile Cajun Band. In 1999, the band released its first album, *La Musique Que Viens du Beaubassin*, which was nominated by the Cajun French Music Association as Best First Recording of the Year. Landry received a nomination for Best Male Vocalist of the Year. (Ray Landry.)

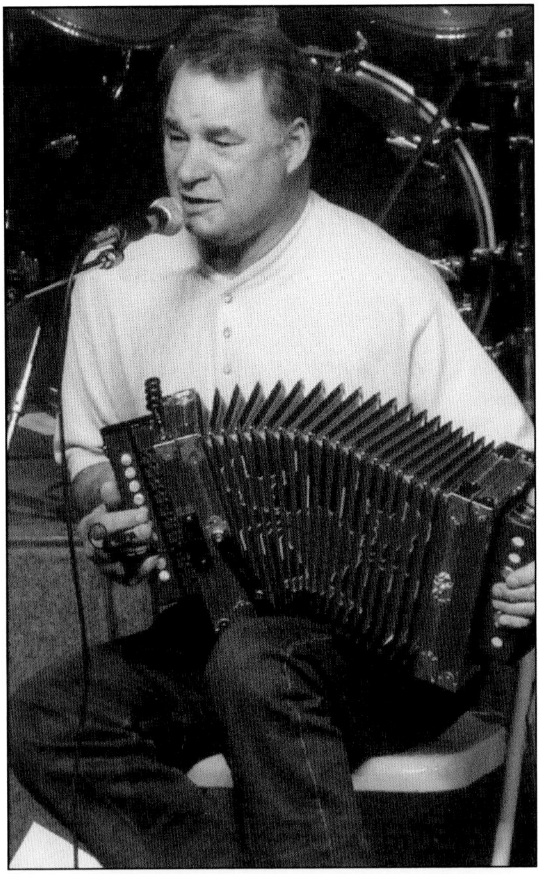

Ron Guidry resides in Carencro. Around the United States, he is known as "Louisiana Lightning" for his left-handed pitching skills. Guidry pitched for the New York Yankees from 1975 to 1988. In 1977 and 1978, Guidry helped lead the Yankees to victory in the World Series. His number, 49, was retired by the Yankees in 2003. Pictured here from left to right are Allen "Coach" Conque, Carencro alderman; Bud York, Carencro contractor; Guidry; Glenn Brasseaux, Carencro alderman; and Carencro mayor Tommy Angelle. (Ron Guidry and Glenn Brasseaux.)

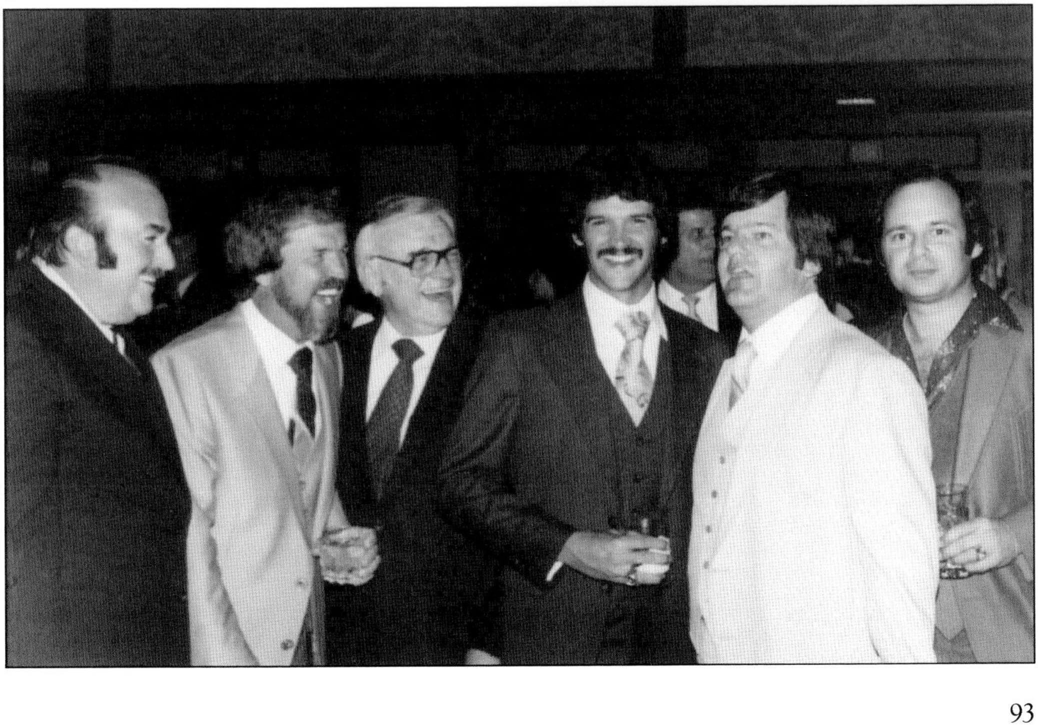

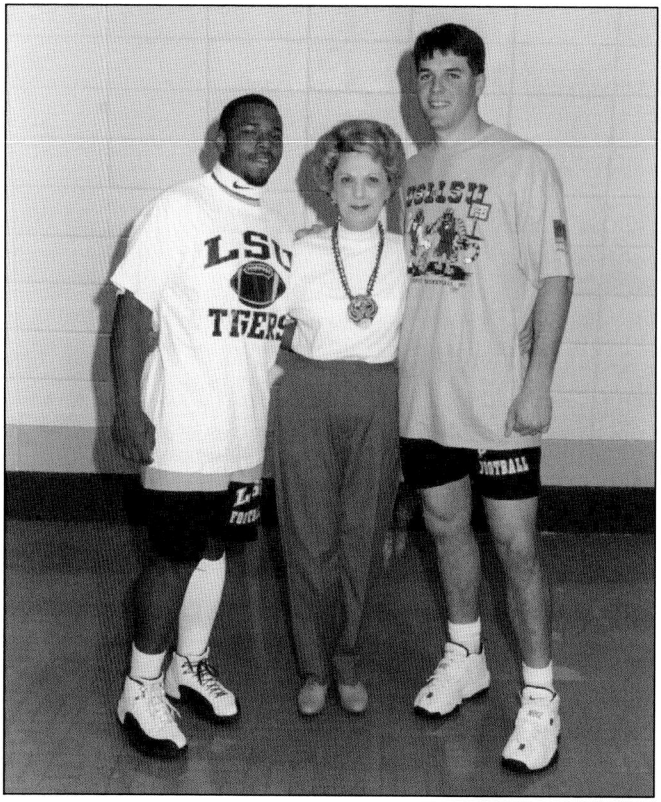

Kevin Faulk, Catherine Brasseaux, and Wade Richey are pictured sporting purple and gold for Louisiana State University (LSU). Faulk helped lead the Carencro High School Bears to a State Championship Class 5A title in 1992. Faulk played college football at LSU and was drafted as a New England Patriot in 1999. As a Patriot, Faulk earned three Super Bowl rings. Richey began his football career at Carencro High School as a kicker. He went on to kick for LSU in college and played for the San Francisco 49ers, the San Diego Chargers, and the Baltimore Ravens in the NFL. (Catherine Brasseaux.)

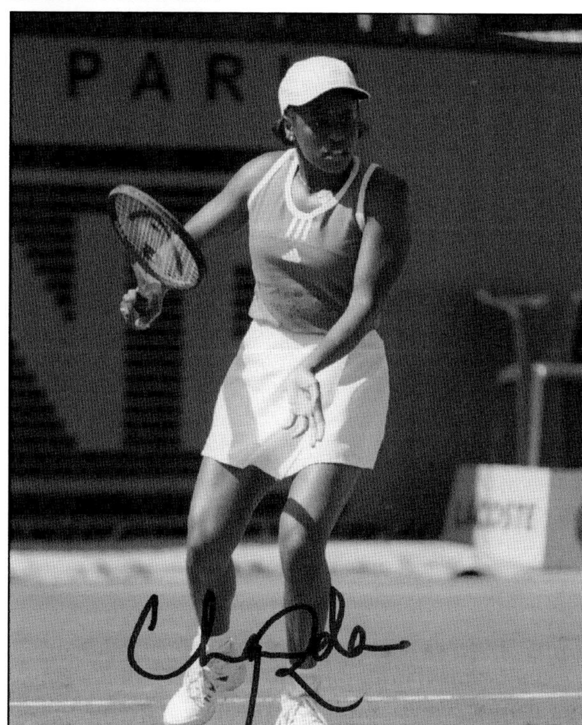

Carencro native Chanda Rubin was inducted into the Louisiana Sports Hall of Fame on June 29, 2013, for her skills on the tennis court. A household name around the country, Rubin has played in the French Open, Wimbledon, Australian Open, Lipton Championships, and other major competitions. In 1996, Rubin was No. 6 in women's tennis rankings in the world. Her work with local and state community events and nonprofit organizations still shines bright today. (Rubin family.)

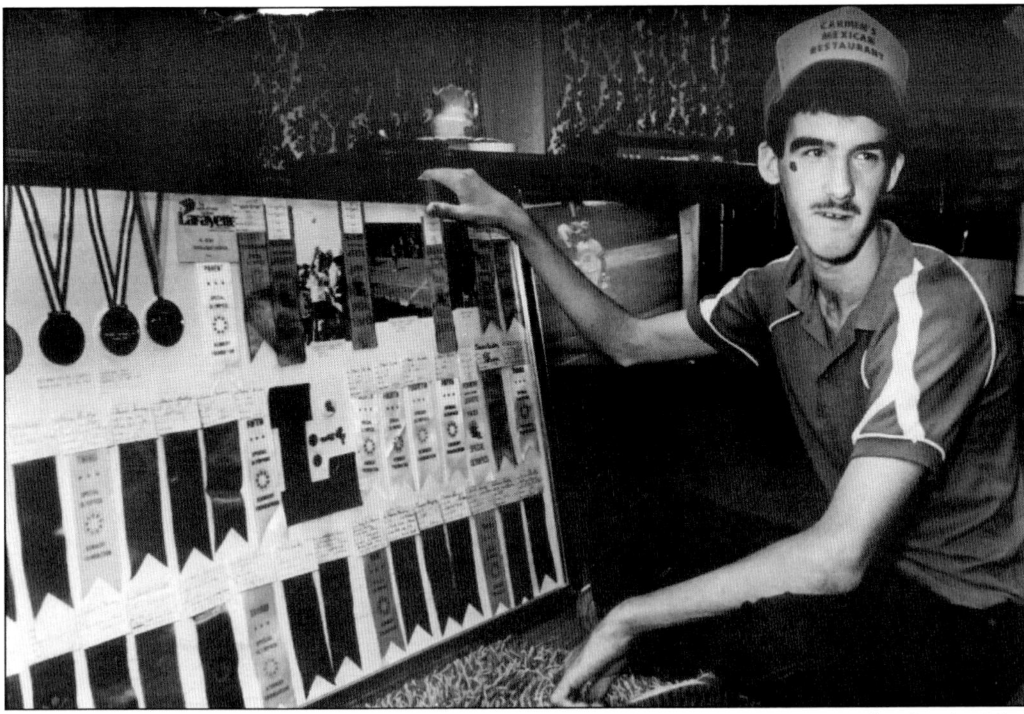

Travis Guidry is the brother of Carencro's Ron Guidry. While Ron went on to play for the New York Yankees, Travis was making a name for himself in the Special Olympics. Travis is pictured here with his many awards earned over the years. (Guidry family.)

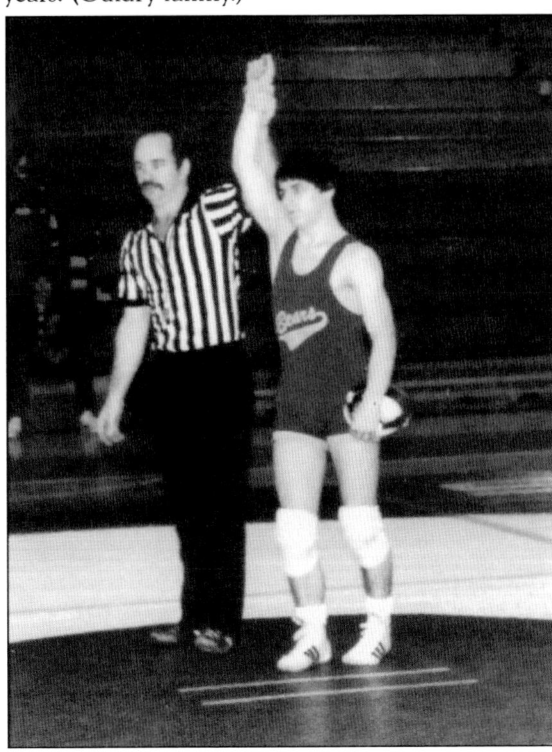

For over 15 years, Greg Lavergne spent his time as a volunteer wrestling coach at Carencro High School (CHS). Lavergne excelled in wrestling while at CHS from 1979 to 1982. When his sons were young, he began coaching them in a youth wrestling league and stayed with them through their years at Carencro High School. When his sons graduated, Lavergne remained as a coach. In February 2013, while coaching at Carencro High School, Lavergne passed away from a massive heart attack. On January 10, 2014, Carencro High School honored his memory by renaming the school's annual parish wrestling tournament, which begins the sport's season, the Greg Lavergne Parish Duals Wrestling Championship. (Lavergne family.)

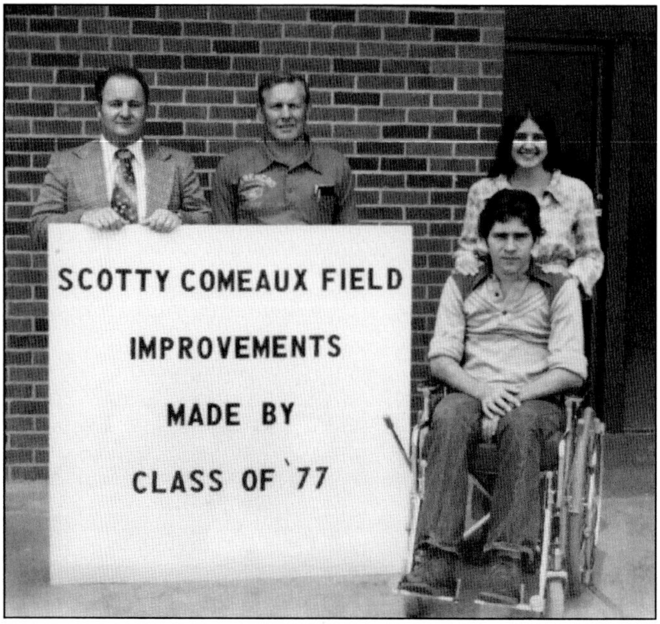

Up until 1977, Scotty Comeaux was an athlete at Carencro High School who played both baseball and football. Comeaux was involved in a car accident that left him in a wheelchair. His classmates, coaches, and school faculty and administration renamed the field in his honor. From left to right are principal Don Bourgeois, coach Jerry Griffith, senior class president Annetta Broussard, and Scotty Comeaux. (Community Chronicles.)

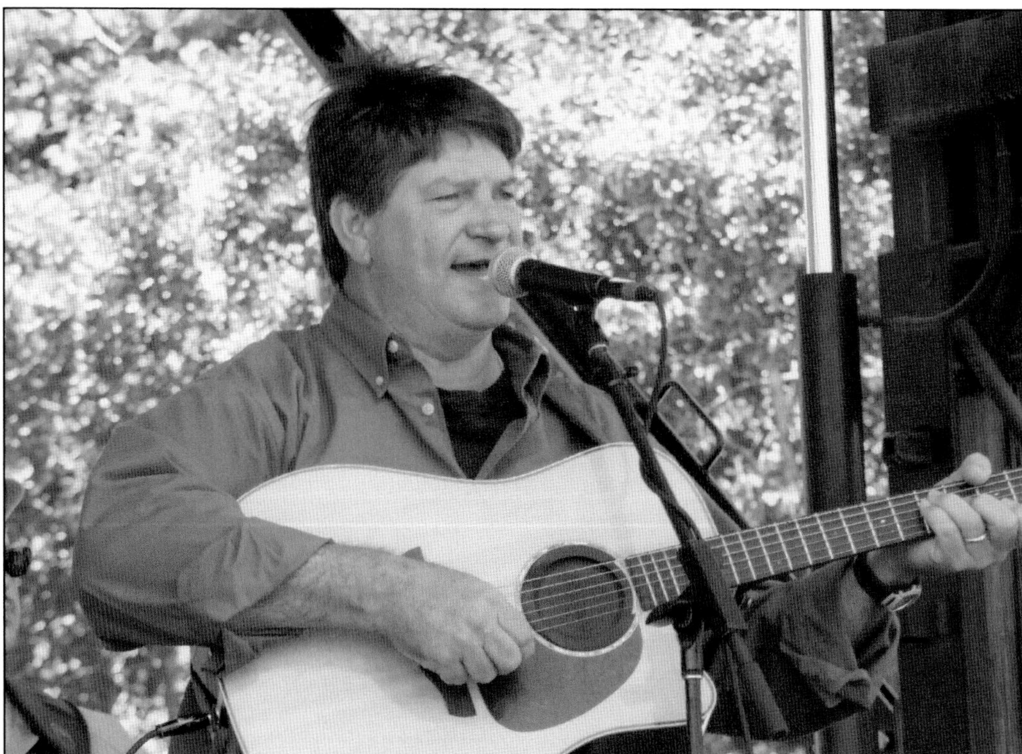

Mark Latiolais started playing guitar and singing at age 16. For 32 years, he has called Carencro home. He has played with Elton Cormier, Reggie Matte and the Church Point Playboys, and currently plays with Jason Frey and Lagniappe and Paul Daigle and Cajun Gold. Mark is also a member of the St. Peter Roman Catholic Church choir along with his wife, Donna Latiolais, and is active in the church. (Latiolais family.)

Eight

Early Businesses

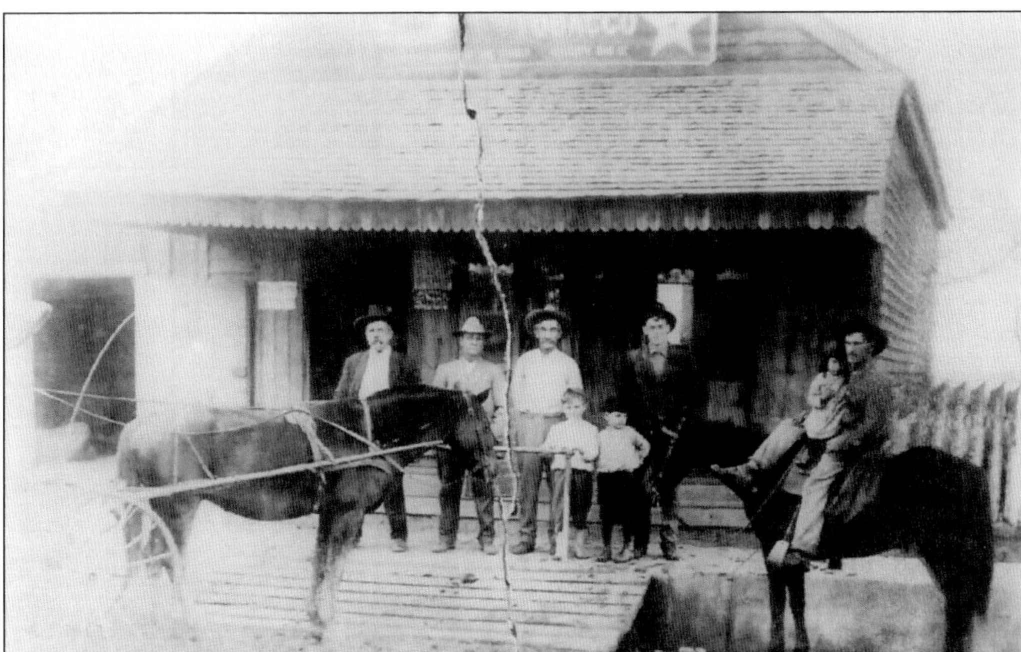

Henry Francez's store was located on the corner of Armand and Church Streets. The downtown area has always been prosperous. At times, many butchers, blacksmiths, and clothing stores were lined up along St. Peter Street. Even though various types of businesses shared the same street, they all did well financially. The street was lined with hitching posts, some of which remain today.

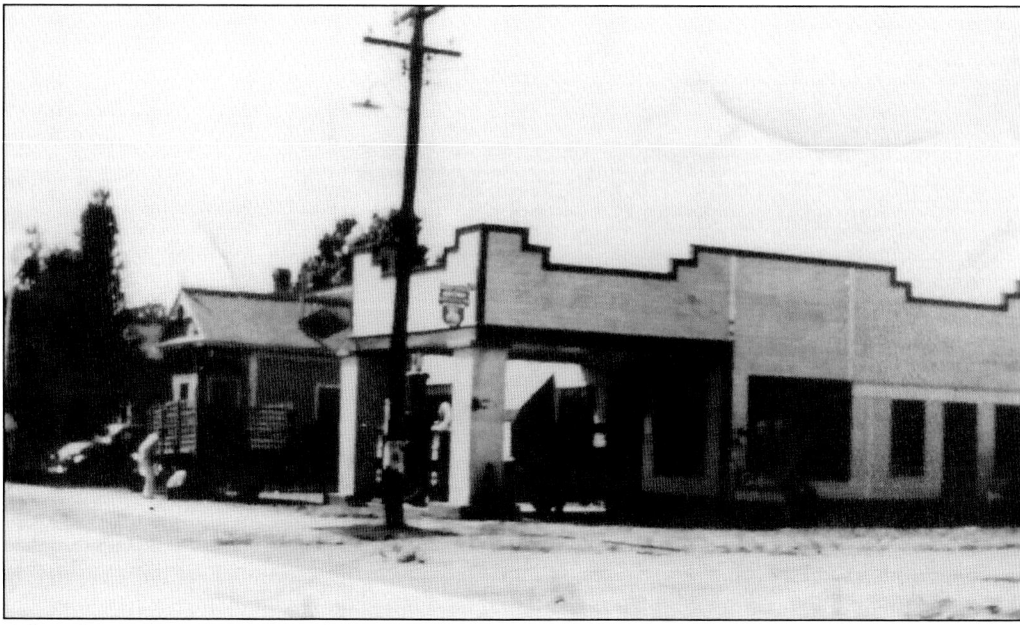

After the Great Depression, the way of life changed for many in Carencro. People were more conservative with their money, food, and way of life, but business eventually resumed in the downtown area. Louis (Bill) Brasseaux opened a gas station under the Pan-Am name in 1936. The station was located across the street from Carroll's, a store that sold a little of everything. (Jimmie Brasseaux.)

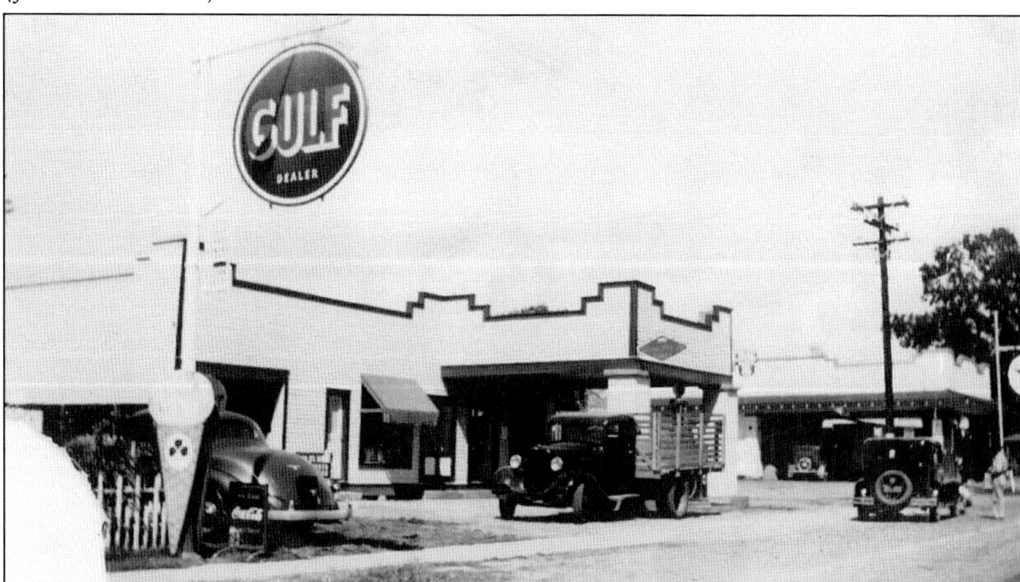

Eventually, Brasseaux moved his station across St. Peter Street to a corner lot off of North University Avenue. This made him neighbors with the Overton Breaux Texaco station. Brasseaux's later became Gulf Oil and operated under Brasseaux until World War II, when gas was hard to come by. The station closed in 1941 when Brasseaux volunteered to assist with national defense. Once the war was over, the station began operating again, but the shortage of parts forced Brasseaux to close again. He then went into the coffee business. (Jimmie Brasseaux.)

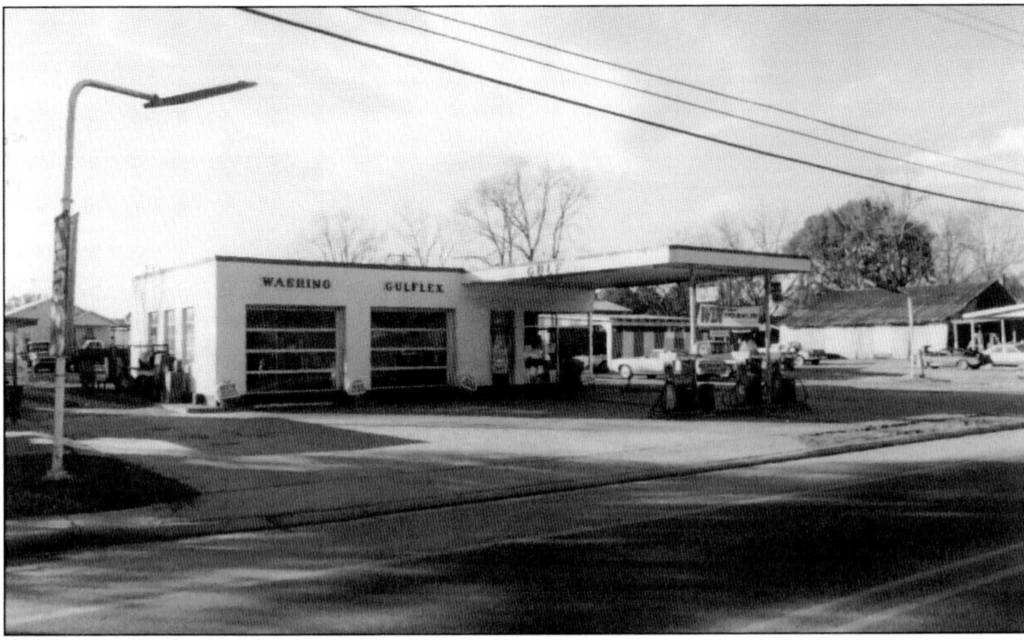

In 1955, Jimmie Brasseaux followed in the footsteps of his father, Louis (Bill), and reopened the gas station after remodeling it. Brasseaux's Gulf Service opened its doors with gas prices at 32¢ per gallon. The corner station served many in the area until Jimmie retired in 1997. It is now known as Carencro Automotive. (Jimmie and Catherine Brasseaux.)

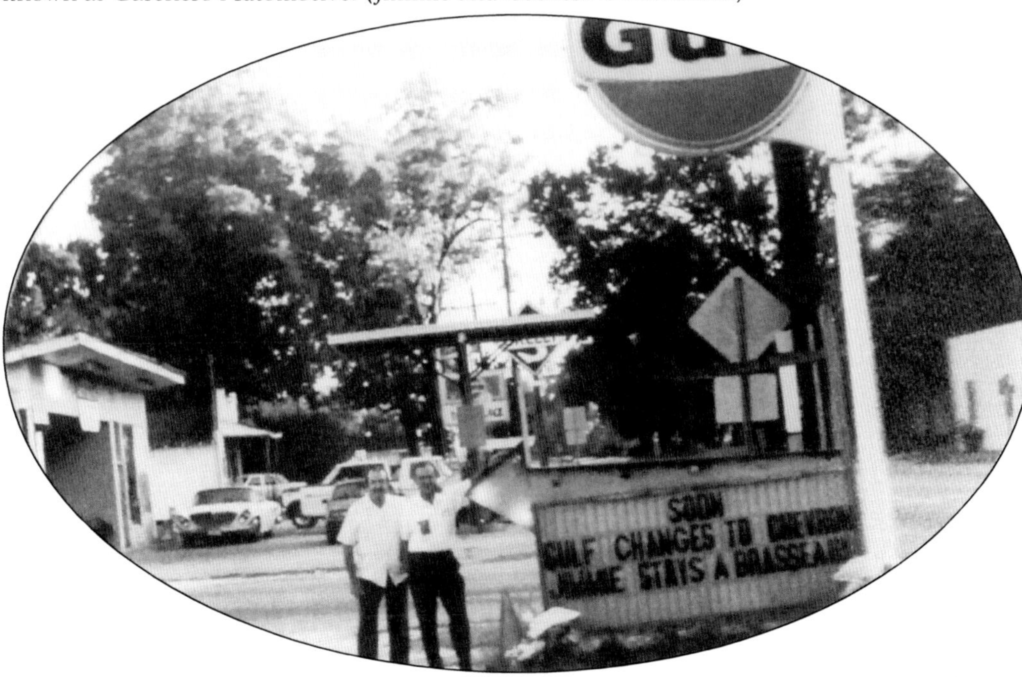

Jimmie Brasseaux is advertising that his station is changing from Gulf to Chevron. The sign reads, "Soon Gulf changes to Chevron Jimmie Stays a Brasseaux." The station sold Shamrock Ice Cream—two scoops for 5¢. Greyhound bus tickets could also be purchased there. A ticket from Carencro to either Lafayette or Sunset was 20¢. (Jimmie and Catherine Brasseaux.)

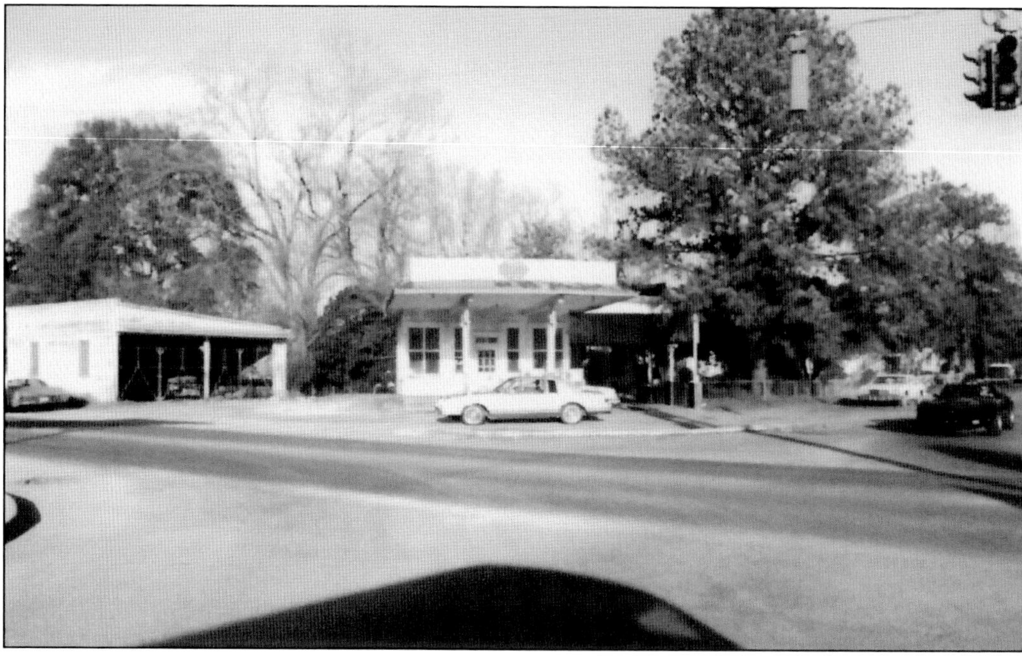

Slim Broussard's station and Lloyd Albarado's garage were on the corner of St. Peter Street and University Avenue. Accounts claim that Red Guidroz, Slim's brother-in-law, and Slim were the nicest old men. They would pump gas, check oil, and clean windshields while talking about the weather or whistling while working. Albarado had a repair shop on the side. Slim's sister Leah and her husband, Lionel Dupuis, owned Dupuis Liquor Store.

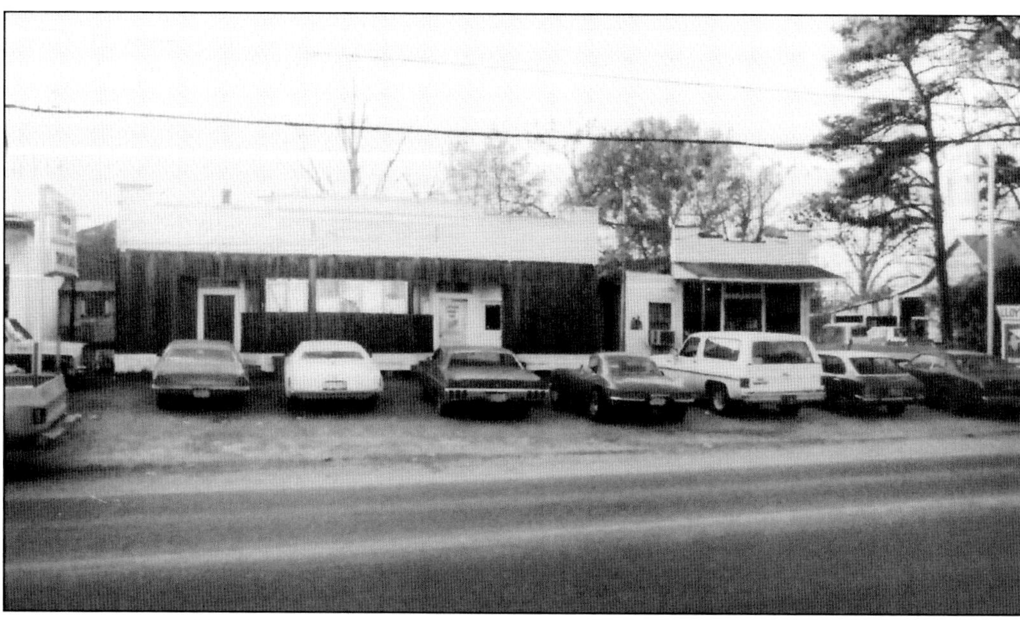

Carencro Bar and Lloyd's Café were located where Auto Zone is now on North University Avenue. (Janet Stemmans.)

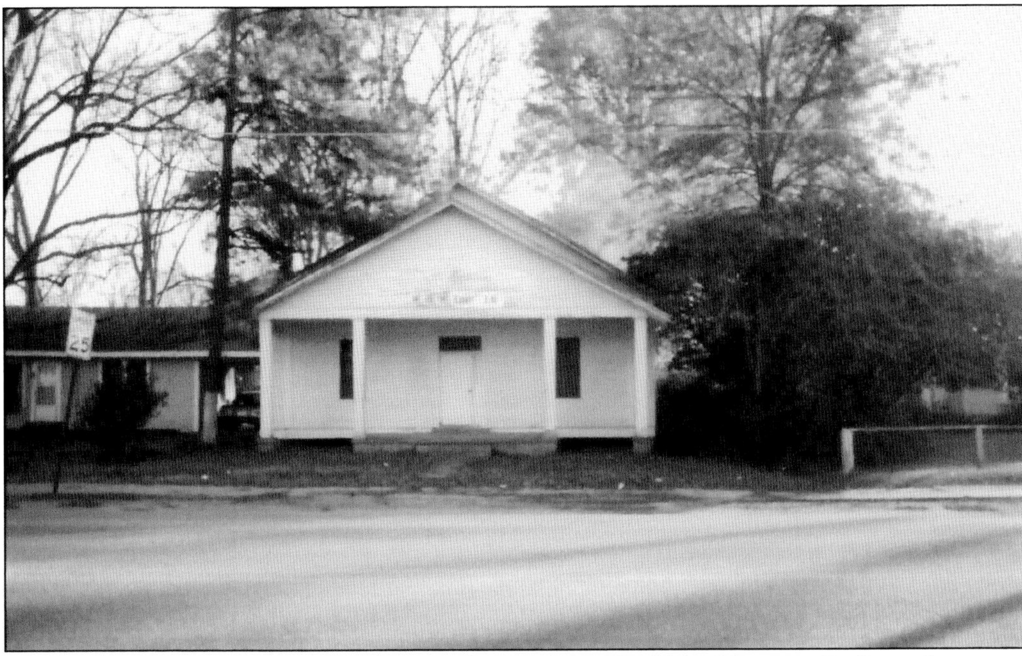

According to Carroll Guilbeau, the Woodmen of the World building on St. Peter Street was first Labbe Bakery. It served the St. Pierre community in the late 19th and early 20th century. The building burned down sometime in the 1900s and was not rebuilt. Woodmen of the World purchased the property and built on it. (Janet Stemmans.)

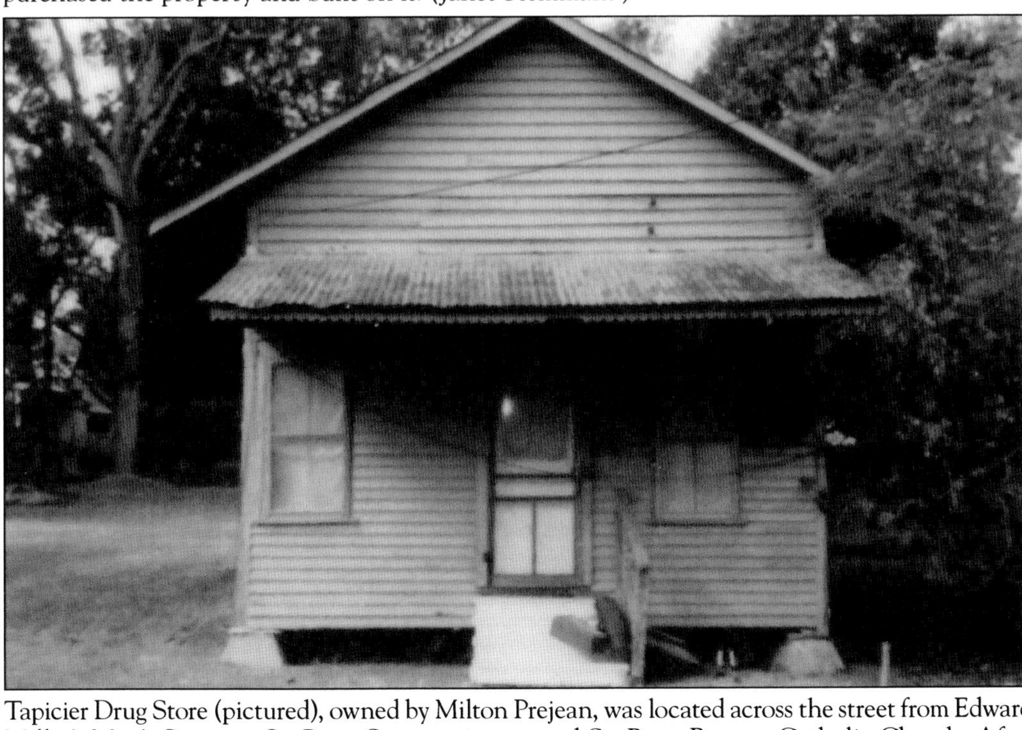

Tapicier Drug Store (pictured), owned by Milton Prejean, was located across the street from Edward Miller's Men's Store on St. Peter Street going toward St. Peter Roman Catholic Church. After Prejean closed his drugstore, he sold it to Jean Crouchet for his barbershop. (Janet Stemmans.)

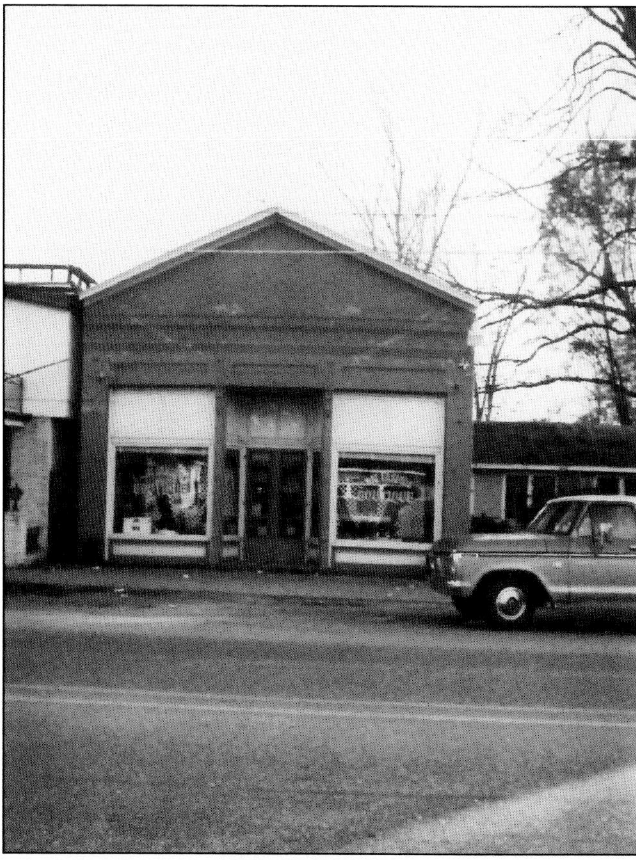

This brick building, which still stands downtown, was once a men's clothing store owned by Edward Miller. Items sold here included an array of clothing, hats, and umbrellas. Leo Mary brought the vacant structure in 1945. It was reopened as a general store for a number of years before closing again. Designer's Faire and C&M Fashions were located in the building at one time but are now closed. The building is now vacant. (Louis Perret.)

Standing in front of Miller's Haberdashery in 1910 are, from left to right, George Mechior, mayor of Carencro and banker; Dr. Eric Guilbeau; and Edward Miller, store owner. (Louis Perret.)

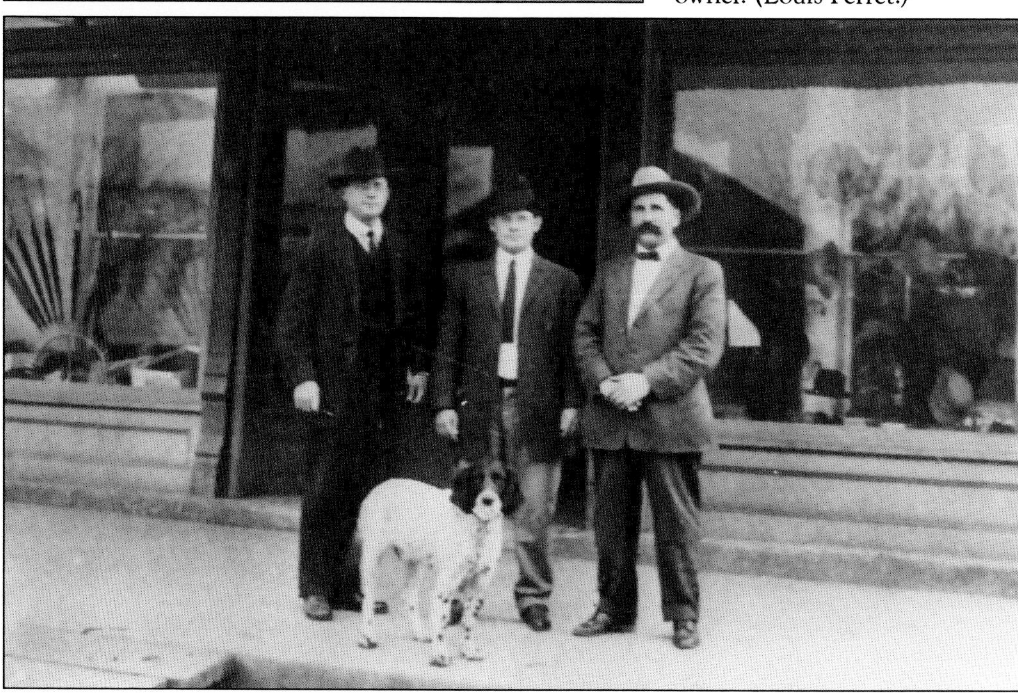

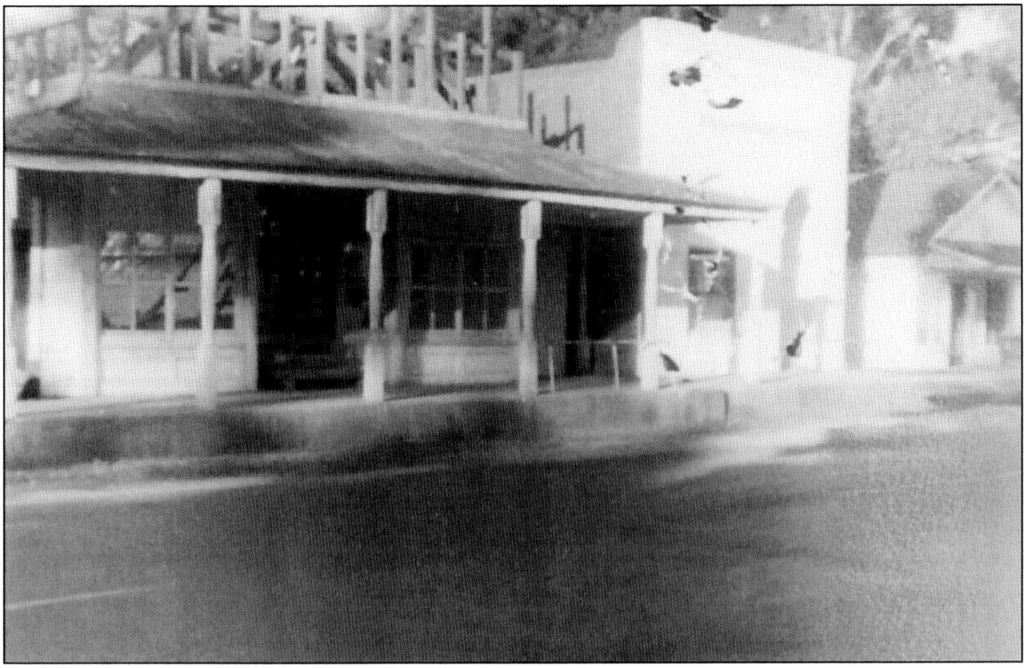

Pictured here are the Felix Martin General Store, Angelle Insurance, and Milton Prejean Drug Store next to each other on the corner of St. John and St. Peter Streets. The picture was taken just a few days before the old Felix Martin store was dismantled in the 1970s.

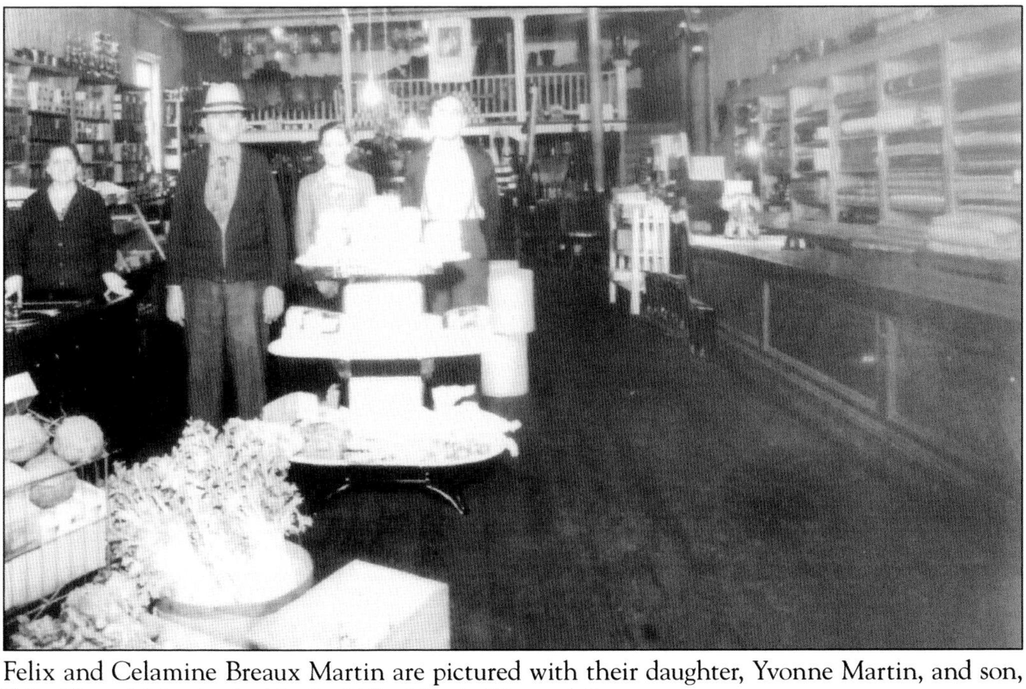

Felix and Celamine Breaux Martin are pictured with their daughter, Yvonne Martin, and son, Felix "Frere" Martin, inside the Felix Martin General Store.

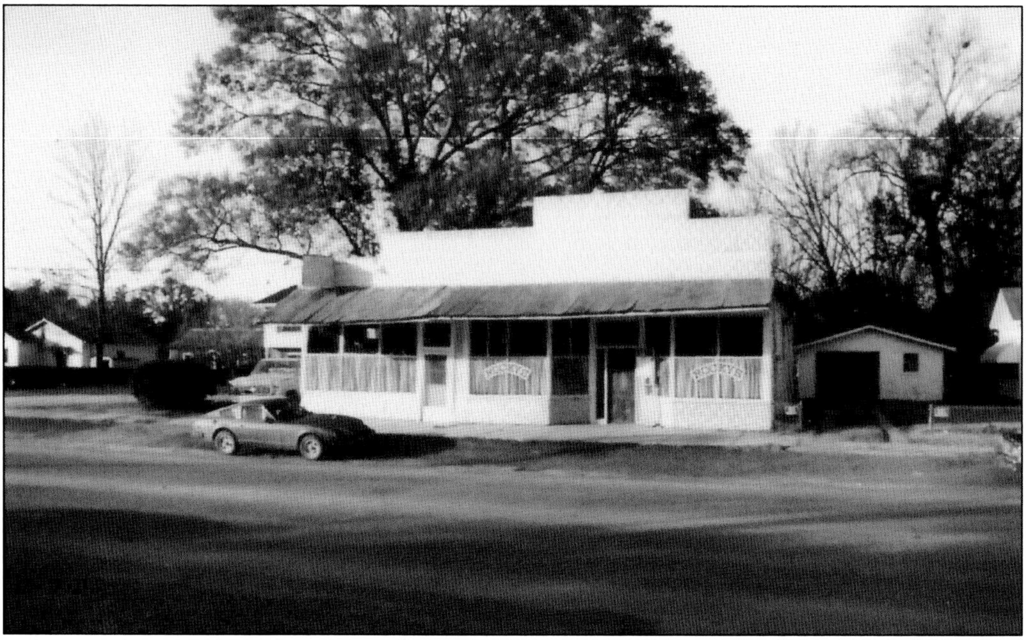

Rocky's seafood restaurant was located across the street from the new city hall on St. Peter Street. This picture was taken in 1981. In recent years, the property has housed a business known as Paul's Pirogue. (Janet Stemmans.)

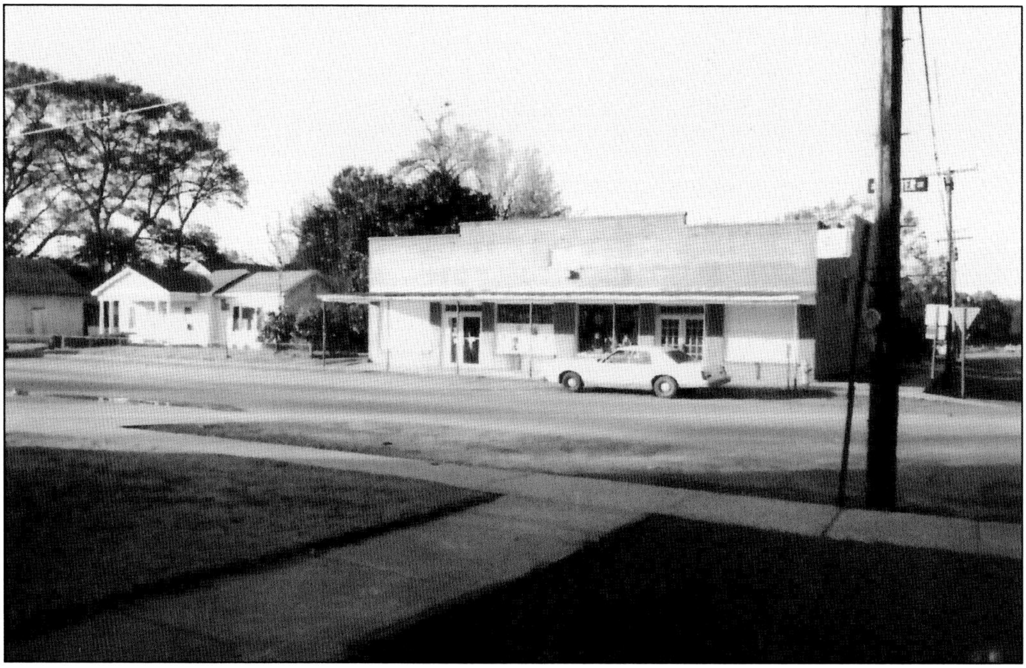

Ethel Broussard Martin owned this store on the corner of St. Peter and Church Streets. Many residents of Carencro may remember Burton Andrus having a store there along with two other occupants. Jules Broussard had a meat market, and Ulger Miller was the owner of a shoe shop. In later years, the store served as a Vick Ashy clothing store, a laundromat, the Carencro Library, and the church gift shop, St. Peter Book Store. (Janet Stemmans.)

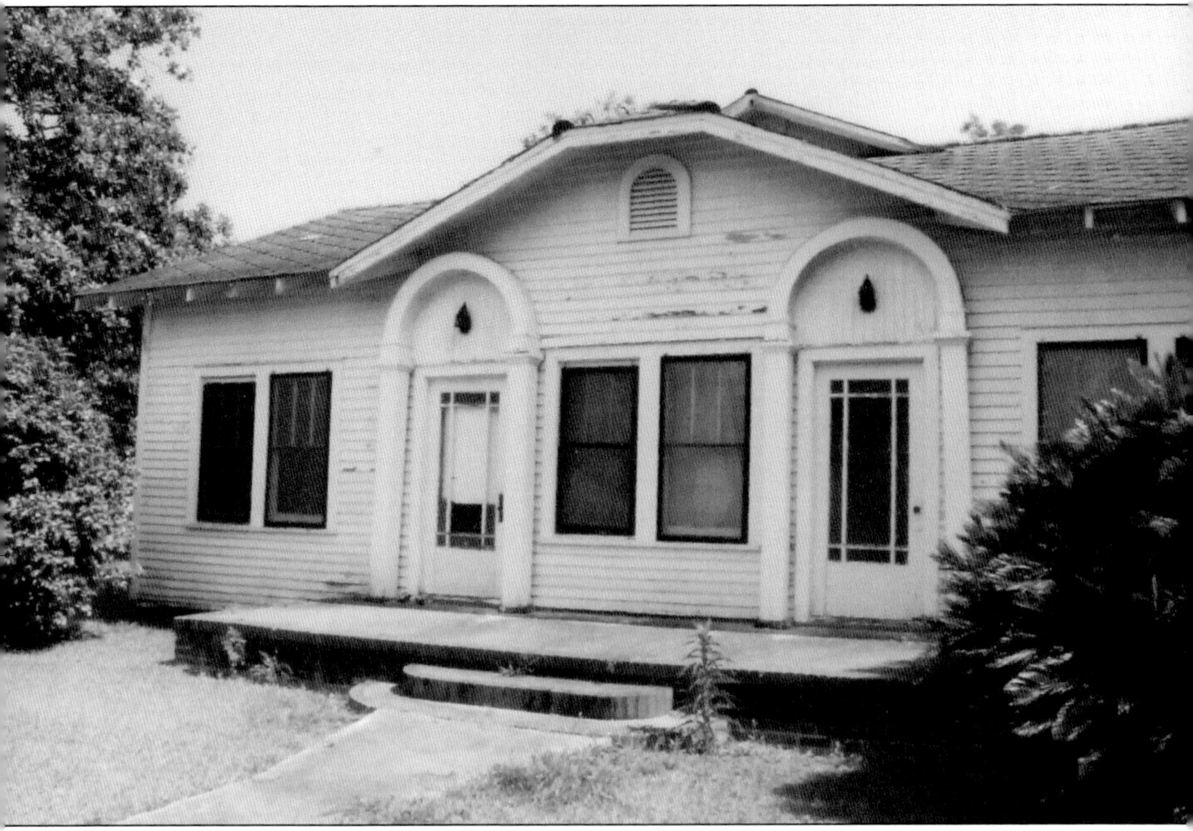

Dr. Eric E. Guilbeau Sr. followed in the footsteps of his grandfather, Dr. Romain Francez, and his uncle, Dr. Cank Guidry, by graduating from medical school. Dr. Eric Guilbeau Sr. earned his degree from Tulane University in 1906. After returning to his hometown, Dr. Guilbeau opened his practice next to his family's home on St. John Street in downtown Carencro. At the beginning of his career, Dr. Guilbeau either saw patients in his office or traveled in his buggy to their home. When he got a car, families would contact him and have someone in a horse and buggy meet him at the crossroads where farmland met the public gravel/dirt road. In 1937, Dr. Guilbeau's first office was replaced with a clinic known as St. Ann's Clinic, which still stands today. At one time, the clinic was manned by both Dr. Guilbeau and his son, Dr. Eric Guilbeau Jr. (Janet Stemmans.)

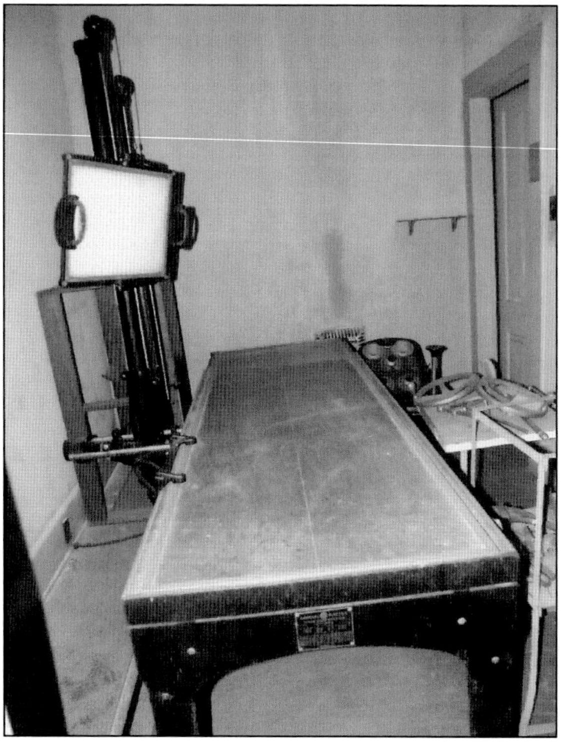

Surgical procedures, setting of fractures, baby deliveries, and the treatment of regular aches and pains were all performed at St. Ann's Clinic. The clinic has been moved to St. Louis Street downtown and remains empty. However, while patients are no longer able to receive services at St. Ann's Clinic, the waiting room, surgery room, laboratory, patient rooms, and X-ray room (which held the X-ray machine that was purchased for $10,000 after World War I) now hold old equipment and other family memorabilia. (Community Chronicles.)

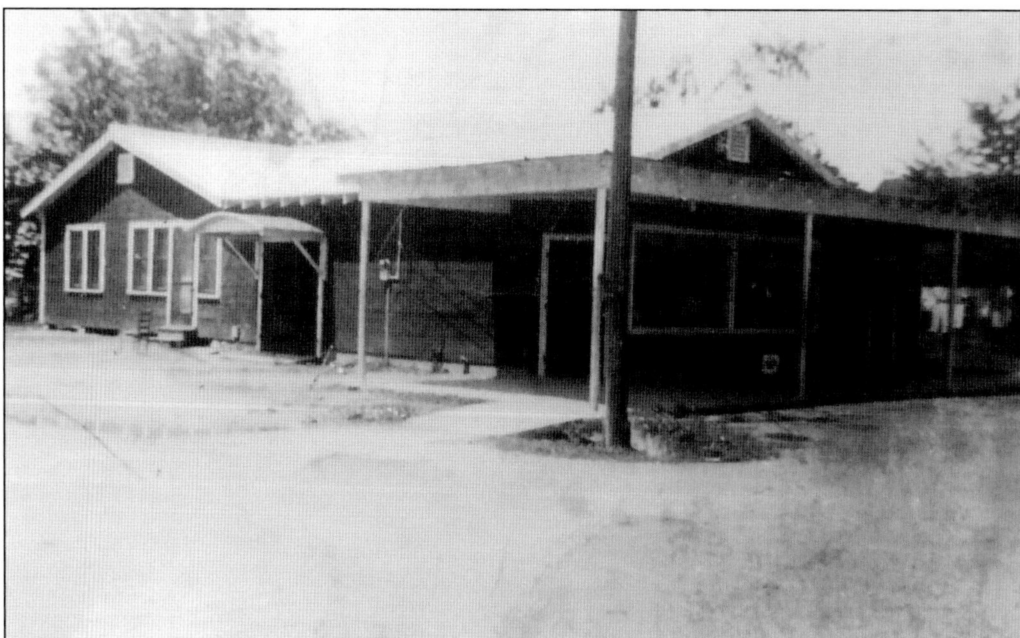

A two-story building belonging to Sam Cuccio once stood on the corner of St. Peter and Church Streets. Cuccio had a general store and shoe shop on the first floor, with living quarters on the second floor. The establishment was torn down during World War I, and David and Sidney Guidry built a new store in the late 1930s. Burton Andrus later purchased the general store. The City of Carencro purchased the property from Burton Andrus to build a sheriff's station and city hall.

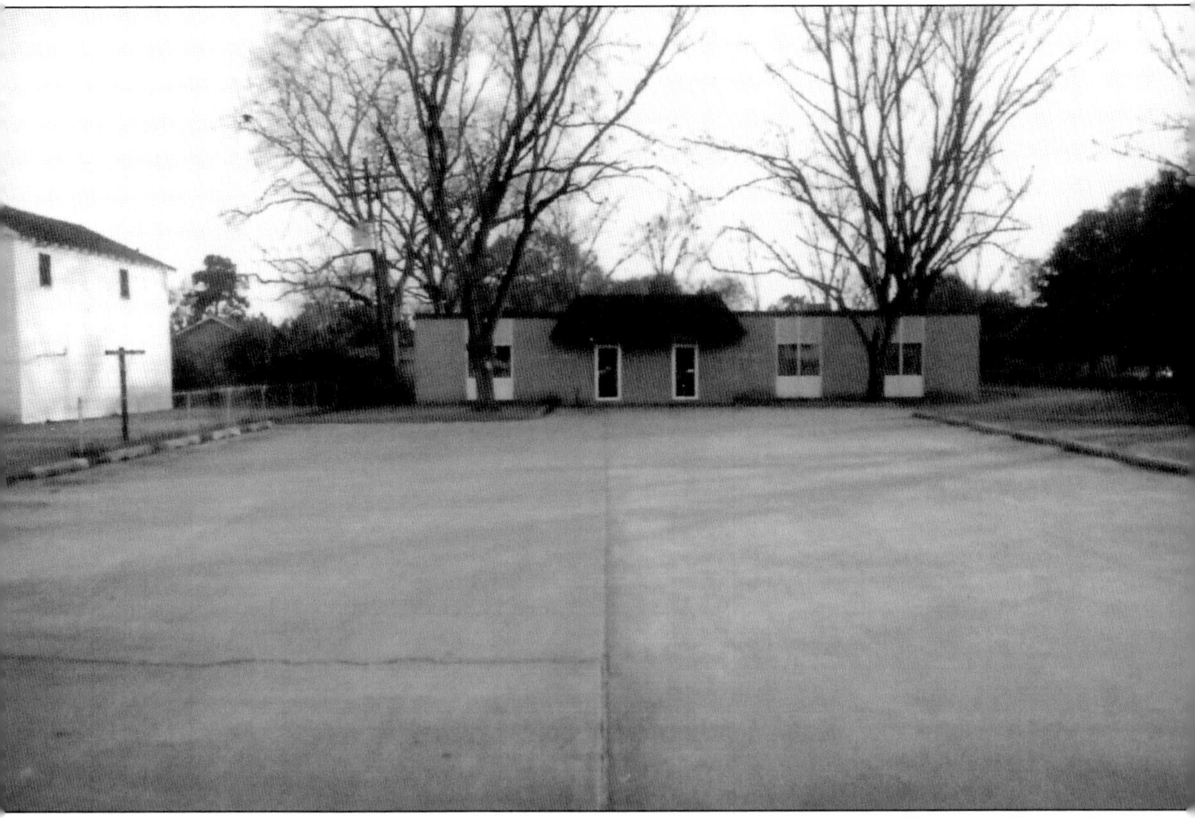

In 1964, Dr. James Clause and pharmacist Paul Guilbeau established a new doctor's office and pharmacy on University Avenue where Pizzaville USA now stands. They eventually relocated their practice to St. Peter Street in 1973. The new location was where the popular bakery, The Bakery, owned by Warren Arceneaux and Caramlite, once stood. The Bakery was well known for its sweet treats and baked bread and doubled as an ice house that sold ice blocks for iceboxes. Although they are both now retired, the practice they established has been carried on by Paul's daughter, pharmacist Sheri Guilbeau, and Dr. Richard Feucht. In reflecting on their practices, Sheri commented: "Both Dr. Clause and my dad practiced in an era where after-hours calls to treat a patient or to fill a prescription were not uncommon. I literally grew up watching my dad's passion for serving the community, which makes it even more special for me to carry on his good work." (Janet Stemmans.)

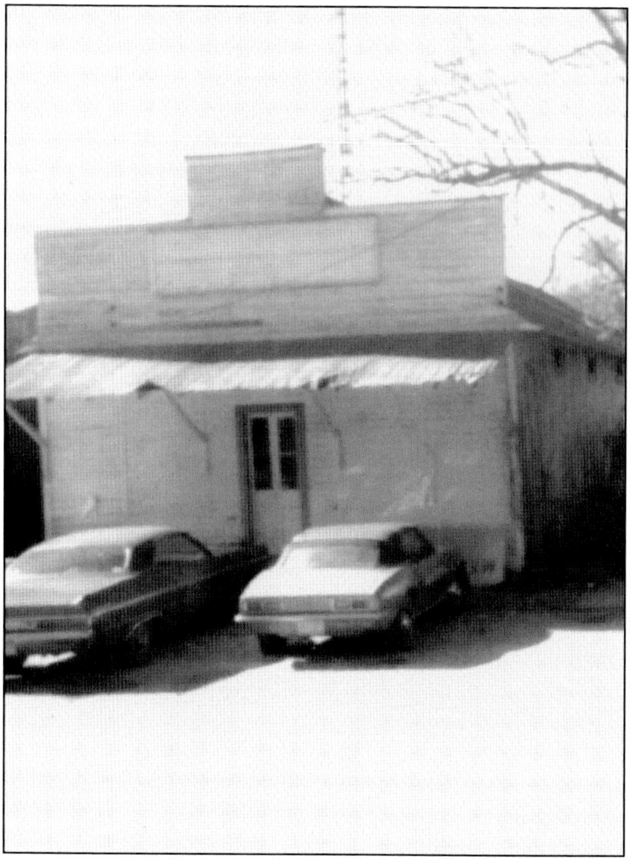

North Church Street contained a blacksmith shop (left), corn grist mill, and embalming business, all owned by Edmond Melancon. In the 1920s, Melancon opened a hardware store (below) vnext door under the name E.D. Melancon and Son, selling only John Deere parts. Farmers who needed their services would buy on credit and pay their bills when the crops were harvested and sold. After World War II, Edmond's son, Ray, convinced his father to sell John Deere tractors. When a larger space was needed, Ray bought a cement-block maker and made 25 blocks of cement every evening after work in order to build a new store next door to the original wooden building (where Cicchiello's Hair now sits). In the 1950s, Ray moved into the new store and established Melancon Implement Company. Twenty-five years later, he built a larger complex on property at the corner of Interstate 49 and Gloria Switch Road. (Both, Jennifer Connolly.)

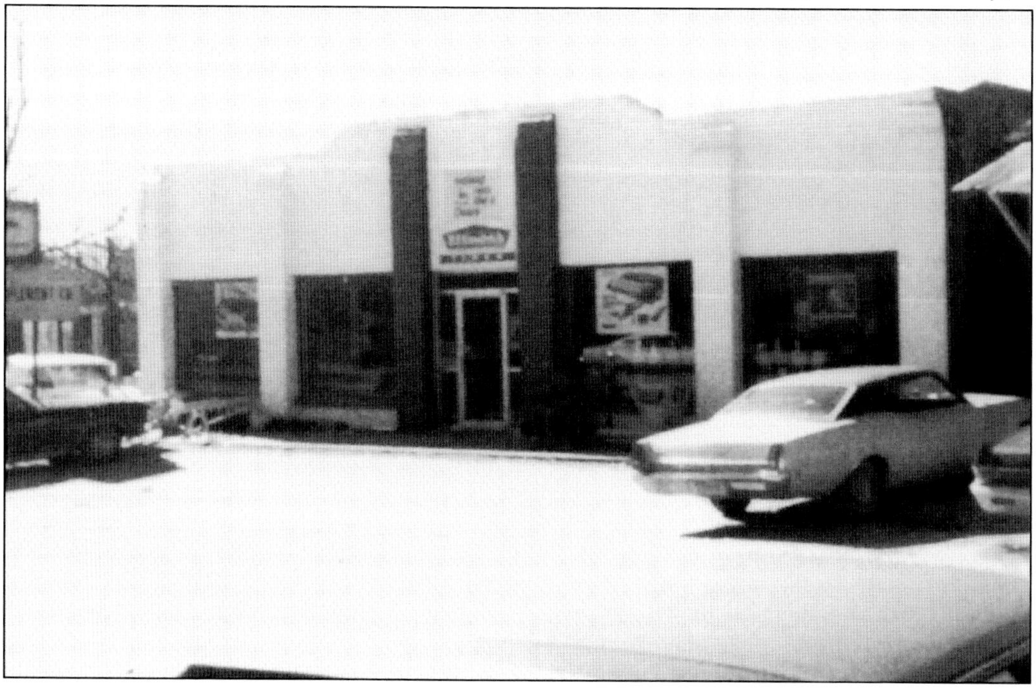

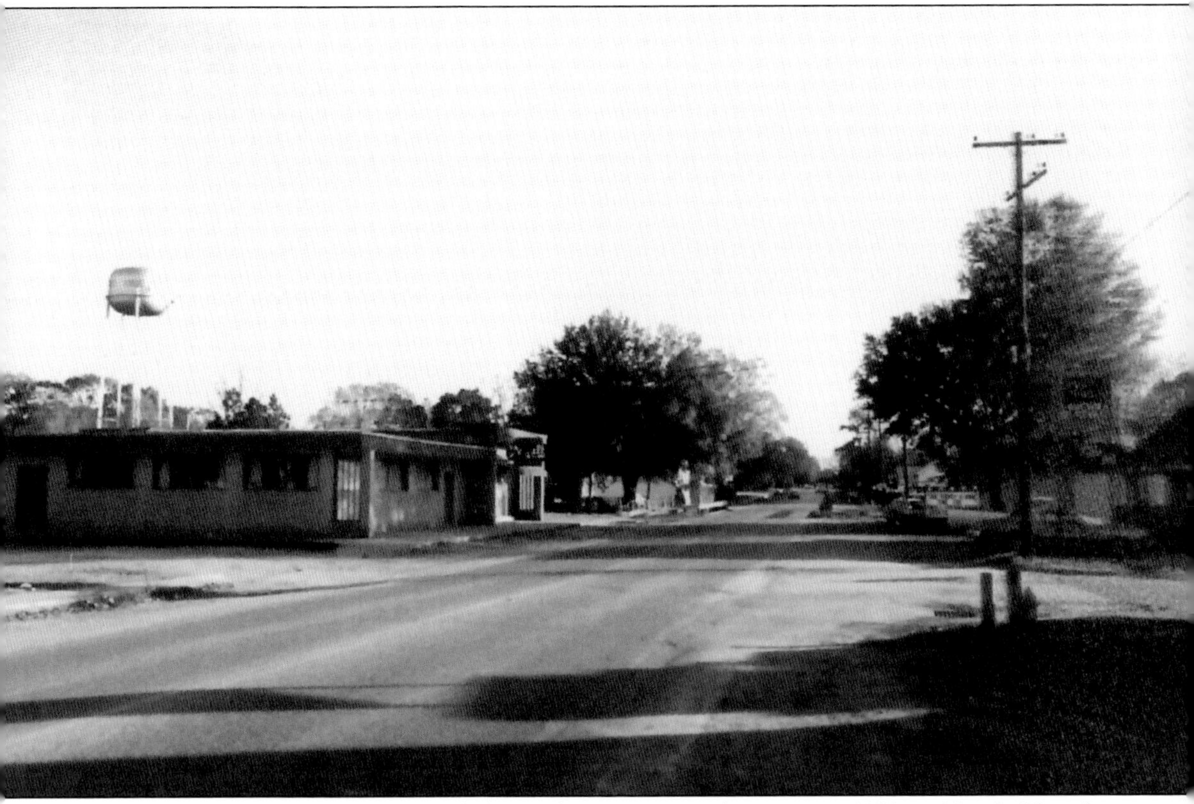

Three Melancon brothers combined their talents to start a business in 1953 on North Church Street downtown. Ed Melancon opened Melancon Pharmacy, Bill Melancon opened his medical practice, and Lester Melancon served as a funeral director. All three businesses being housed in one location allowed for residents to have easy access to a doctor, pharmacist, and funeral hearses, which also served as ambulances. According to Ed Melancon III (Eddie), who now owns Melancon Pharmacy with his brother David, the three brothers were available 24 hours a day to meet the needs of their customers and clients. (Janet Stemmans and Eddie Melancon.)

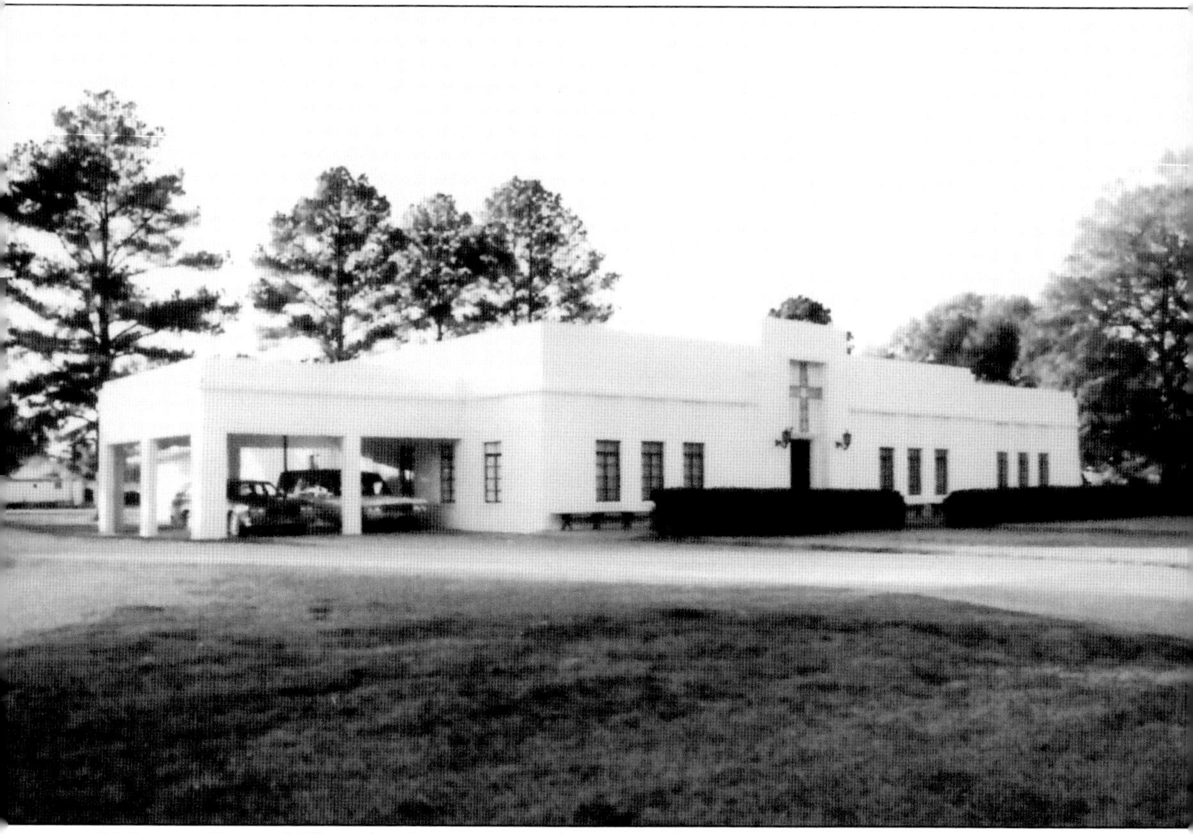

Melancon Funeral Home has been a trusted name in Carencro since 1907. As a third-generation funeral director, Gerald Melancon is carrying on his family's legacy. His great-grandfather, Ophe Melancon, began in the funeral service in the late 19th century. His grandfather, Edmond Melancon, then stepped into the role as funeral director. Gerald's father, Lester Melancon, became the funeral director in Carencro and remained in that position for many decades. Gerald and his brother, Lester Melancon Jr., have both carried on the family legacy. Gerald's family serves as the leading force behind Melancon Funeral Home, and Lester's family runs the Melancon Marble & Granite Works on North University Avenue. Melancon Funeral Home has expanded over the decades and now has two locations in Carencro, as well as locations in Arnaudville, Opelousas, and Grand Coteau. (Jennifer Connolly.)

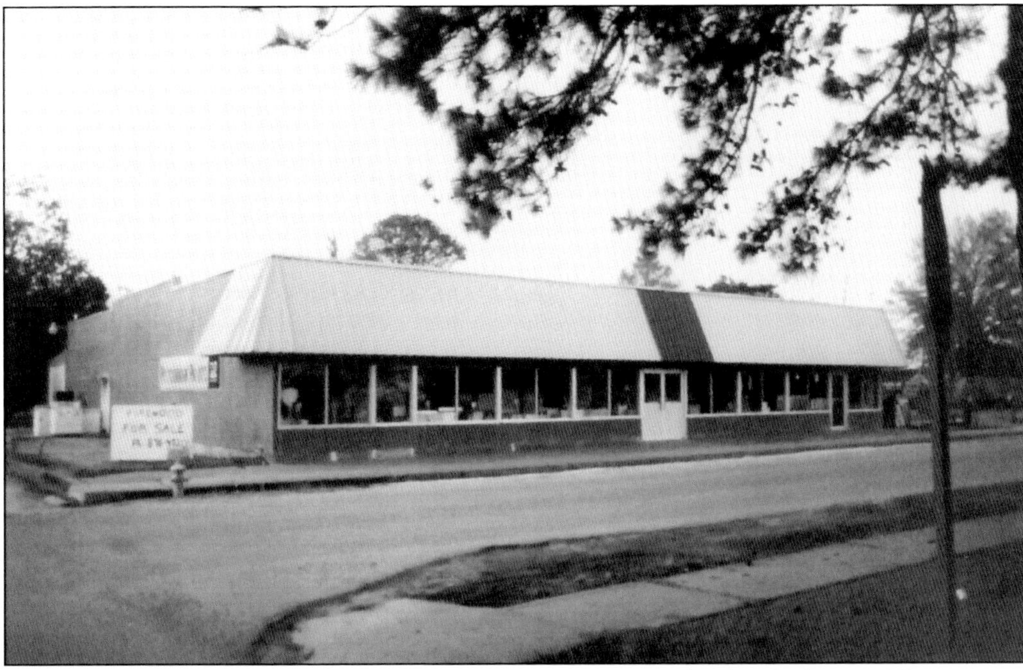

C.J. Richard Hardware sold everything from sacks for cotton to lumber for homes. The company also served as a builder for homes across Carencro and Lafayette. Robley Richard III ran the family business until it closed its doors in 2010. He commented, "I can remember at the age of eight unloading the railcars of West Coast lumber, brick and other materials. While we spent many hours working in the lumberyard, we also had lots of time to make memories with our friends. The lumberyard was the best place to play a good game of hide and seek."

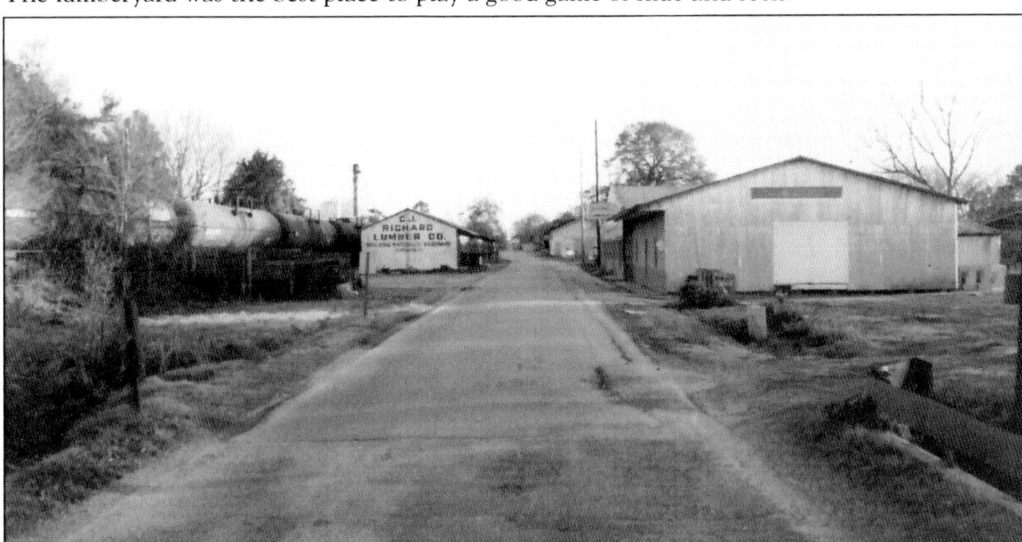

According to Robley Richard III, a hardware business that had been in the Carencro Prairie in the 1800s was sold to C.J. Richard in the early 1900s. The name changed to C.J. Richard Lumber Company, and the business was located near the railroad in the village of Carencro. C.J. Richard's son, Robley "Bobby" Richard, wanted to buy the business from his brothers and sisters, but they bought him out instead, and he opened Carencro Builder Supply in 1946.

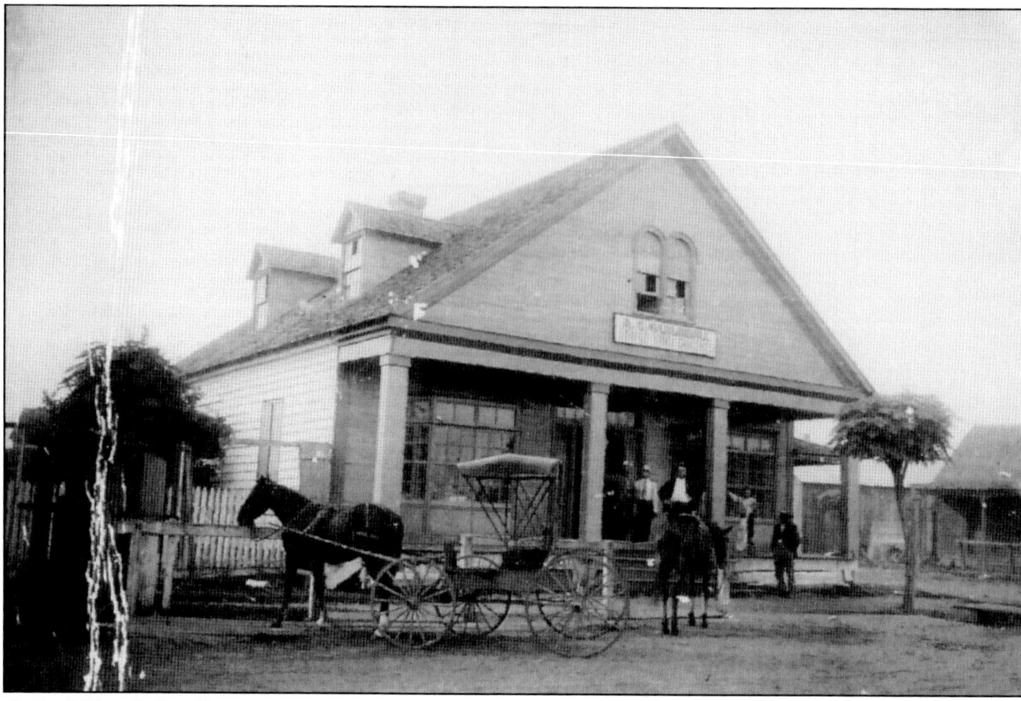

A.C. "Chap" Guilbeau's store was on the corner of Clara Street (Veterans Drive) and North Church Street.

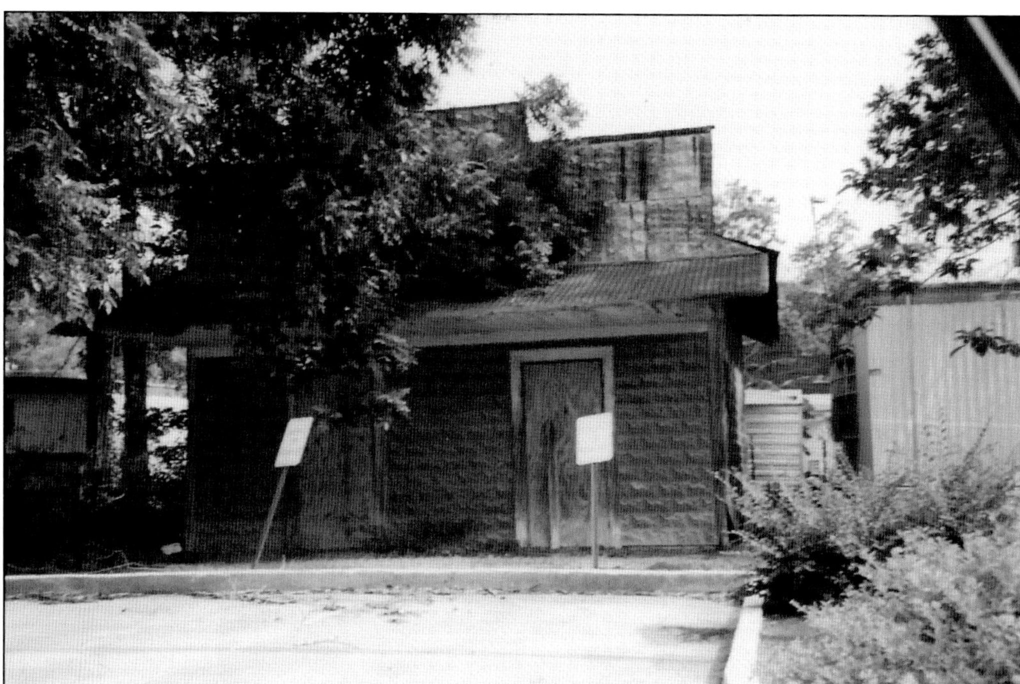

Alcee Brasseaux's grocery store was behind the home of Lucille Breaux Guidroz. The grocery store faced Carencro Middle School. Before school lunch programs were offered, many students either brought their lunches from home or bought them from Brasseaux. (Janet Stemmans.)

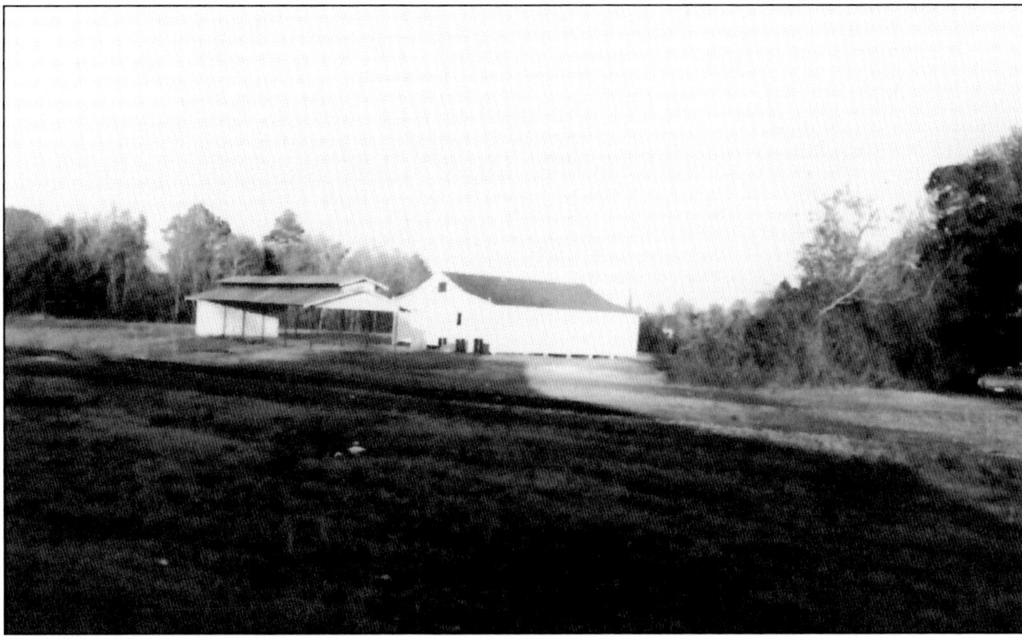

According to Jennifer Connolly, Wilbert Lacombe joined the Navy in 1956 and came home in 1962. He is now serving his seventh term as commander of the Carencro veterans group, which meets at Carencro Veterans Hall. The group was organized in 1947 by returning World War II veterans. Today, all branches of service are represented. Monthly meetings are held in the hall, which the public can rent for functions such as bridal showers or family reunions. (Janet Stemmans.)

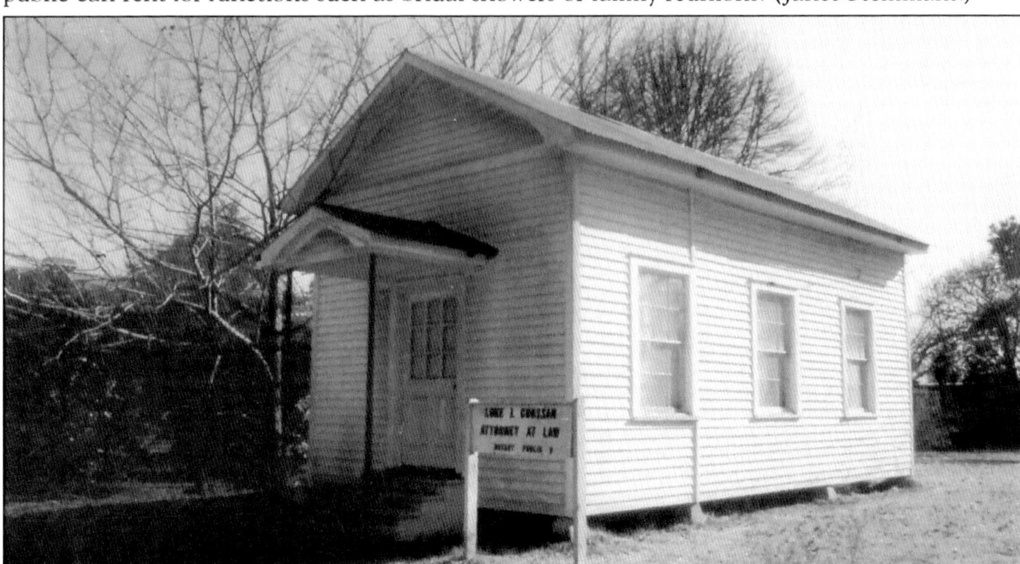

Dr. Andre Prejean's dentist's office was located on Church Street. Dr. Prejean also served as mayor of Carencro for two different terms. Carroll Guilbeau recalls, "The building, which is still located in the downtown area, was a one-room establishment without running water. The front and rear doors would remain open for air flow. Everyone passing in town could stop and take a look at Dr. Prejean either treating a patient or taking a nap." It later became a lawyer's office as shown here. Today, the building is used as a home and can be found on St. Anne Street.

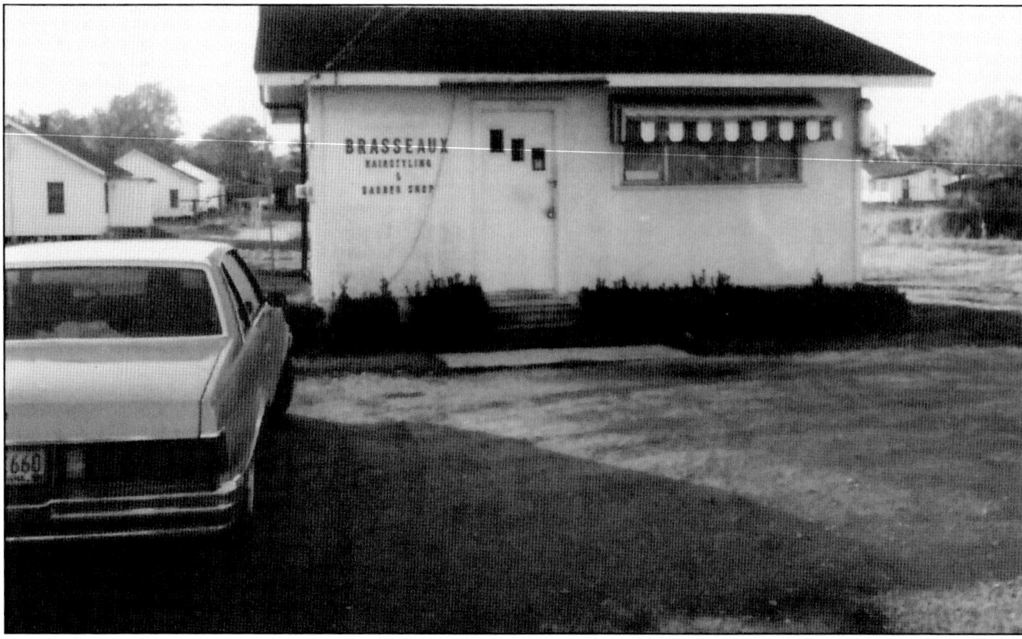

Noah Brasseaux had a barbershop next to Theo Breaux's bar. Many of the barbers had mugs and shaving brushes for each of their clients. Many of the elderly men in Carencro still have their personal mugs and brushes in their homes. (Louis Perret.)

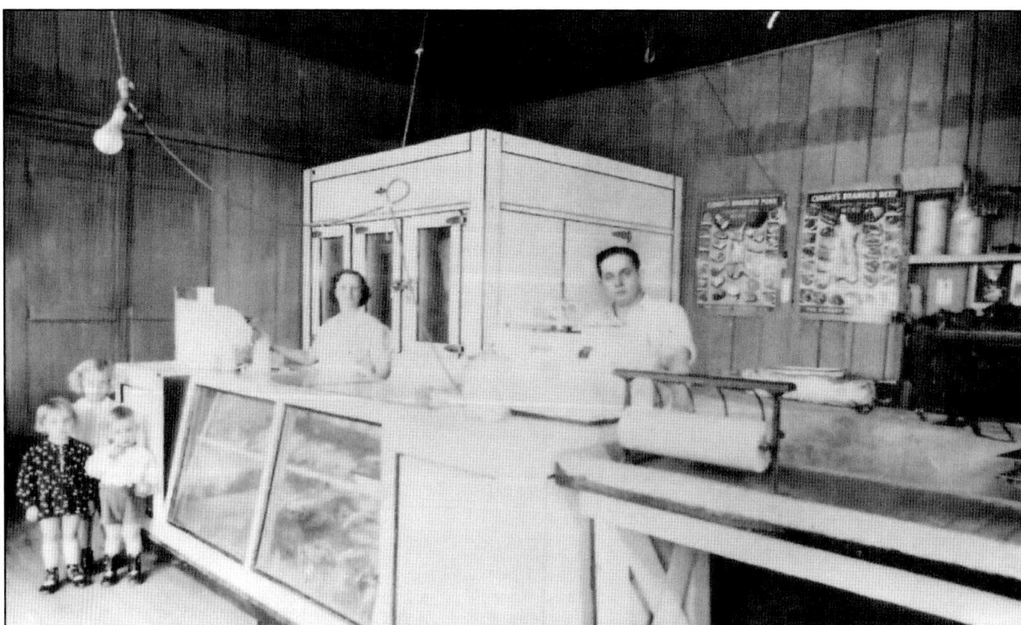

Prejean Market was owned by Elie Prejean and was located on the corner of Bernard and North Church Streets. It was managed by Clay Begnaud when this photograph was taken in 1940. Pictured behind the meat counter are Maud and Clay Begnaud. The children are, from left to right, Jeanelle, Olga, and Donald Begnaud. At one time, Clay Begnaud owned and operated You Need A Butcher on Surrey Street. (Louis Perret.)

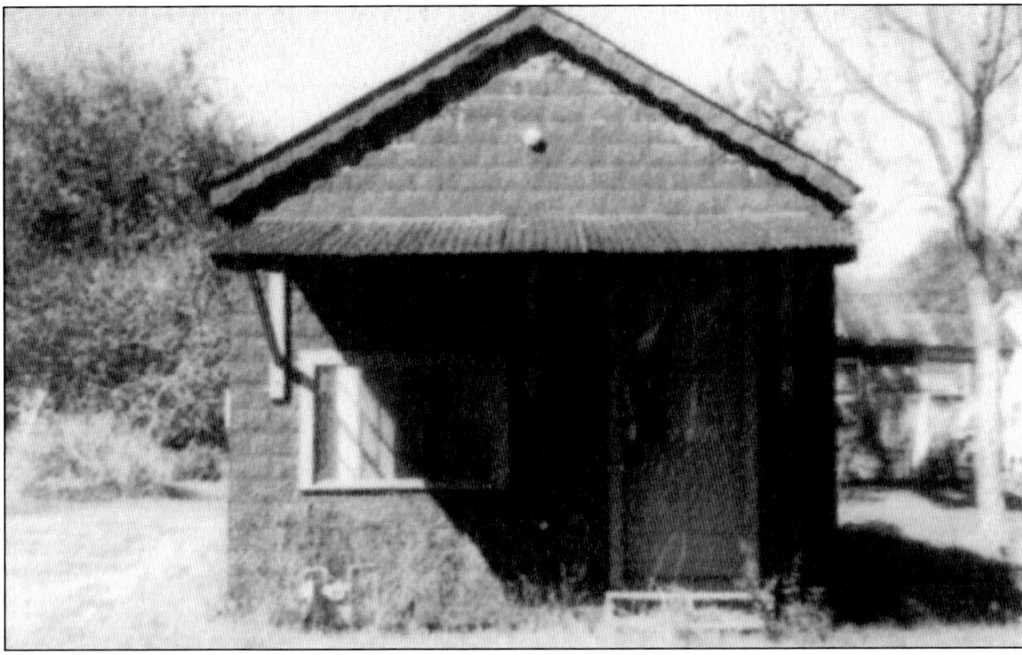

Lodger Guchereau Pressing Shop was owned and operated by Lodger Guchereau and was located on the corner of Church and St. Louis Streets. The Guchereau home was between the Guchereau Store, which they also owned, and the pressing shop. (Janet Stemmans.)

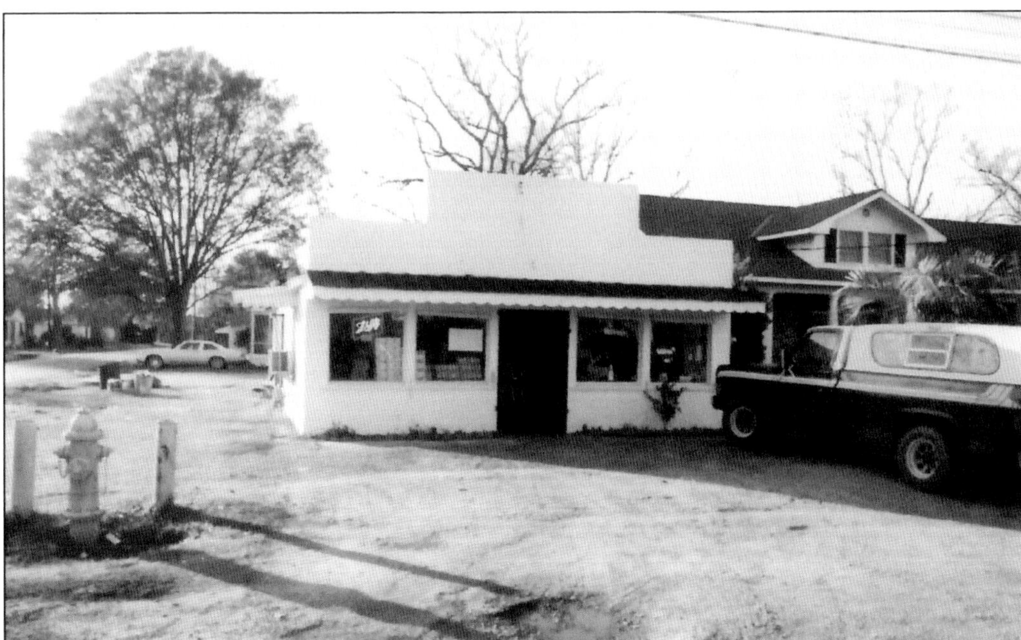

Guchereau Store was also known as Lionel Dupuis Liquor Store. It later became Flap's and Cajun Cro Cafe. (Janet Stemmans.)

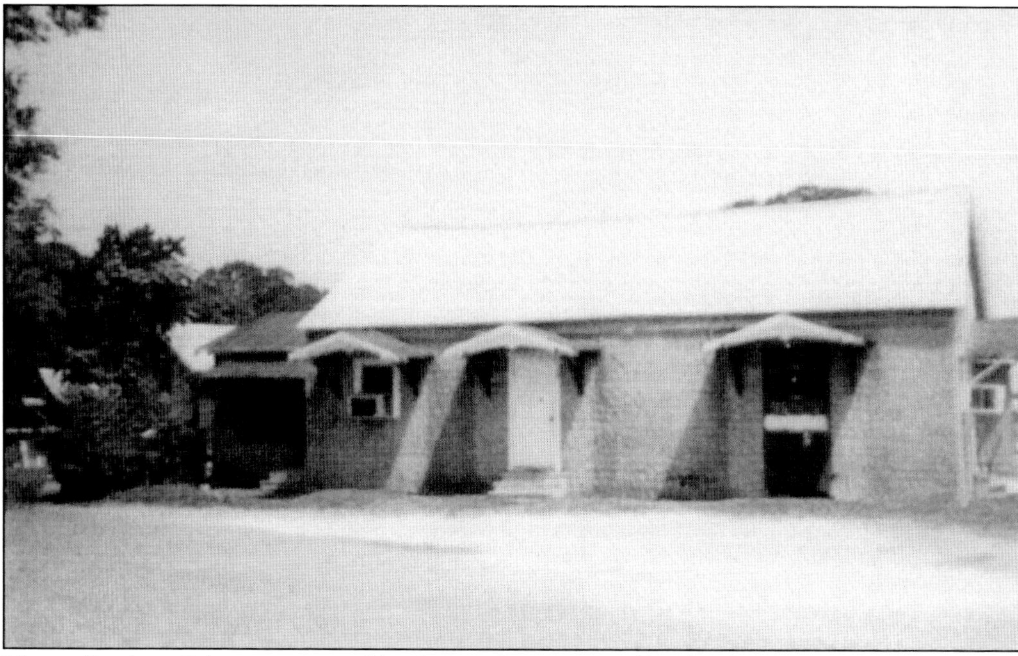

Martin Brothers Saloon was owned by George E. Martin and his brother, Rousseau. A barbershop was attached to the back of the building, and the only access was from the outside. The saloon was located across from the A.C. "Chap" Guilbeau Store on Clara and North Church Streets. (Janet Stemmans.)

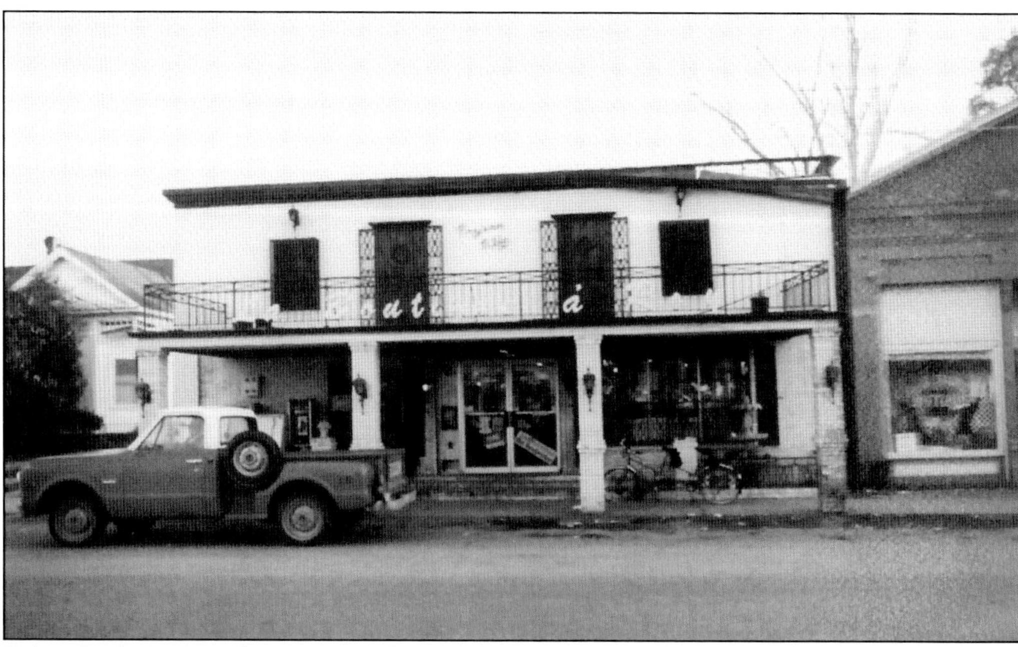

Odon Guidry's general store sat in downtown Carencro. The store offered some of everything, from livestock feed to groceries. The old general store was torn down and replaced with the building that is now home to Advance 2000 Tax. (Janet Stemmans.)

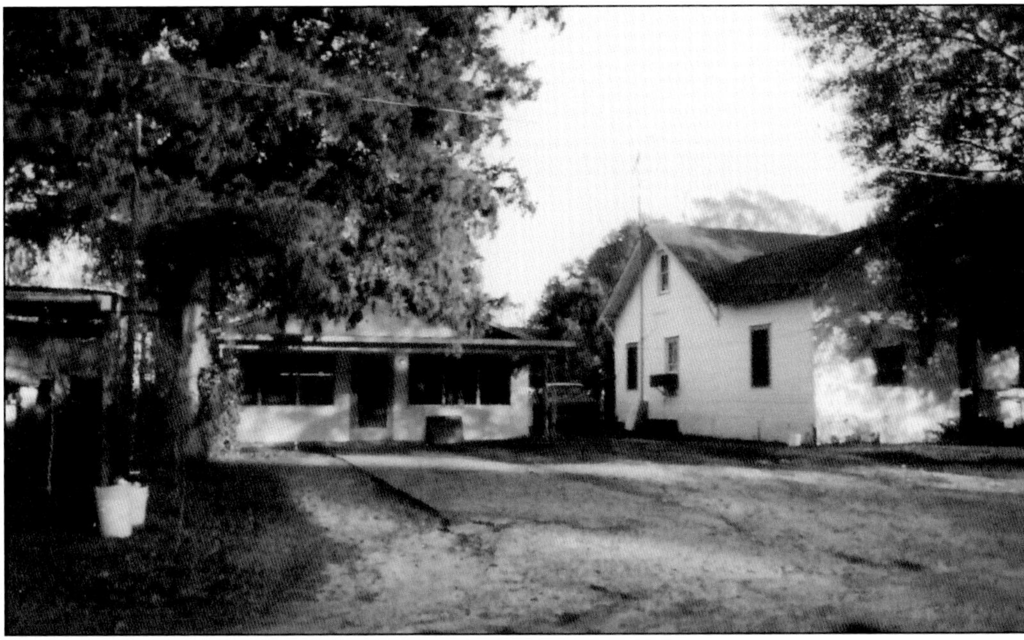

Breaux's Flower Shop, on the corner of South St. John and St. Anne Streets, was started by Anna Mae Breaux in 1965. Breaux lived next door to her flower shop downtown. She passed away in May 2009, and the shop is currently owned by Kaddie Taylor, who purchased the business in the fall of 2009. Taylor is carrying on a tradition by supplying the city with ribbon for all ribbon-cutting ceremonies. (Janet Stemmans)

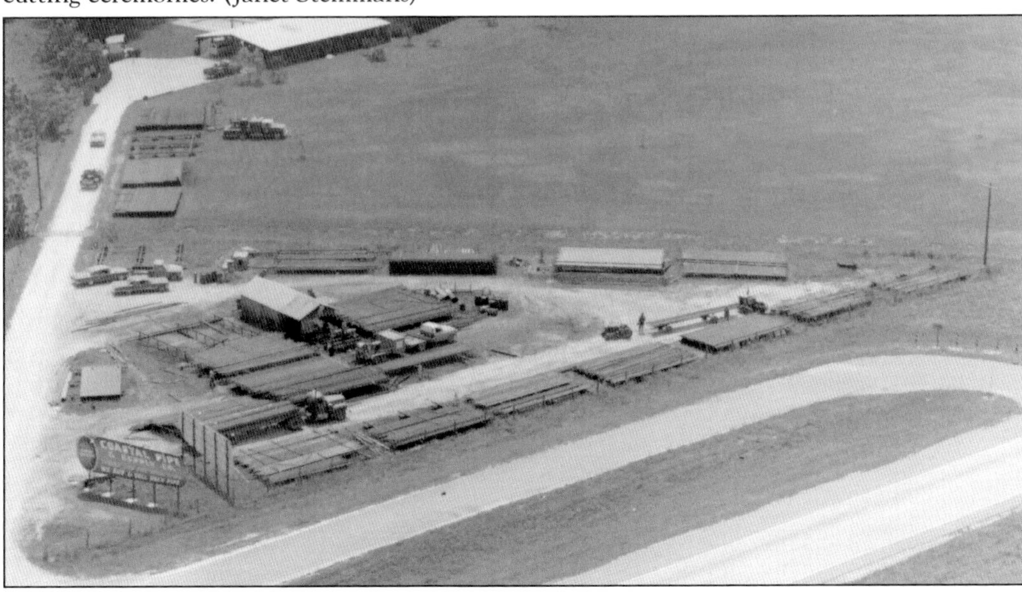

Coastal Pipe was opened in 1957 by N.J. "Buddy" Yentzen. It was once located across the street from where it now sits on the interstate before Interstate 49 was even constructed (as shown here). Yentzen sold the business during the oil boom in Louisiana. When the recession hit in 1985, the new owners closed the business, and Yentzen once again purchased Coastal Pipe. Today, Coastal Pipe is owned and operated by Yentzen's son Doug, Doug's wife (Tanya), and their three sons, Jonathan, Jake, and Jordan. (Community Chronicles.)

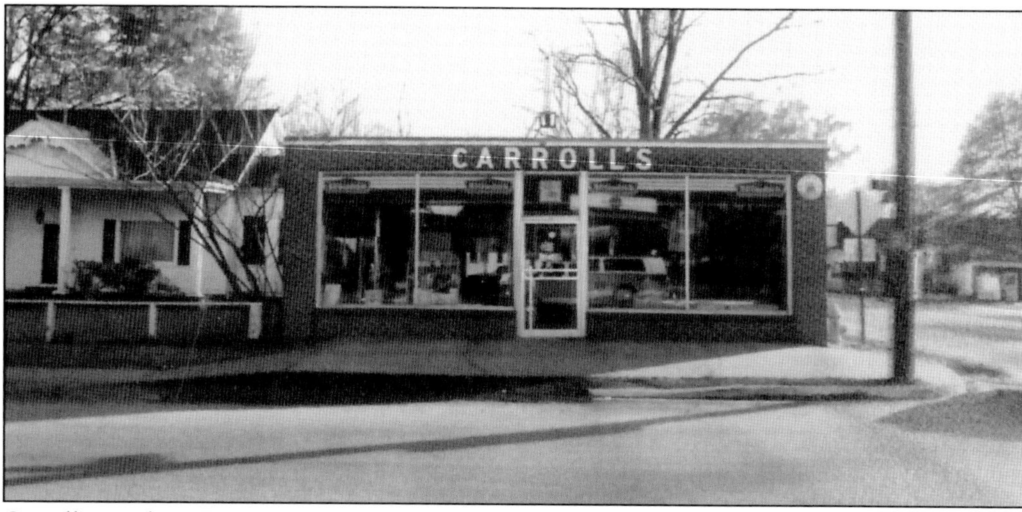

Carroll's sat where Esteve Martin's Drug Store was once located on the corner of North University Avenue and St. Peter Street. Carroll Guilbeau opened a store in 1946 that served the area for five decades. At first, the business sold a little of everything—as did most stores in the area. Guilbeau said, "From small home appliances to larger ones, one could fill up the needs of a home in my store. TV sales were a hot commodity for the store at one time. Also, Carroll's became well known for TV and antenna repairs. After Hurricane Audrey, my sons and I fixed 20 to 30 antennas a day for months. When larger department stores became popular, Carroll's began to sell automobile parts and tires." After closing in 2000, Carroll's sat vacant until a pottery shop known as Emily V's opened in 2012. (Janet Stemmans and Carroll Guilbeau.)

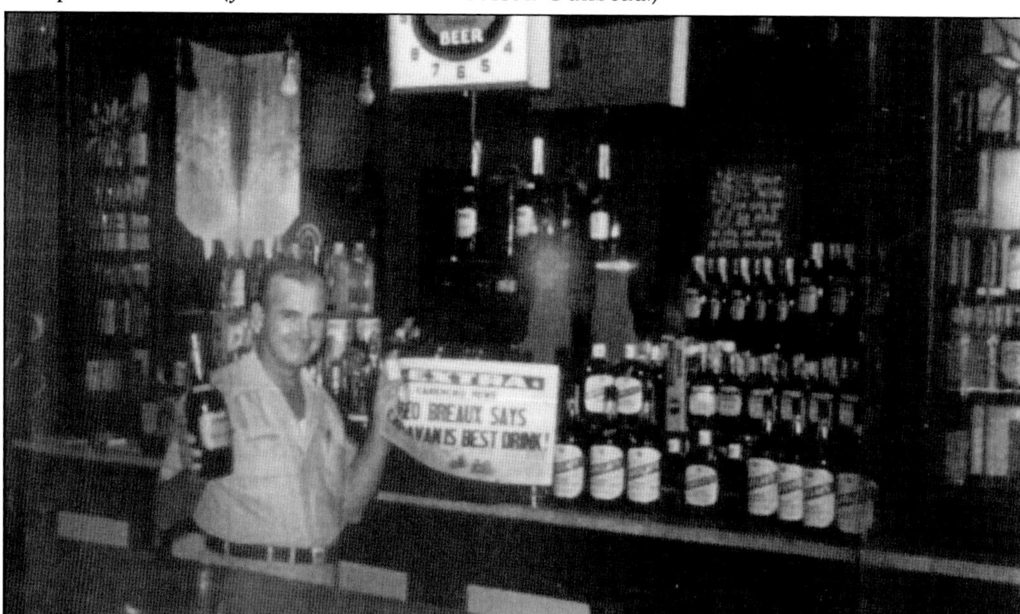

Theo Breaux owned a dance hall and bar. In the South, dance halls have always been a place to mingle with friends and family. In Carencro, there has never been a shortage of them. Some buildings are still standing but are now home to other businesses, while some have been torn down. Do not worry, though, about having a toe-tapping good time in Carencro—many businesses still offer live music, so Cajun dancing and fun can still be enjoyed with others. (Janet Stemmans.)

Nine

Pieces of the Past

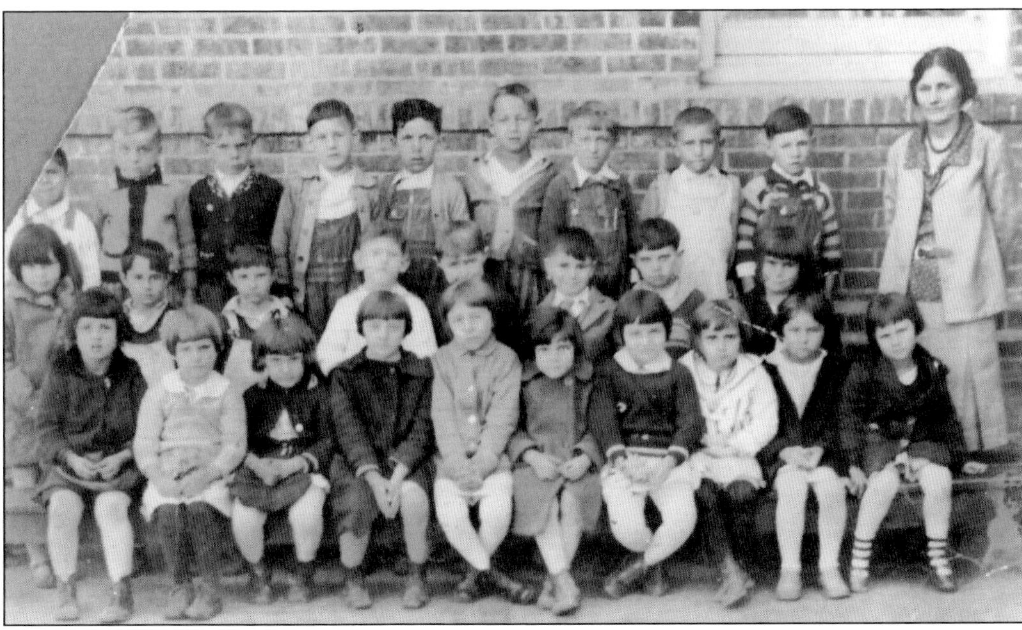

Students of the Carencro Elementary School are pictured here in 1930. In 1970, the last graduating class from the original Carencro High School completed their years of study before the high school moved to its current location on Butcher Switch Road. Other high schools combined and changed their names—Scott and Judice High Schools became Acadiana High School; Milton, Youngsville, and Broussard High Schools became Comeaux High School. The residents of Carencro fought to keep their high school's name for many years. Although they were not able to keep their beloved name of St. Pierre, Carencro High School remained as the community gathered to fight for the "home of the Golden Bears." (Louis Perret.)

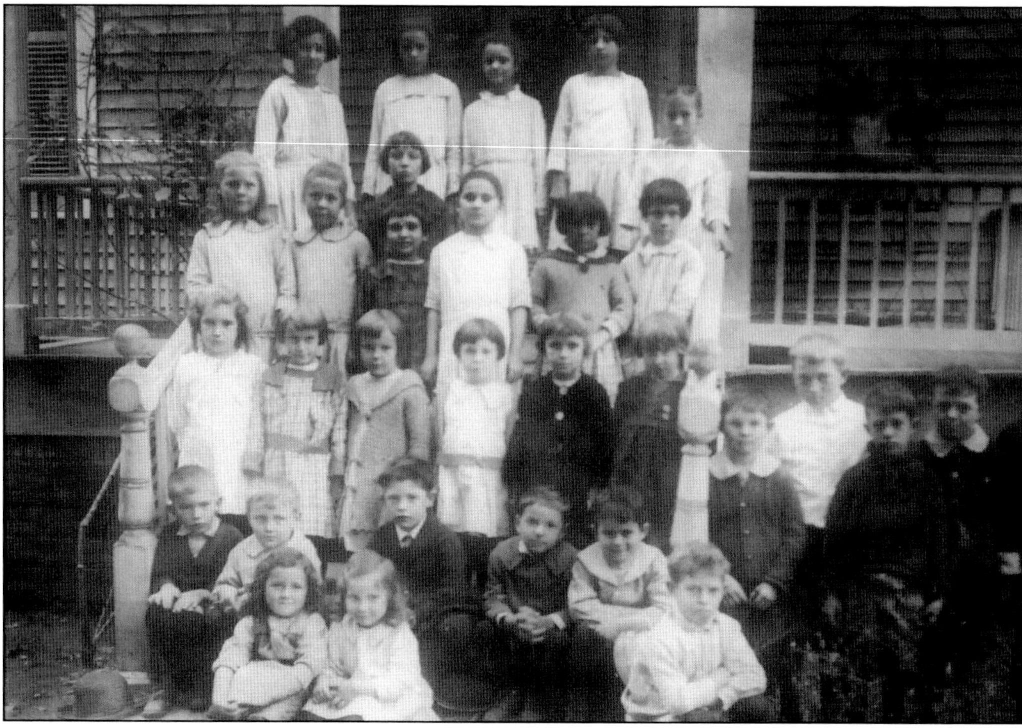

This picture was taken on the steps of St. Ann Convent around 1923–1924. The students are, from left to right (first row) Flo Colomb and Anna Grace Martin; (second row) unidentified, Eugene Villard, Leo Mary, Doucet Coussan, A.G. Domingue, and unidentified; (third row) Leota Prejean, Henrietta Breaux, Billie Breaux, Lillian Crouchet, Mattie Breaux, Anna Mae Andrus, Julo Conque, Stanley Clause, Stephen Albert Coussan, Raoul Arceneaux, and unidentified; (fourth row) two unidentified, Uta Domingue, Aline Clause, and two unidentified (Augustine "Poon" Begnaud is standing directly behind Uta Domingue); (fifth row) all unidentified.

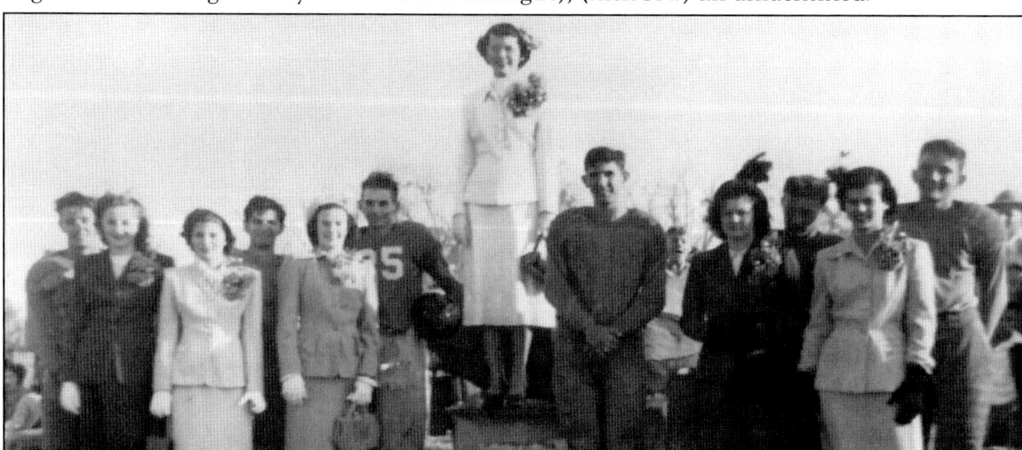

Carencro High School's homecoming court is pictured in 1949. From left to right are Alfred Comeaux, Delores Comeaux, Rowena Guilbeau, Roland Bernard, the Arnaudville queen, the Arnaudville captain, Carencro queen Delores Ann Roy, Carencro captain Nolan Guidry, Jane Greene, Allen Guilbeau, Betty Jean Domingue, and Merlyn Arceneaux. That year, the Bears football team only consisted of six men. (Louis Perret.)

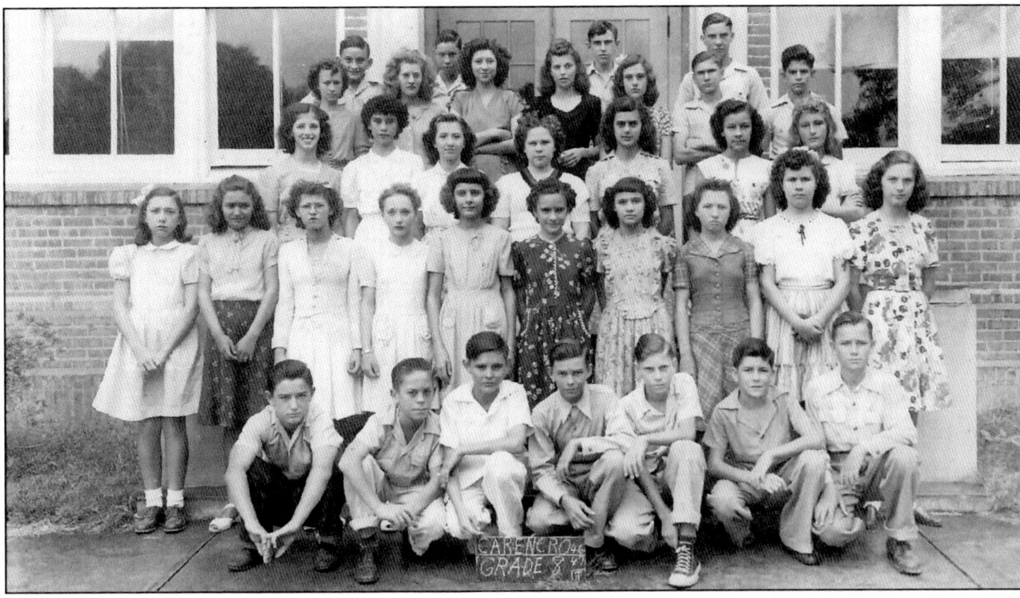

Pictured here are members of the eighth grade class of 1947. From left to right are (first row) Alfred Comeaux, Charles Mamer, Avery Bergeron, Curley Allemond, Anthony Miller, Bernard Prejean, and Malcolm Latour; (second row) Barbara Parker, Theresa Chiasson, Vitalis Marie Robin, Sadie Belle Trahan, Doris Louise Grand, Eva Delle Begnaud, Jane Greene, Beatrice Chassion, Gloria Brasseaux, and Catherine Arceneaux; (third row) Emerdine Menard, Juanita Roger, Mabel Delhomme, Geraldyne Andrus, Betty Jane Domingue, Claire Sonnier, and Mary Ruth Guilbeau; (fourth row) Mary Ann Hebert, Hilda Roger, Mary Alice Bergeron, Lucille Leger, Elsie Mary Prejean, Carroll Prejean, Roland Bernard, Merlyn Arceneaux, Willis Carriere, Earl Patin, and Allen Guilbeau.

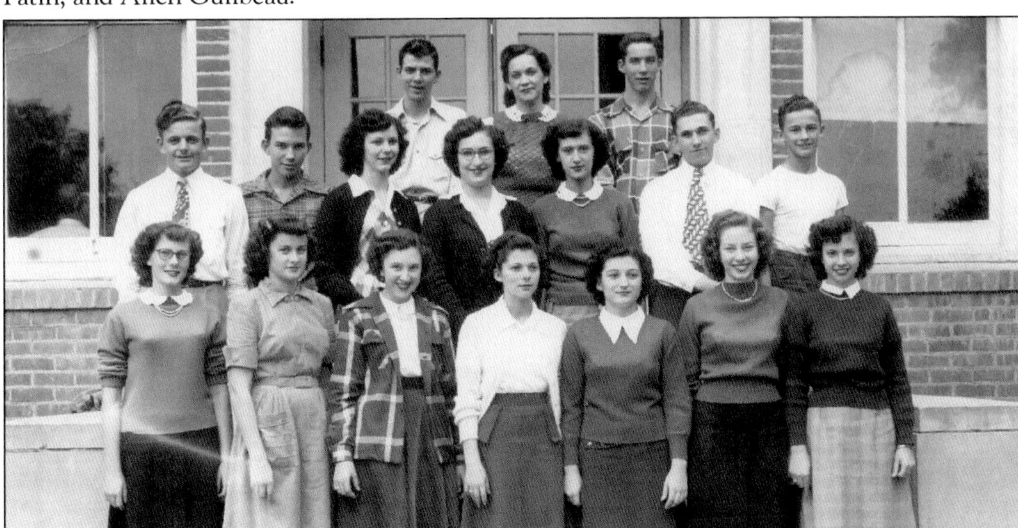

The education system before 1950 only required 11 years of school to graduate. The class of 1950 was the first to complete the new requirement of 12 years. Among the students pictured here are Earl Clavelle, Norma Miller, Eva Joyce Patin, teacher Miss Dagmar Francez, Ruby Domingue, Rowena Guilbeau, Jerry Kirsh, Adam Guilbeau, Carrie Guilbeau, Benn Wiser, Dallas Hebert, D. Menard, Bella Bourque, Evely Benoit, Barbara Hernandez, and Theresa Bernard.

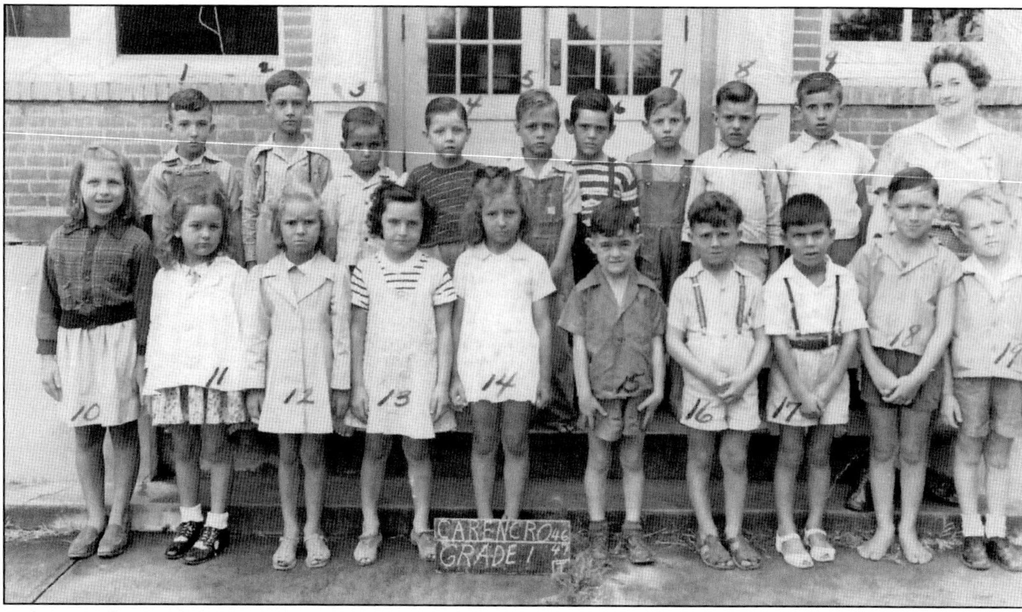

Taken in front of the Carencro lower grade area is the first-grade class of 1946–1947. From left to right are (first row) Joan Dugas, Dolores Lanclos, Rose Mary Marmottin, Shirley Ann Brasseaux, Lizzie Anna Dugas, Raymond Noel, Preston Breaux, Russell Lee Boudreaux, Floyd Kennerson, and Carol Paul Lacy; (second row) Dallas Wingate, Olan J. Guilbeau, Raymond Latiolais, Reyland Carriere, Waydell Latiolais, George Paul Roach, Aurelie Jacneaux Jr., Frank Prejean, Ursin Leger, and teacher Noida Brasseaux. (Russell Boudreaux/Liz Sonnier.)

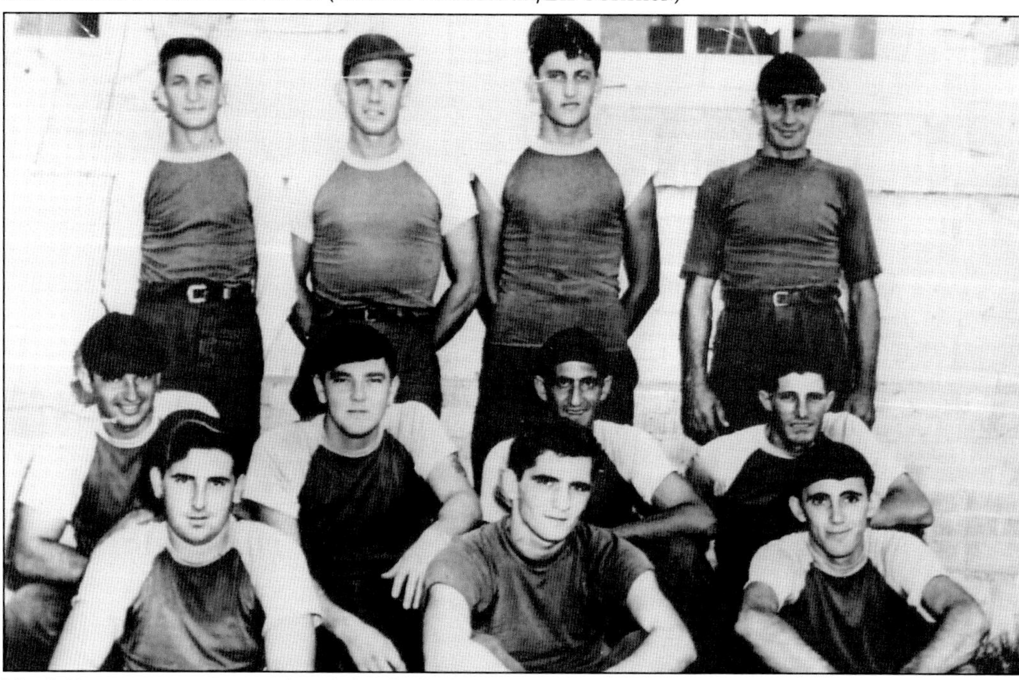

Noah Brasseaux is pictured with his ball club in 1946. The players include Sosthene Arceneaux, Sidney Dugas, Adolph Babineaux, Harold Prejean, Gerald Richard, Elton Cormier, Arius Royer, Newton Meche, Irey Breaux Jr., William Guidry Jr., and Ulysee Cormier. (Louis Perret.)

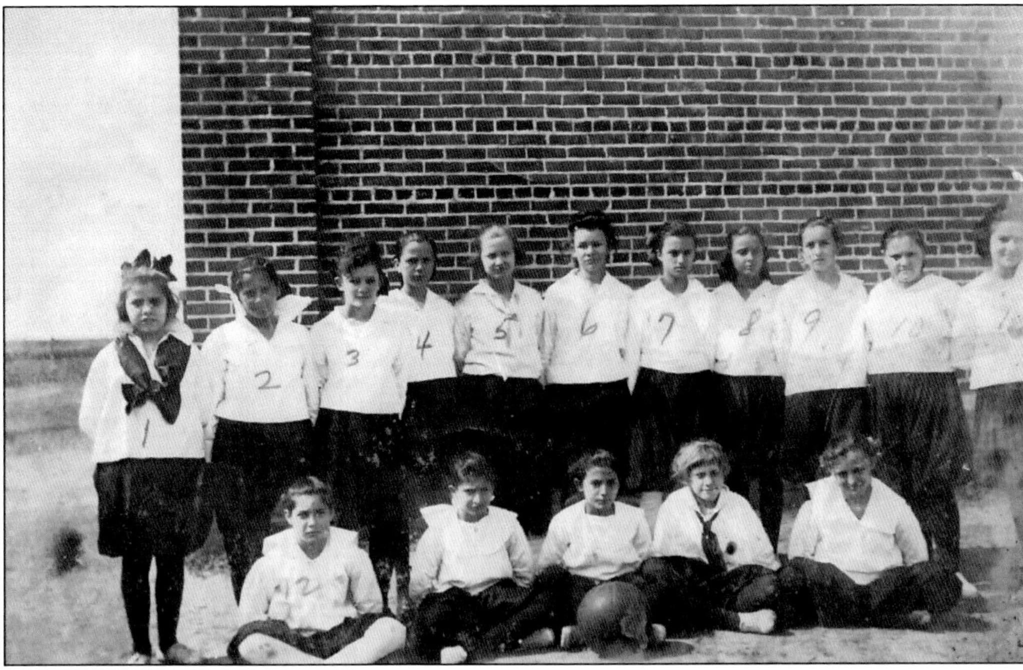

The Carencro girls basketball team mostly consisted of residents of the downtown area of Carencro, formerly known as St. Pierre. In fact, Carencro and St. Pierre were two totally different entities. For those who loved St. Pierre, they never stepped foot in Carencro. Teams from both areas competed against each other. Carencro is said to start near where the ARC resale shop sits near the bridge. St. Pierre included St. Peter Roman Catholic Church. (Louis Perret.)

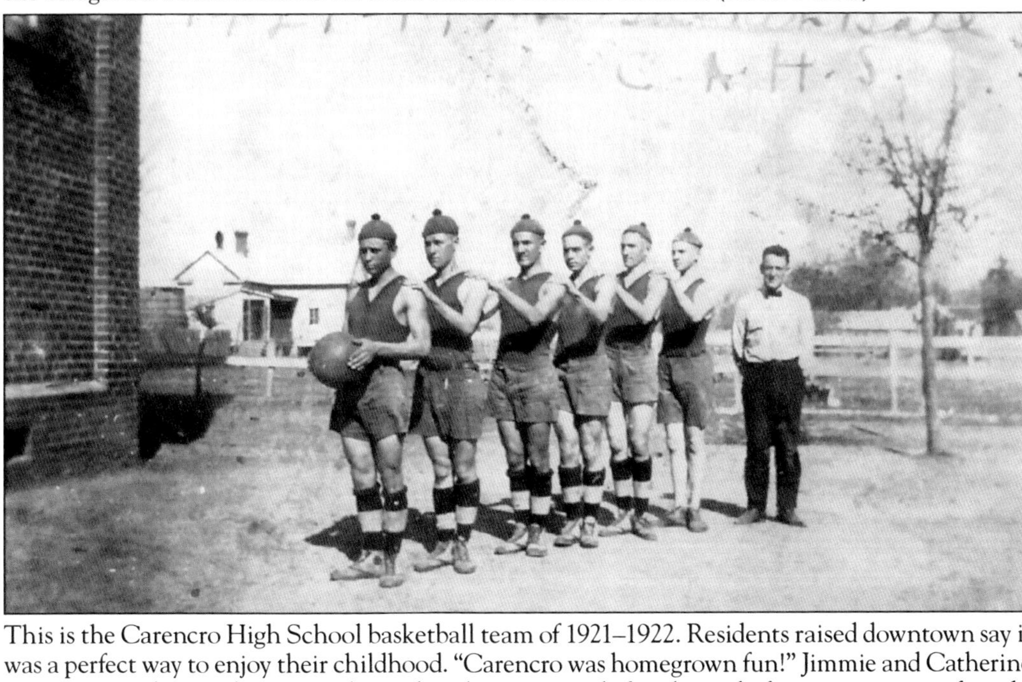

This is the Carencro High School basketball team of 1921–1922. Residents raised downtown say it was a perfect way to enjoy their childhood. "Carencro was homegrown fun!" Jimmie and Catherine Brasseaux said. "Sundays were about church, eating with family, and afternoon visits to friends. Coffee in pretty cups to a game of marbles, Carencro was home and has always been."

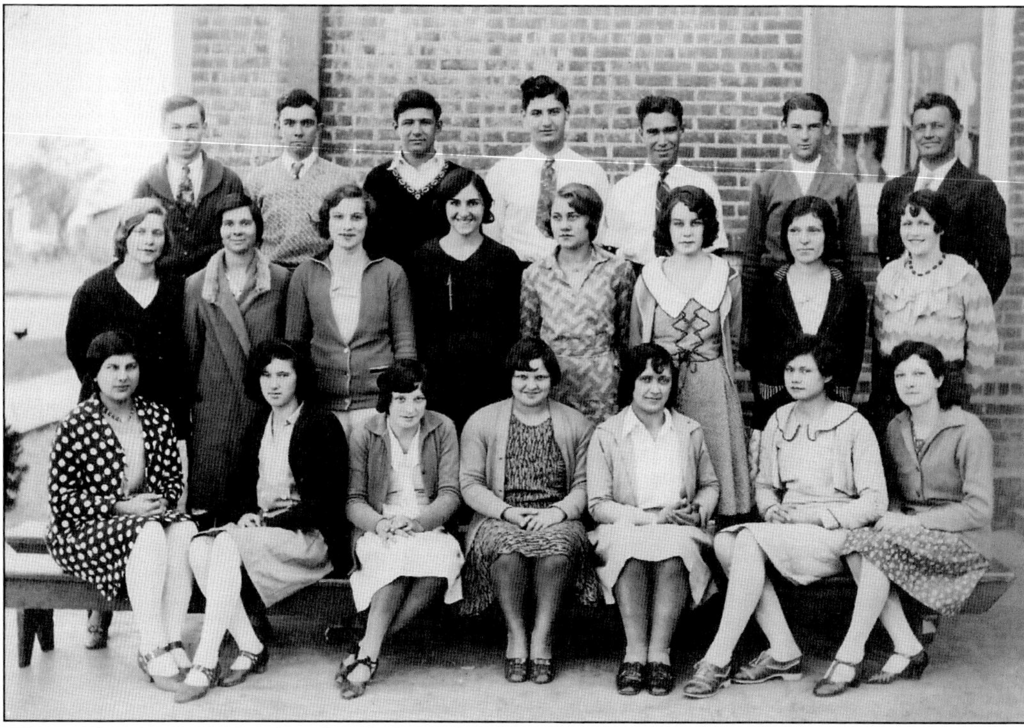

This is the Carencro High School class of 1931. From left to right are (first row) Jeanne Anne Conques, Ethyl Comeaux, Elsie Ruth Martin, Lena Marie Conques, Yolande Breaux, Kathleen Frances Miller, and Sophie Guidry; (second row) Louise Guilbeau, Viola Prejean, Editha M. Prejean, Inez Matthieu, Florine Melancon, Anna Francez, Florence Guilbeau, and Elsie Mary Andrus; (third row) Charles Connolly, Ledel Dupuis, C. Riolan Coussan, Oray E. Dodge, Ray Roger, Thomas Crochet, and principal Odon Hebert. Pictured below is the third grade class in 1922.

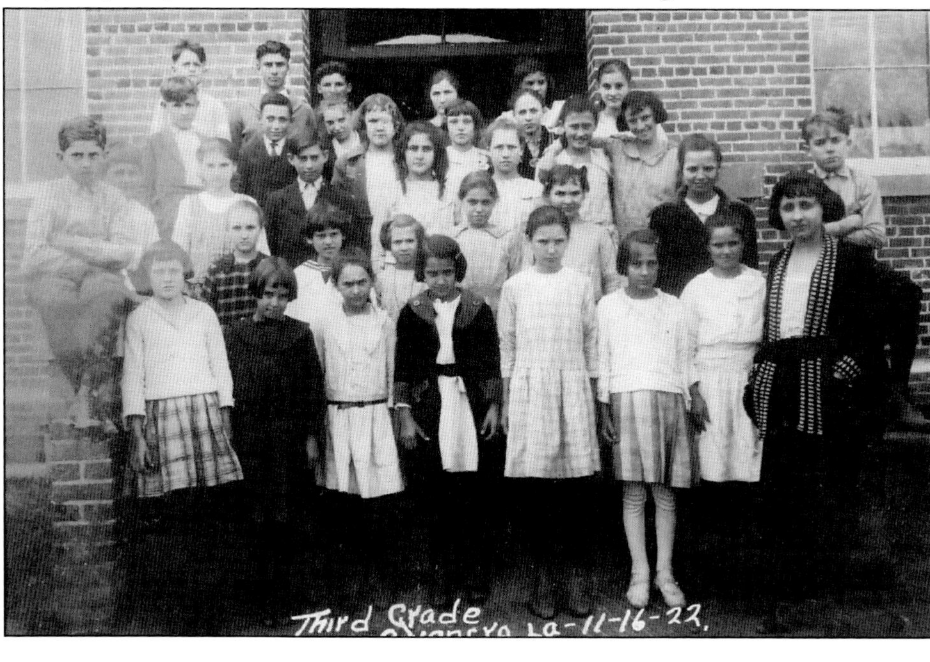

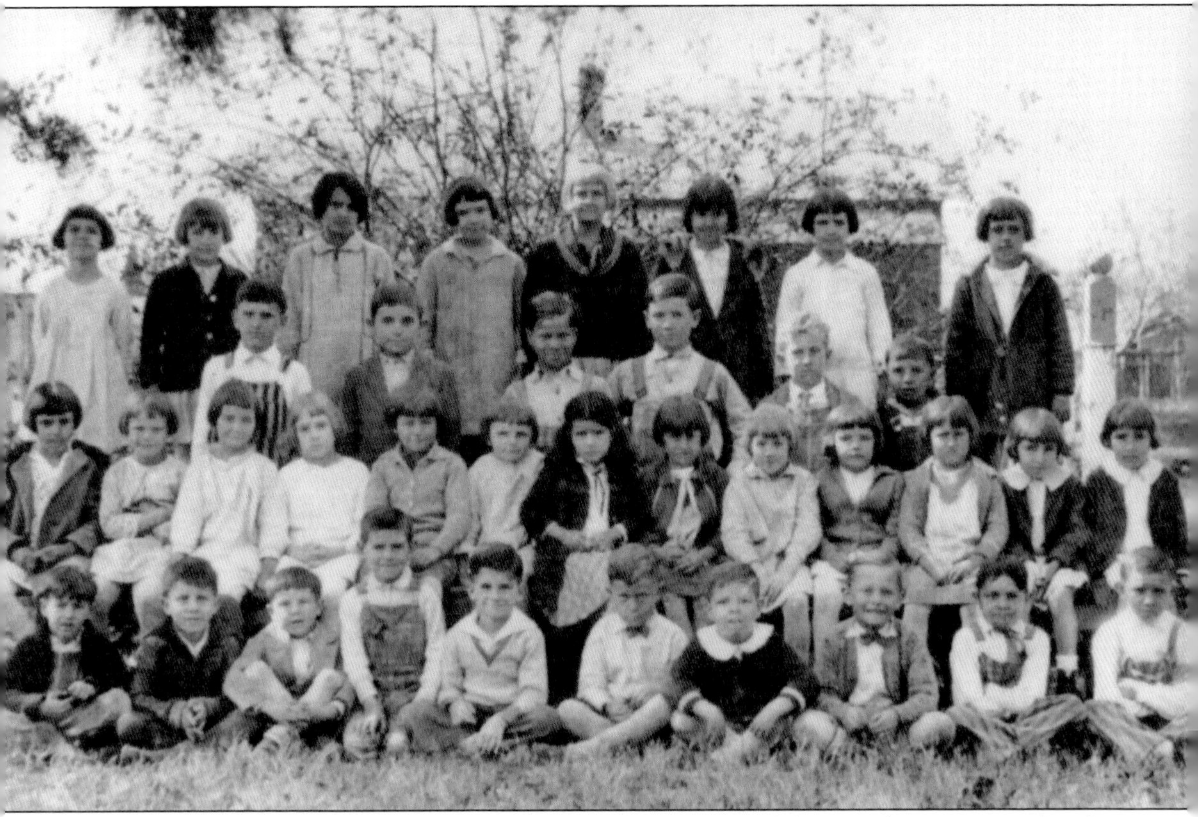

This 1930 photograph shows St. Ann Convent students. Many of these students went to church every Sunday at St. Peter Roman Catholic Church with their families. In those days, many families had an assigned pew. Strange looks could occur if a family entered church and someone was sitting in their pew, as families would actually pay for their pews once a year. For example, Catherine Arceneaux Brasseaux's family would sit in pew five, while the family of her husband, Jimmie, had pew nine.

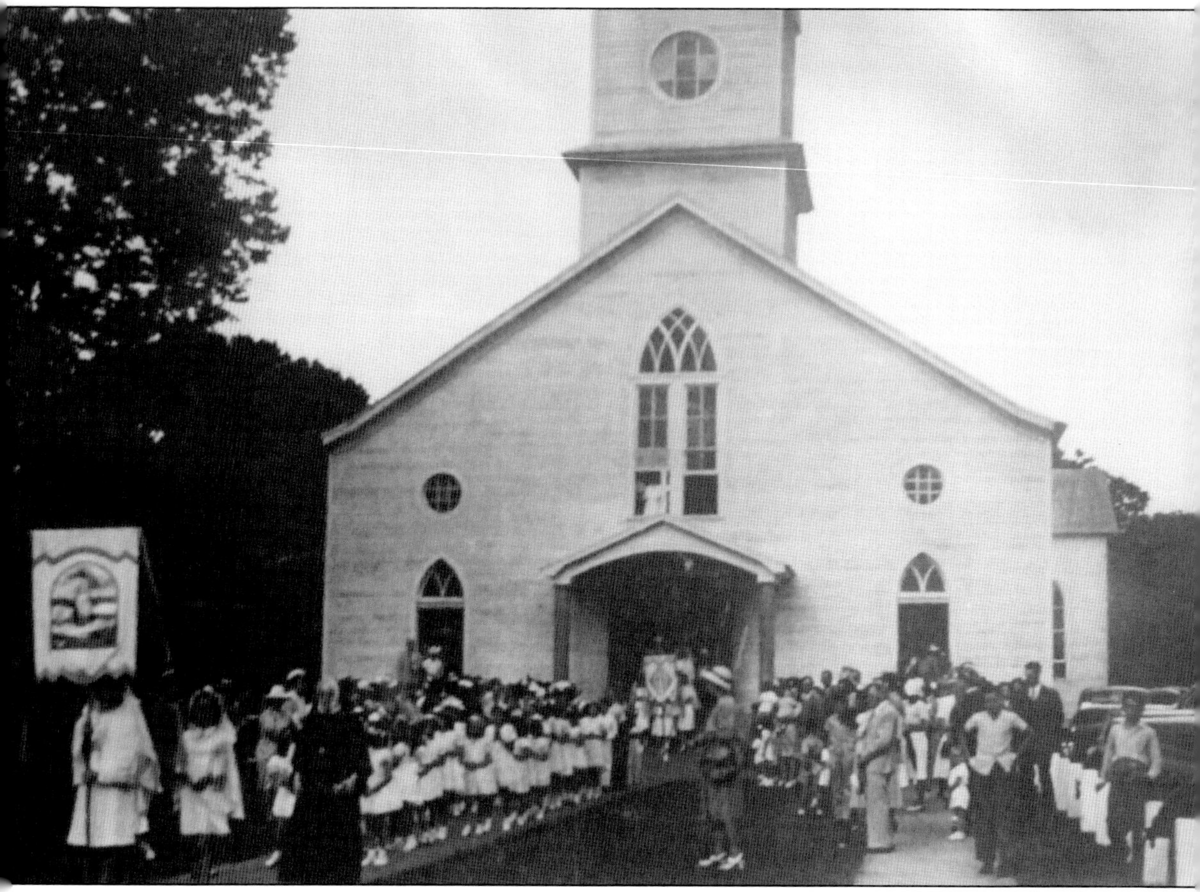

First Communion at St. Peter Roman Catholic Church was always a day filled with family and friends. On any given Sunday, everyone dressed in their best. Women wore hats, gloves, and dresses that would not show any bare skin on the arms. Men would wear their best suits. For the faithful, it was a day for God followed by a day spent with loved ones. Carencro began its tradition in faith with the early settlers in the 1700s. Today, faith and family are still a huge part of the city of Carencro.

Bibliography

Connor, H.N. *The Diary of 1st Sergeant H.N. Connor.* www.wtblock.com/wtblockjr/diaryof.htm.

Dafford, Douglas. *A Short History of Carencro Prairie*. Printed by Douglas Dafford, 1989.

Guilbeau, Charles. *The History of St. Pierre*. Carencro: Printed by Charles Guilbeau.

Kenneson, J.A. Claude. *Historical Narrative of Carencro: Its Inception Through World War I.* Printed by J.A. Claude Kinneson, 1989.

About the St. Pierre Genealogical Society

The St. Pierre Genealogical Society was established in 1998. The nonprofit group is an organization that desires to preserve pieces of the past for future generations. The group's quarterly meetings are held at the North Regional Library (a branch of the Lafayette Public Library) in Carencro.